Tibet: Land of Snows

photographs by Wim Swaan, Edwin Smith and others

Contents

TRANSLATOR'S NOTE ON THE
REPRESENTATION OF TIBETAN WORDS

The spelling generally adopted in this book is an approximation to the spoken values of standard Central Tibetan. It therefore differs widely from the strict *transliterations* of Tibetan orthography which are used when writing for specialists familiar with the written language. These more scientific forms give the uninitiated layman no guidance to pronunciation and accordingly, except in the case of a few words already too widely familiar to change, have been relegated to a table of equivalences that scholars may consult.

It is hoped that the system will be reasonably self-explanatory for English readers. Initial *ch-* and *sh-* have their English values whilst in the 'aspirated' initials *kh-*, *chh-*, *th-*, *ph-*, a slight puff of breath follows the consonant (which should not be the case in *k-*, *ch-*, *t-*, and *p-*). *ng* has the value we give it in 'sing': if the *g* is to be sounded separately in the middle of a word, *ngg* is written. For the vowels, we have borrowed the spellings *ö* and *ü* from German, *é*, *è* and *ê* from French.

TIBET Land of Snows

by Giuseppe Tucci   translated by J. E. Stapleton Driver

𝔰𝔡 Stein and Day / Publishers / New York

Stein and Day / Publishers / 7 East 48 Street, New York. N.Y. 10017
Istituto Geografico De Agostini S.p.A. - Novara 1967
Printed in Italy

List of Plates

Jacket illustrations:

front: Detail from a Tibetan thanka: a Buddhist saint, possibly Da-charwa, a Buddhist Tantric adept.
back: Part of the gilt surround of an image, showing Śāriputra, one of the Buddha's two principal disciples.

Front endpaper:
Tibetan inscription on stone.

Back endpaper:
Portion of a bone 'apron'.

Illustrations in the text

Acknowledgements

The Publishers would like to thank the staff of all those museums and individuals for their kind assistance in the collection and photographing of the illustrations to this book. The objects photographed are acknowledged to the following collections:

Museo Nazionale d'Arte Orientale, Rome: 1, 26, 42, 55; E. M. Scratton Collection, Ashmolean Museum, Oxford: 2, 25, 65, 82, 105; Author's Collection, Rome: front of jacket, 14, 15, 16, 17, 18, 22, 27, 28, 29, 34, 36, 37, 38, 43, 44, 51, 52, 53, 54, 63, 64, 66, 70, 71, 72, 75, 76, 77, 78, 79, 84, 85, 89, 90, 91, 96, 98, 99, 102, 103, back endpaper, back of jacket; Signorina Bonardi: 19; F. Spencer Chapman: 67; ex. coll. Sir Charles Bell, lent by Lt Colonel A. F. Bell, City of Liverpool Museums: 68, 92; Richard Townley: 80; Major and Mrs P. Richard Knight on loan to the Ashmolean Museum, Oxford: 81; Victoria and Albert Museum, London: 100; Horniman Museum, London: 101; India Office Library: Figs 1, 2, 3 (reproduced by courtesy of the Secretary of State for Commonwealth Affairs); British Museum, London: 4, 5, 6, 7, 8, 9.

The photographs are acknowledged to the following photographers:

Wim Swaan: front of jacket, 14, 15, 16, 17, 18, 19, 22, 26, 27, 28, 29, 34, 36, 37, 38, 42, 43, 44, 51, 52, 53, 54, 55, 63, 64, 66, 70, 71, 72, 75, 76, 77, 78, 79, 84, 85, 89, 90, 91, 95, 96, 97, 98, 99, 102, 103, 106, back endpaper, back of jacket; Edwin Smith: 2, 25, 65, 67, 68, 80, 81, 82, 92, 100, 101, 105; the Author: front endpaper, 7, 8, 10, 11, 20, 31, 32, 39, 40, 41, 86, 87; Pietro Mele: 3, 4, 5, 13, 21, 35, 45, 46, 49, 50, 56, 83, 88, 93, 94; Marco Pallis: 6, 9, 58, 59, 61, 62, 69, 73, 74; the late Rev. Arthur Hopkinson: 57, 60; Camera Press: 12 (China Photo Service), 23, 24 (120227), 30 (88415), 47 (China Photo Service), 48 (120149), 104 (NCNA); Adventure: 33.

the weight of their burdens nor the long marches could quench. At the end of each day's journey camp was pitched near rivers, springs or nomad encampments, in inhabited or desert places, in the neighbourhood of villages or monasteries. Then the first noisy contacts were made: after the local authorities had sent their customary offering of tsampa, butter or meat, all the men, women and children came flocking to pry and question. It was hard to get any peace before nightfall, since everyone wanted to come into the tents to see how they were made and what was inside, and how life went on in the camp. Although this curiosity could sometimes be rather a nuisance, it was so spontaneous and respectful that it would have been unfair to take offence. At hand to control this traffic, in any case, was the caravan leader, practically my stand-in, whom I always chose with care. On my journey to Lhasa I had the invaluable companionship of Tenzin, who was soon to climb Everest. Both courteous and energetic, resourceful and multilingual, he grasped the purpose of my research at once, and supported it ably and wisely in dealings with the civil and religious authorities. He has given evidence of this understanding in the sketch of myself he dictated to Ullman in his book, *Man of Everest*, where he shows a balance of judgment for which I am grateful to him. On each of my journeys, in addition, I took a lama along. I recall in particular a very erudite astronomer of Sakya monastery, and Sönam-sengé, a Mongolian geshé to whom many doors were open at Lhasa, and who I am told is now abbot at Ulan Bator.

Traversing much of the country in this way, I was able to build up a rich collection of Tibetan books; to reconstruct in part at least the course of Tibetan art, and reveal the various influences it has undergone; and to study the ruins of many monasteries which, particularly in western Tibet, are wonderful monuments to artistic sensibility and religious fervour built in a country now largely deserted. Later on, in the region of Yarlung south of the Tsangpo, I studied the tombs of the first Tibetan kings, and some inscriptions that go back to their time.

I must add that when events made it impossible to pursue them further, these researches in a way inspired my later more specifically archaeological work. For it was the mysterious figure of Padmasambhava—who consecrated the temple of Samyê in the eighth century when Buddhism was proclaimed the official religion—that suggested excavations in Swat, where that master is said to have been born. I wanted in fact to find out what artistic and cultural connection existed between Swat (then called Uddiyāna) and Tibet; what remains there were of the particular school introduced to Tibet by Padmasambhava, who was considered by the Tibetans its most brilliant representative; and why Swat, now in Pakistan, is holy ground to the Tibetans.

Tibet has thus played a leading role in my academic work, and has stimulated a lot of my research.

The impact of arriving there for the first time is one I shall never forget. Yet it was repeated with equal intensity every time I crossed the frontiers, whether by way of Kashmir; of Ladakh; of Simla, along the Sutlej valley and the Shipki pass; of Almora and the Lipulekh; or by the more-used route through Sikkim, and Kampadzong or Yatung as the case might be. As the sub-Himalayan landscape changed and the influence of Indian ways grew less and less, as happens in all the border lands, it was not just a different landscape that greeted me, but an unfamiliar human world.

Description can never equal a first-hand encounter. Only those who have been in Tibet know the fascination of its huge landscapes, its diaphanous air that scarfs the icy peaks with turquoise, its vast silence that at once humbles man and uplifts him. Flights of mountain ranges flow on endlessly like the elaboration of a single musical theme in some oriental melody. But every so often the rhythm is broken, as a pass, which had seemed an obstacle, opens upon a sudden new wealth of colour and light; cliffs tumble one upon another and rear up abruptly in fantastic shapes; sudden patches of yellow, turquoise, violet and red creep out over the gilded backcloth of the rock. When you least expect it, a hint of green shows on the far horizon, and in its midst, as one draws closer, the eye rests on the whiteness of houses. Monasteries stand out huge against the hills, their golden roofs glittering in the sunlight. It is a glorious play of colours to which nature, man, mountains and sun alike contribute.

A bond of sympathy was set up from the first, in spite of the profoundly different life. There were no police, passports were not demanded, one felt at home straight away. Bountiful hospitality, constant good humour, attentiveness to the stranger, sincerity of religious beliefs yet sensible tolerance, at once brought to the fore the human qualities of a nation whose inaccessibility has sometimes led to misleading accounts of it.

Given the dominant role of religion, the success of any relations the visitor could establish with people depended largely on his attitude towards religion and on the opinion the populace at large had of him. Above all one had to try not to do anything that displeased the monks or made them suspicious, for they, because of their prestige, determined the lay-people's response. Not to have taken this into account would have meant meeting with a wall of incomprehension that prevented any useful contact. In other words, the best way for the visitor to achieve his aims was to present himself as I did, as a pilgrim visiting the sacred places. This was no lie, either, in view of my Buddhist leanings, and furthermore my purpose was precisely to enter all the monasteries and study their artistic importance as well as the abilities and training of the monks inhabiting them. Like every other pilgrim, I lit votive lamps (*chhömé*) on the altars, distributed suitable sums for the tea-offering (*mangja*), knelt as the rite prescribes before images or monuments the Tibetans held in special veneration. When I was admitted to the Dalai Lama's presence, it was not in the capacity of a foreigner but of a believer: prostrating myself head to the ground three times, and receiving His threefold laying-on of book, statue and *chhörten* upon my head. Any book handed to me, in the same way, I accepted with respectful ritual, both hands outstretched, and then raised it to touch my forehead in order for the sacred volume to bestow blessing (*chinlap*) on me by this contact. It was well to seek this blessing, respectfully, of any Lama generally esteemed for learning or sanctity that one met en route or in a monastery. In this way suspicion and resistance disappeared and the monasteries, with their libraries and artistic treasures without number, became accessible. Acquiring books also became a possibility—for because of the sacred character imparted by their religious contents, they were not always easy to buy. How much less so the statues and objects of worship carefully listed in the monastic registers, whose disappearance would be bound to involve severe penalties for the monk responsible for their custody. In private chapels it was just the same: desire for gain would never have overcome the reluctance to trade in sacred things were the owner not certain they were going to one of his own faith.

It should not be supposed that I draw a romantic picture of Tibet; I record things and persons as I saw them and I cannot falsify in any way the feelings they roused in me. Naturally someone fascinated by the marvels of *homo oeconomicus* and *homo politicus* might have had a different set of impressions, for life in Tibet was lived on another plane, a kind of miraculous mediaeval survival behind the sheltering, isolating mountain-belt.

To enter Tibet was not only to find oneself in another geographical world. After crossing the gap in space, one had the impression of having travelled many centuries backward in time. By this I do not mean the absence of certain commodities, skills or discoveries that make our life easier, or more complicated, than that of the Tibetans: or of the tools and gadgets science is ever more bountifully, and dangerously, placing at our disposal. Some of these had reached Lhasa, and other large towns, where they aroused interest and were even sought after (gramophones and records, or cameras, for instance); but the way they were regarded and made use of was different from ours. They remained a curiosity, a toy, and perhaps this is the only way to beat the fearful tyranny of the machine. No; what belonged to the past was a particular psychological situation—the shared outlook, the very distinctive manner of viewing things and the world—which we happen to think of as mediaeval. It was rather like an atmosphere everyone breathed, and we too were gradually steeped in it. It was a single, over-all, immediate impression, felt rather than demonstrable, springing from everyday contacts, and appearing, if one tried to analyse it, as the inevitable meeting-point to which the many aspects of the Tibetan spirit tend.

I think the most distinctive characteristic the Tibetan derived from his Buddhist faith was a sense of the fundamental vanity of things. From caravaneer to abbot, from peasant to lord, all shared the conviction that the world is *tongpanyi*, emptiness: an emptiness stripping all substantiality from what we think of as 'being', which is nothing but appearance. But the presence of this void did not cast a veil of grief over things so much as restore them to proper proportions, comparing and relating them with one another. It is not in practice a factor leading the Tibetan to a painful, pessimistic view of the world, even though it was the Truth of Universal Pain that the Buddha made the foundation-stone of his doctrine. The void must be conceived of as a relativity. If everything is empty, so is pain; pleasure and pain are illusory appearances. This illusiveness strikes at the roots of all we suppose real, yet the fact is that such reality remains valid till we have turned our whole scheme of life inside out; and that comes only after long experience, as the maturity won over many lifetimes. And so there is no cause for grief; on the contrary, the outcome of these assumptions is a certain lightness, an easy skimming over things, since at bottom nothing is conclusive. The same may be seen from the Tibetans' different way of looking at death, which is not for them a clean break between a now and a hereafter. No doubt this life is a great risk, since our next is staked on its outcome, but that in turn does not last for ever: it is a scrap of time in which, even whilst we reap the fruits of today's good or evil action, limitless possibilities open up to man's free choice. Death is not the door to nothingness or to eternity, but the joining of two links in an endless chain, or a definite passing away for ever from the illusion of time and being. In consequence imagination, which tends to carry less and less weight in our busy matter-of-fact life, occupied a prominent place in Tibet. Moreover the fact of sharing in a transcendent reality is present, conscious or not, within each of us; for each is of the same substance or essence as the Buddha-nature. This belief turned man into an ambiguous creature—partaking of an atemporality which defies every definition, yet caught up in a time-span that measures his own illusoriness and that of all he does.

Perhaps the Tibetans' affability sprang from this state of affairs—a certain laughing, convivial serenity alongside the more solid religiousness. There was no trace of the *contemptus mundi* that cast its gloom over other countries of Asia.

A curious mixture of sacred and profane, faith and commercialism grew out of this. The dividing line between reality and legend was not fixed; one shaded over into the other. In the monks you met learned theology and dialectic one moment, immersion in the void or magical exaltation the next.

The sense of the void inculcated by Buddhism, let me add, was rekindled by the immensity of space. Man is truly overwhelmed by the landscape's pitiless vastness: a physical void reflecting religion's metaphysical void, and a solitude into which the Tibetan frequently plunged either for trading purposes or for the pilgrimages he liked making to sacred places. Through the crystal brightness of the air, the traveller would see a small dark spot taking shape in the distance, on the horizon of one of those broad corridors between the mountains that dash themselves against the sky; would see it gradually grow larger and take on the ever more definite appearance of another solitary traveller. Just two points, two nothings lost in space. Finding himself so inexorably alone man's sense of emptiness grew sharper: there was no relation between the two small creatures and that vastness, empty as a dead planet. Nature had the upper hand, as in those Chinese paintings where the human figure is only introduced to emphasize its fragility or insignificance. But the Tibetan sensed in that solitude the presence of innumerable forces—now hostile, now benevolent, most often indifferent, yet capable of swift reaction to any act of his, enmeshing him in an invisible society under whose surveillance he completes his journey.

In the Tibetans, by and large, I found that seemingly discordant thoughts, moods and feelings lived peacefully side by side, conducive to the greater simplicity, rather than complexity, of their spirit, with none of the harshness that comes from unyielding certainty. Buddhism forbids the killing of living beings of any kind, but it does not follow that the Tibetan is a vegetarian: he may merely leave it to butchers, avoided as impure, to kill animals, and refuse to be present when they are at work. The conviction that everything is an illusion, and the only reality the elusive and indefinable void, makes the Tibetan admire the ascetic and regard his life as the ideal; but that is not to say that he renounces the world himself.

Above all, I found a great openness in everyone: to me the Tibetan seemed frank, less inclined to the insincerity that sometimes makes Orientals hard to understand. Finally he was rather independent, perhaps because communal life was so meagre, and from ancestral custom.

Such, for the most part, was the Tibetan as I came to know him through long association. 'Was'—and I shall often have occasion to express myself in the past tense—because this Tibetan 'culture', based on religious and social forms that were still intact when I was in Tibet, has been profoundly altered by events since then: what was valid up to a few years ago is certainly no longer so today.

Fig 1. Title pages from two Tibetan manuscripts.

1. Part of a fresco from a temple in Western Tibet, showing the Buddha preaching his first sermon in Sarnāth, c. fifteenth-sixteenth century.

2

History

We have only to glance at a map of Asia to see Tibet clearly marked off by encircling mountain chains that, in addition, criss-cross its interior. It stretches from east to west, shaped rather like a heart resting upon the diaphragm of the Himalayas to the south, and may be divided into several large, vaguely bounded areas whose outlines have reflected the course of political events. First, from the western end, comes *Ngarikorsum*, the three districts of Ngari, adjoining Spiti and Ladakh on the west: both of these are culturally Lamaistic, with strongly Islamic pockets in the latter case, and with almost completely Tibetanized indigenous populations. Ngarikorsum includes Purang, with its principal centre at Taklakot not far from the Nepalese frontier, and Gugé, an ancient independent kingdom subject to Tibet from the seventh century (it regained its freedom after the fall of the royal dynasty and was reincorporated in Tibet in the seventeenth century). Here rises Tisé, the mountain sacred to Tibetans and Indians, which the latter call Kailāśa, Śiva's legendary, inaccessible abode. South of Kailāśa, like a huge turquoise set in a circlet of peaks, sparkles lake Mapham, the Indians' Manasarowar. On these two converge pilgrims of three religions: Hinduism, Buddhism, and Bon (the ancient religion of Tibet). This point is the source both of the Indus, which winds northwestwards and then descends to water Pakistan, and of the Sutlej, which cleaves its way through narrow valleys to India. From here the Tsangpo begins its long course, crossing Tibet from west to east, turning southward after Kongpo and then southwest, to reach Assam where it takes the name of Brahmaputra, 'son of Brahma'.

After Ngari comes *Tsang*, with Sakya, Shigatsé, and Gyantsé. At the centre is *Ü* —the Middle region—with Lhasa. Eastward on the Chinese border lies *Kham*, where four great rivers run parallel—the Salween, the Mekong, the Kin-sha kiang (later becoming the Yangtze kiang), and the Ya-lung kiang—vast spouts of water that pour down from the roof of the world, to irrigate the lands of the south.

Northeast of Kham is *Amdo*, through which the Yellow River pursues its leisurely course along the Bayankara chain; and then the great lake Koko Nor. In the north is *Changthang*—the Northern Plateau — inhabited by nomadic races.

The indigenous name for Tibet is *P'ö* (spelt *Bod*), or *P'öyül*, and more poetically, the 'Land of Snows': a succession of uplands and valleys with an area of over one and a half million square miles, thirty times that of England. On all this territory lives a population of two or three million, according to what I could gather on my travels: less than two inhabitants per square mile. There were certainly more in the past, as may be inferred from surviving traces of intensive cultivation and from irrigation works in now almost deserted places. At Öka, for example, which at one time had appreciable political importance, there remain but a few houses near the ruins of ancient fortresses; in western Tibet at Tsaparang, once capital of Gugé and now seat of a Dzongpön, live a handful of families who turn nomad on the adjacent plateaux in summer, but the Portuguese missionary D'Andrade, who stayed there in the

2. Bronze gilt statuette of Chenrèsik (Avalokiteśvara)

seventeenth century (1624-36) and was received with tolerant sympathy by the king, speaks of a population of five hundred families. His information hardly seems exaggerated to anyone who knows the place, an enormous troglodytic town peeping from empty caves, cut in a mountainside that stands out yellow against the valley. It is the same story at Dawazong and other places in the province which, after long political independence, succumbed first to Ladakh and later to Lhasa.

This means that wars, followed by the decline of what had been a flourishing trade with India, and later invasions and plundering by the armies of Raja Gulab Singh of Jammu (1835), left the country with no strength for recovery and repopulation. In most places, other than in well-watered valleys, cultivation is not easy: it depends on irrigation, involving all the farmers in constant maintenance work.

The above division is the one Tibetans usually make of their country. But it is a general one that may be added to by subdivisions into smaller districts: Yarlung, Kongpo, Lhari, Poyül and so forth, each with its own historical and cultural traditions, though these usually converge in due course.

Apart from border regions, and leaving the ethnic components of the present Tibetan population out of account, the country is culturally and linguistically fairly homogeneous, though a proverb affirms that every Lama has his own method of teaching, each valley its own mode of speech.

The ethnic origin of the Tibetans is complex. There were the *Ch'iang* (Tibeto-Burmans), whom Chinese sources record from very early times, with their neighbours to the west, Indo-Europeans like the *Yüeh-Chih*: when these were pushed westwards by the Chinese, some of them ended up in Ch'iang country and were absorbed. There were the *T'u yu hun* (Turco-Mongols), assimilated after their conquest in the seventh to eighth centuries; the *Hor*, largely of Mongol origin, but in their turn Tibetanized; the *Dards* of western Tibet, together with outlying Austronesian groups; and a whole zone of different peoples in the south assigned by Tibetans the blanket term *Mön*, who are to be regarded as aboriginal in some areas. But the fact remains that this ethnic complexity has been overlaid, for all the variety of dialects that persists, with a linguistic unity ideally exemplified by the dialect of Lhasa; and above all, with the cultural unity of religion, which not only enjoins respect for various doctrines, but also inspires a special way of life, and of conceiving and arranging society.

Though they turned to agriculture quite early on in the irrigable valleys, the Tibetans have long continued to be stockrearers and shepherds as well. The two forms of life often co-exist, for property is not solely in land; monasteries and well-to-do families have an abundance of flocks and herdsmen, which considerations of grazing and often of climate will not allow to remain in the immediate neighbourhood of the cultivated fields.

Yaks, sheep, goats, *dzo* — offspring of yak and cow—and horses of several breeds are raised. In the wild state we find the *kyang*, a kind of ass, which along with the yak plays a noteworthy part in epic tradition. Cultivation is not very varied because of the climatic and soil conditions. The main crops are barley, grown as high as 13,000 feet or more, and corn; occasionally too, in some parts of the south, rice, sorghum, potatoes (a recent introduction), turnips, peas, millet, and a root called *droma* (*Potentilla anserina*). Fruit-trees grow there too: apricots, apples, and walnuts. In short, Tibet offers a reasonable variety of natural produce, despite its mountainous character.

3. The Monastery of Trashi-lhünpo, fifteenth-century residence of the panchen ('Trashi') Lama.

Diversity of terrain occasions varied ways of life, so much so that the people following them are known by special names: inhabitants of the *drok*, upland plains where pastur-

4

5

age is the exclusive occupation, are called Drokpa, as distinct from those of the narrow valleys, the Rongpa. Although vast, almost uninhabitable desert areas are the rule because of the altitude, rich wooded tracts are found in the south and in the eastern districts. Even in the heart of Tibet, where nature is usually more arid, one comes across unexpected green oases, for example, the hermit city of Yerpa, near Lhasa. North of Samyê, in valleys where the castles of Tibet's first kings stand, the scrub is dense enough to give a tinge of green, contrasting with the relentless yellow of the dunes to the south of that famous monastery, which undulate down to the banks of the Tsangpo.

The variety of landscape, then, naturally has its influence on social habits, but it does not violate the fundamental unity I have mentioned. The climate, too, is less extreme than some travellers have described it. Obviously at these altitudes the winters are hard. The cold is piercing on the passes over which the track toils. On the plateaux an icy wind springs up about noon each day and blows violently till sunset, obliging the wayfarer to pull down the flaps of his fur hat for protection, and the women to grease their faces. But snow rarely falls in the valleys, and when they are shielded from the winds the sun makes the air there agreeable even in winter, as well as extremely healthy, being so pure and dry.

Inhabited centres are widely separated from each other. Villages, the little clusters of houses scattered over the better-watered valleys, cannot expand into great cities: it would be impossible to provide for the needs of a large population. Riots not infrequently broke out when Chinese garrisons were sent to Lhasa and Shigatsé, because the sudden flood of new inhabitants brought scarcity of provisions and higher prices. The difficulty of communications and the lack of rapid means of transport obliged every town or village to rely upon its own sources of supply.

Large cities, consequently, do not exist in Tibet. Lhasa itself, as I knew it, had a population of no more than 40-50,000 inhabitants. Even this is an approximate figure, since there was neither municipal register nor national census and since, as in any holy city, the population increased and decreased according to the flow of pilgrims and the contingencies of the religious calendar. Other cities of note are Shigatsé, Gyantsé, Jyekundo, and Dergé. The remainder are unimpressive clusters of humanity, in the higher places no more than a few houses. Then, on the plateau-lands, are the Drokpa, and over Changthang, the black tents of its great nomad encampments, sometimes veritable moving towns—temporary halts in an eternal wandering.

Tibetan history begins when we have reliable contemporary records of events. Particularly important are the fairly precise Chinese sources that record China's first contacts and conflicts with Tibet, as soon as the latter appeared at her frontiers as a threatening political power in the last years of the sixth and the early years of the seventh century A.D. (Kai-huang period, 581-600). Then there are Tibetan legends put into writing in later times, handing down glimmers and echoes of antiquity in the epic manner—not so fanciful, however, that the historian can gain no light from them. Chronicles, of the barest kind, start with the first king, Songtsen-gampo (died 649 or 650), who continued the work of his grandfather and his father by uniting the whole country under his control, and began wars of conquest. Year by year the essential facts are entered: births and deaths of kings, shiftings of the court, wars, rebellions of chiefs and their suppression; but all with the utmost brevity. Even in the earliest times Tibet was not completely shut off from the rest of the world. Certain words suggest ancient contacts with Iranian-speaking peoples; some objects,

4. The Potala Palace, Lhasa.

5. Chhongyê in the Valley of Yarlung, birthplace of Ngawang Lopsang-gyatso, the fifth Dalai Lama.

23

prior to the fully historical period but otherwise undatable, recall the style and subject matter of Luristan bronzes. Being chiefly herdsmen, the Tibetans had to move with the season, like neighbouring pastoral and nomadic populations. Such was the case in the districts nearest China and in those bordering upon countries within the Indian orbit. Geographical remoteness is consequently not matched by a rigid cultural isolation; outside influences could make themselves felt at any point.

Tibet emerges split up into vast territories, each under the control of one family boasting divine descent: its ancestor was supposed to have come down from the sky, or was identified with an awesomely sacred mountain. In many instances the family's name and that of the region it lived in were identical. It owned that country — its property took the form of irrigable lands, pastures and livestock. Exchange and barter went on, as they still did in recent times, on traditional sites, at convenient meetings of the ways. Hunting too was practised by the chieftains' families, and others of lesser standing but possessing wealth of their own: it was not merely a sport or means of livelihood, but a ritual performed after propitiation ceremonies. The hunt was a necessary custom in this social context, serving to develop warlike virtues and a fighting spirit and keep men at the ready. There was no shortage of artisans, especially metalworkers making arms or ornaments from both local and imported materials.

An essential feature of this society were the shamans and exorcists. With their techniques of ritual, divination and other magic practices, they kept the human world in touch with that of gods and demons, carrying out the necessary sacrifices, journeying into the beyond to bring back the souls of the sick or dying, visiting heaven and directing funeral rites.

The spread of agriculture was slow from the very nature of the terrain, and started with the technique of irrigation. The two ways of life, pastoral and agricultural, remained complementary.

The division of Tibet between great families naturally caused conflicts: grazing limits were not laid down with precision, and it was to be expected in a still fluid society that disputes would arise from their violation. The normal dwelling was the tent, but groups of houses were not unknown. The Chinese, when they begin to have direct knowledge of the Tibetans, report the existence of square, flat-roofed houses which foreshadow those of today. The chieftains lived in fortified hilltop castles. In winter the cold restricted grazing and, where the nature of the land allowed, the herdsmen would take refuge in caves hollowed out of the mountain, often at high altitudes. Access was by way of ladders and steps cut in the walls, easily removed if necessary.

A tradition that we have no reason to doubt relates that in the sixth century the lords of Yarlung, south of the Tsangpo, succeeded in bringing much of Tibetan territory under their sway: the first to embark on this task was Namtrhi, but the real founder of dynastic power was Songtsen-gampo. The latter imposed a new order and compelled the various families to recognize his sovereign power, at the same time appointing their heads to ministerial office or noble rank. The state thus established was run in accordance with a military structure that divided Tibet into a centre, two wings (*ru*), and a supplementary wing facing south or south-west. Each chief responsible for his own territory had to furnish a set number of officials and soldiers grouped in decimal units, on a pattern that is met with amongst the Mongols and the Turks and that was in vogue as early as the Achaemenids: myriarchs, centurions, captains of ten. The reforms of Songtsen-gampo (and of his father) were most probably accompanied by changes in political and religious customs. It was usual for the king to surrender power, or simply be eliminated, as soon as his son had reached the age

6. Likhir Monastery, Ladakh.

24

7

8

of thirteen and was capable of riding; until the thirteen-year-old successor reached his majority, power was in practice entrusted to his mother or maternal uncles. This led to frequent clashes and palace conspiracies that sometimes put the lives of the kings and their heirs in jeopardy. We are not told that the royal family always succeeded in asserting its own authority over the leading families that opposed it.

Although the Tibetan state was firmly established as a power in Asia and soon began to expand at the cost of China and other neighbouring countries, there was an inherent weakness in its internal make-up. One king tried to carry out reforms aimed at a fairer distribution of property, but we have too little evidence to gauge what real substance there was in this attempt; at all events, the reform was not followed up. In their exercise of power the kings were normally assisted by ministers. They usually chose to marry into the great families, and during the period of regency the queen or her family was in power. Since Tibetan kings were polygamous, the court often felt the effect of power conflicts between the various groups: their persistent rivalry progressively enfeebled the dynasty. This does not entitle us to say that the Tibetan regime was feudal. The term is not applicable, since the great families were owners of territory in which they had been established from time immemorial, and received no investiture from the king, though in the event of rebellion or disobedience they ran the risk of having their chief punished and their goods confiscated. On the other hand, owing to the ascendancy of one family over another, and the scale of its own heavy military commitments, the dynasty was forced to look for support to at least a section of the nobility; this brought about an unstable balance of power that was often on the point of collapsing.

The chronicles written after the triumph of Buddhism celebrate Songtsen-gampo as its patron, and indeed as the incarnation of Chenrêsik (Avalokiteśvara) (cf. pl. 2), the merciful deity who protects Tibet. But there is more to his greatness than that: with him begins Tibet's expansion in the four directions, in which, according to the ancient tradition, lay the kingdoms threatening her fortunes. In 634 Tibet attacked and worsted the T'u yu hun, encamped in the Koko Nor region. Then Shangshung, corresponding more or less to the region between Kailāśa and Ladakh and the northern highlands, was subdued; and after reducing Nepal to vassalage, Tibetan troops reached northern India. Wars against China were not infrequent.

The death of Songtsen-gampo, in 649 or 650, did not interrupt the rapid conquest. The great cultural and commercial centres strung out along the prosperous caravan-routes of Turkestan—Khotan, Kucha, Karashar, Kashgar—were removed by degrees from Chinese sway, and came under Tibetan control after 666. All this was the handiwork not only of the kings but also, perhaps chiefly, of the Gar family, which for some time supplied the dynasty with its most commanding and effective prime ministers, in particular Tongtsen Yalzung, who was sent to China to seek a royal princess Wên-ch'ing (generally called Kongjo in Tibetan), as a wife for Songtsen-gampo. But the rise of this powerful family represented danger, which Songtsen-gampo's greatgrandson, Düsong, finally eliminated by forcing Gar Thinding to commit suicide (698).

Tibetan armies penetrated the Chinese frontiers several times, but these were not lasting conquests. Over a long period there was a succession of advances and retreats, with several feeble attempts at agreements and treaties. In 694 the Tibetans lost the four cities in Turkestan; Nepal rebelled in 703; the Arabs were at the border and Tibet was dragged into the unstable situation to which their incursions brought the whole of Asia. Mé Aktsom was able to conclude a treaty (730) with China, allowing

7. Tibetan women weaving.

8. Novices reading pages of the scriptures.

the Tibetans to give their attention to other parts of the frontier; king Trhisong-detsen, who came to the throne in 755, resumed the military expeditions; the Tibetans, profiting from China's momentary weakness, even succeeded in capturing the capital, Ch'ang-an (763), and putting a new emperor on the throne. But it was a success that lasted less than a month.

Trhisong-detsen, who died at the end of the eighth century or the beginning of the ninth, was succeeded by Rêpachen, during whose reign Indian Buddhism made its greatest penetration. He succeeded in concluding a treaty with China (821-2), the text of which is inscribed on a pillar at Lhasa. After him the collapse began. In 838 he was succeeded by his brother Langdarma who, according to tradition, re-instated Bon and persecuted Buddhism, but after a year and a half's reign (according to most sources) he was killed. The empire begun under Songtsen-gampo crumbled. Revolts and clashes broke out within the country.

Tun-huang was lost in 831 and about the end of the ninth century nothing remained of the Tibetan conquest. The royal family itself, after the two sons of Langdarma had disputed the possession of the country and divided it up between themselves, was split into minor branches.

This summary of names and dates is the bare skeleton of much more important events that were going on at the same time. In less than two centuries Tibet attained a consciousness of her own unity, even if she did not fully succeed in bringing that unity about; various tribes merged, Tibet came out of isolation and entered the history of Asia as a political and military power of the first order. Furthermore, contact with other peoples, whether in peace or war, widened cultural horizons, and introduced new ways of living and thinking which, though leaving the Tibetans' native propensities unaltered, civilized him nonetheless, and made him sensitive to the appeal of older and more complex traditions. From China, from the cities of Central Asia energetic in trade and artistically alive, from India, whether directly or through Nepal and Kashmir, Tibet welcomed Buddhism and made herself familiar with the subtleties of its thought; she compiled an alphabet of Indian origin and committed to writing her own chronicles, her own epic traditions, mythologies and cosmogonies. For reasons of government, trade or religion, or simply out of curiosity, many Tibetans learned Chinese, Sanskrit, and the tongues of Central Asia. Songtsen-gampo compiled a code of laws that survived him by centuries. Tibetan scholars attended in China the schools where the Chinese *literati* were trained, and others familiarized themselves with the recondite abstractions of Buddhist doctrine. Other religions, too, such as Manichaeism, Nestorianism, and Zoroastrianism, must have been encountered by the Tibetans when they flooded towards the Central Asian caravan routes where Occident and Orient had met for centuries. Their admiration for the monuments seen in the countries they visited gave a spur to their art. At first, unable to execute works of equal splendour on their own, they invited foreign artists to their country.

Besides the distress and uncertain fortunes of war, all this was a significant outcome of the Tibetan dynasty, however short its duration and frail its structure.

Of these events the most important was undoubtedly the acceptance of Buddhism and its rapid triumph. One of the factors that favoured it is to be found in the desire of the court, and the families loyal to it, to free themselves from a religious tradition that limited the power of the king, who, circumscribed within a sacred *majestas*, could not break away from the weight of custom and the ascendancy of the priestly class unless he had a very strong personality. This explains the eagerness with which the royal dynasty received the apostles of Buddhism.

The Buddhists brought not only a religious creed, a philosophy and an art, but also a new conception of the world and of royal authority. As soon as the first monasteries were founded in the time of Trhisong-detsen and the first monks ordained (779), Buddhism caused a considerable change in economic and administrative organization. Following Indian practice, grants of land and of retainers were made to the monasteries, and they were exempted from taxes and *corvée*: they thus constituted a new power. Buddhism, protected by the court and later officially adopted, represented a new outlook for society as well as the spirit, by investing the king with a new spiritual sovereignty. As patron of the new religion, he was proclaimed *chhögyel*, the king of the Law, personifying the Buddha's Law or Dharma, and, in theory at least, its defender on earth. Relations with China were improved and a treaty of peace concluded in 783. Buddhism continued to spread under Rêpachen (815-38).

The Bonpo priestly class could not sit back while its prerogatives and prestige were being curtailed, and they were soon joined as allies, on the pretext of defending the old traditions, by those aristocrats who resented the power of the king and of the noble families supporting him. Their resistance smouldered for a long time before it exploded little more than half a century after Trhisong-detsen's edict which proclaimed Buddhism the state religion. Langdarma (838-42) prohibited Buddhism, persecuted its followers, and brought back the old religion, only to meet his end after a short time at the hands of a Buddhist monk, who killed him, both to save the religion and, say the chronicles, out of compassion for his sins. Indeed Buddhism, respectful of life as it is, does not rule out manslaughter when there is no other way to save the sinner from committing greater sins.

But the revival of Bon was half-hearted, and Buddhism, on the other hand, declined and became corrupted. It had been supported by the court's favour and, above all, invigorated by the frequent arrival in the Land of Snows of monks and missionaries from China, India, Nepal, Kashmir, Central Asia, Swat—all places where invasions and political upheavals, and the ever more massive advance of Islam, made life difficult for the community and cut down the activities of the Buddhist universities. Many temples had been built, many books translated into Tibetan from Sanskrit, Chinese and other languages, and real schools of translators faithful to the letter and the spirit had been set up. But after Langdarma's persecution, without the constant life-giving contact with Buddhist centres in India, Central Asia and China, Tibetan Buddhism degenerated. There survived mainly treatises on magic, and certain scriptures of a magico-gnostic character. These have a double meaning, the one literal and the other esoteric, the value of the latter depending on its being correctly understood or inwardly experienced by virtue of the enlightening word of one's master.

The downfall of the dynasty introduces the second period of Tibetan history, which might conveniently be called the Tibetan Middle Ages. A political upheaval began, of which the course of events is still not known in much detail. There was in a sense a return to the pre-dynastic situation, with the difference that many of the families among whom Tibet was now divided were new, and not those who had supported or opposed the rise of the dynasty. Many of the latter had been swept away in the crash, but this did not result in much alteration in the country's social structure.

Thus fragmented politically, Tibet was forced by the historical situation to shut herself in; but the cultural isolation was short-lived. Langdarma had not succeeded in suppressing Buddhist resistance: he had silenced its voice, but not its spirit. Following his murder a number of monks succeeded, after various difficulties, in reviving the flame of the faith in Kham with the cooperation of certain Chinese *ho shang*, and in reconstituting the community based on regular ordinations. The most important figure in this revival is Gerapsel (died 915 or 975), whose disciples branched out into Kham and Central Tibet. In the tenth century a dynasty that united western Tibet and much of western Nepal under its rule embraced Buddhism with renewed vigour.

Up to this period documentary evidence is scanty: we have only genealogical lists of the families ruling in various parts of Tibet. Even the chronology is doubtful till 1027, when a new reckoning was instituted, substituting the sexagenary cycle for the cycle of twelve years used in the ancient chronicles. There are gaps in the intervening period. From here onwards the history of Tibet is no longer, or only in an indirect and secondary way, a tale of feats of conquest; it is, above all, the narration of the progress and spread of religion. Histories in fact are now called *Chhönjung*, which signifies 'the way the Law was born', i.e. how it was revealed in India and how it subsequently spread in Tibet and elsewhere. They tell of the lives of saints and teachers, the foundation of monasteries, their rivalries, and the age-long struggles for economic and political supremacy, growing more and more intense.

We have already mentioned Gerapsel and his successors. The 'second introduction' of Buddhism, as Tibetan historians call it, was also the work of two other men, a Tibetan and an Indian. The one was Rinchen-sangpo (958-1055) who was born in western Tibet; the other was Atīśa (982-1054), one of the luminaries of the monastery of Nālandā. The former went to study in Kashmir, whence he returned full of wisdom and loaded with manuscripts. That Buddhism should have been revived through the influence of Kashmir is easily accounted for. Commercial relations between the two countries had never been interrupted; and Buddhism, as well as flourishing in its own right in Kashmir, had left far from negligible traces on Hindu thought. It was natural that the King of Gugé, as western Tibet was called, should turn to the Kashmiris to give new life to his faith; and in Kashmir the exuberance of certain Shaivite schools threatened inauspicious times for the Buddhist community, already showing signs of decadence, and encouraged the exodus of teachers to more hospitable countries.

Atīśa, on the other hand, was a Bengali, and had been invited to western Tibet by king Changchup-ö. He brought dialectical experience acquired in the great Buddhist university of Nālanda, and at the same time that proficiency in Tantric liturgy on which the Tibetans were especially keen. After a stay in western Tibet, which Rinchen-sangpo had strewn with temples—that of Toling is particularly famous—Atīśa moved on to central Tibet, where he had many pupils, and died in the monastery of Netang, not far from Lhasa.

It is proper to insert these marks on the revival of Buddhism in a chapter devoted to history because the expansion of Buddhism and the diffusion of religious communities caused a considerable alteration in the country's social structure. It was some centuries before the great monasteries acquired their maximum power. At first, small communities gathered around a shrine, a *lha khang* of modest proportions, like those still found scattered over western Tibet—or even central Tibet, though there are fewer there because they were either destroyed during the many wars or enlarged and modernized from time to time on account of their fame.

So for a long time Tibet remained fragmented. It was not until the Mongol invasion that the chiefs joined in council to decide with one accord how to behave in the face of danger; a sort of *quriltai* or *jirga* then charged a layman and a monk to treat with the new power that had appeared on the Tibetan borders.

9. General view of Leh, showing the Castle of the Ladakh Kings.

Slowly but steadily, the building of the great monasteries began. The retreats

9

10

11

where ascetics and teachers of great prestige had lived or meditated were enlarged; the teachers and their lay helpers formed a symbiosis. Whilst the former, famed for their spirituality, attracted disciples and pilgrims, the latter were at their side laying the foundations of future political power. Shalu, which was to be famous for the great encyclopaedic scholar, Putön, was founded in 1040, Sakya in 1073, Thil in 1158, Drigung in 1179, Tshê in 1175, Tshurphu in 1189: these are only some of the early instances of this temporal power built upon religious prestige.

These names appear from now on among the major centres of the spiritual and cultural life of Tibet, but above all as determining factors in Tibet's political history, which in this new phase begins with the name of the Sakya-pa and their adversaries, the Drigung-pa, and ends with that of the Phagmotru-pa, after which the institution of the Dalai Lamas was finally confirmed.

Power brought an economic and military structure as its consequence: the monasteries owned large land-holdings, had their own armed men, and waged war among themselves. New political groupings centring on these institutions consequently took shape. The authority of religion and the power of the monasteries led the laymen to link their own fate with the latter's fortunes. They became patrons of the great abbatial institutions in name, but in fact depended on or were controlled by them.

Even though power later returned to laymen, such as the kings of Tsang and Neudong, they still had to reckon with that of the monasteries they were connected with. The Phagmotru-pa family, which reigned at Neudong, entrusted religious authority to the abbots and political authority to laymen, but they all belonged to the one family. Often power was centred in one and the same person, the king-abbot, but this solution did not eliminate the family's internal struggles: it encouraged them.

The fact remains that when the Mongol Empire arose, after Genghis Khan's conquest of the Hsi Hsia kingdom, and threatened to swallow Tibet (he probably made a foray into Ü in 1206 or 1207), the first authorities with whom the Mongols dealt were the heads of monasteries. These sought the protection of one or other of the various Mongol princes, who were not always in agreement among themselves. The Karma-pas (of Tshurphu), Sakya-pas and Drigung-pas all tried to ingratiate themselves with the powerful dynasty. Khubilai, after some hesitation, showed an unmistakeable sympathy for Buddhism and in the end chose the Sakya-pas as his protégés. The Drigung-pas put their trust in Hulagu, but their monastery was burnt by the Mongols led by Khubilai's son (1290). So at first only the Sakya-pas emerged victorious from this rivalry between contending monasteries and princes at the Mongol court. In order to establish some divisions in the course of Tibetan history for convenience's sake, we shall call this the Sakya-pa period, beginning with Khubilai's concession of the title of *Ti-shih* to Phakpa ('Phags pa, 1235-80), and ending in 1350 when power was assumed by the Phagmotru-pa, Changchup-gyentsen. Tibetan sources speak of missionary activity by the Sakya-pas, of course, but in reality Tibet was having to cope with a political situation brought about by Mongol expansion. With Phakpa who, as a small child, had followed his grandfather Sakya Penchen (1182-1251) when the latter visited Godan, the relations between Tibet and the Mongols are clearly defined. The youthful Phakpa initiated Khubilai into the mysteries of a famous Tantric cycle, the *Hevajra*, became imperial religious tutor (*Ti-shih*), contributed to the growth of Buddhism in the Yüan court and received the investiture over the three districts (*chhölka*) into which Tibet had been divided. But the emperor set limits to this investiture by nominating the *Pönchen*, Tibetan dignitaries with mainly military responsibilities who were accountable to appropriate offices at the Chinese court. The

10. Itinerant monks playing religious music on a large drum, and cymbals; others with long trumpets and small horns.

11. Peasants in Western Tibet.

33

latter had meanwhile made arrangements for taking a census of Tibet and subdividing it into thirteen *Trhikor*, myriarchies, reviving a division at once territorial and military and a terminology already favoured in the days of the ancient dynasty. The Mongols proclaimed themselves 'patrons' of the Sakya-pas: the latter in turn were their chaplains, and by reason of this office were invested with temporal authority over Tibetan territory. Thus began the supremacy of China over Tibet; but Tibetan autonomy remained and was respected.

The myriarchies coincided with the territories owned or controlled by the families or hierarchs who had risen by now to the top flight of the country's political life. All China did was to grant an investiture which confirmed an existing state of affairs, ratified by an imperial decree.

This situation encouraged dissensions, because the greater monasteries during the Yüan period (with Sakya and Drigung the most powerful) vied among themselves for supremacy. The secular arm of the Sakya-pas consisted, in theory, of the Pönchens appointed by the Mongols; among the Drigung-pas the Gomchens discharged this office. After Drigung was burnt down in 1290 the Sakya-pas retained the primacy for a short while, but the loyalty of the Pönchens towards them began to weaken when the Mongol Empire first showed signs of collapse, and the new power of the Phagmotru-pas was asserted. It was centred on the monastery of Densa-thil, which a great Kagyü-pa ascetic had chosen as his abode and later on the monastery of Tsethang on the south bank of the Tsangpo.

The founder of the Phagmotru power was Changchup-gyentsen (1302-73), who rebelled against the Sakya-pa hegemony and after many vicissitudes—both fighting, intriguing and profiting from the double dealing of certain Pönchens, as well as from the decline of the Yüan dynasty—succeeded in overcoming the Sakya-pas and taking their place. Thereupon the Phagmotru-pas too were granted investiture by the Chinese. Their power steadily grew after this, while the Sakya-pas lost their political authority for good, although retaining influence in western Tibet and at Dergé.

The clash between Sakya-pa and Phagmotru-pa was not merely the result of the ambition of a proud and able prince like Changchup-gyentsen; really there were other causes of equal importance at work. First and foremost, it was the conscious expression of a conflict already latent between Ü and Tsang. Ü—which means 'centre' — with Lhasa as capital, had never forgotten that it was the starting-point of the expeditions which had unified Tibet, extending Tibetan power to the heart of Asia and elsewhere. When we speak of Ü we mean a much larger area than the traditional territorial division. The name is used to include the surrounding lands which came under its influence: such as the monastery of Samyê, which had been the cradle of Buddhism; and Yarlung, where lay the tombs of the Tibetan kings who had started out from there to conquer their empire. Tsang was more on the fringe, almost a border region where even the dialect differed from the *lingua franca* of central Tibet. But it must not be supposed that the history of Tibet from the fourteenth century onwards boils down to this opposition alone. Around this age-old rivalry struggles flared up between the various powerful families, not to speak of the great monasteries. The latter, profiting from the prestige they enjoyed with the nobility, skilfully exploited the situation, inciting disputes and alliances. In consequence Tibet became for nearly two centuries the field of continual struggles between opposing factions. The conflicts became sharper and the situation more complex when the Phagmotru-pas invested a number of families from their own domains with the title and office of *dzongpön*, or prefect. Since such titles passed from father to son, a new aristocracy was created.

12. The staircase in the Potala Palace, Lhasa.

34

These men, too, soon entered the theatre of intrigue and conflict, with energy which was in proportion to the size of their lands and forces, or their individual daring; and, in fact, the administrative system of Tibet imposed by the Mongols was undermined by their activities. With the fall of the Mongol dynasty Chinese authority was limited to the nominal conferment, or the confirmation, of diplomas and titles and Tibet enjoyed effective independence; but peace and unity were far from being recovered.

The vigorous attempt to re-unite Tibet in this fourth, Phagmotru-pa, period of Tibetan history failed, therefore, because of the revival of the conflicts and opposing interests of the nobility and of the more independent monasteries. Talung, Öka, Nel, Cha (Bya), Gyantsé, Penam, Yargyap, Chonggyê, Drigung, Rinpung, Samdruptsé, are the names that constantly appear in this period of struggles. At length the hegemony of Phagmotru, which was under constant threat, gradually declined, while the chiefs of Rinpung, formerly their powerful vassals and allies, grew in strength and in the end allied themselves with Tsang, where a dynasty supported by the Karma-pas had become established. This sect, a subdivision of the Kagyü-pa (bKa' brgyud pa) school, consisted of two groups, the 'black-hats' and the 'red-hats'. The branch in Tsang was especially widespread, and not only asserted the autonomy of this part of Tibet but also stubbornly resisted the Phagmotru power and set their sights on Lhasa, which in fact was controlled by them for some time. Political rivalry, in a country where the monasteries and religious communities had acquired such wide spiritual and economic power, led necessarily to a clash between the sects, with the 'red-hats'—the Karma-pas or other Kagyü-pa sects, and their allies, the 'ancients' (Nyingma-pa)—lining up against the 'yellow-hats', a new sect that had quickly received widespread recognition. This 'yellow-hatted' school, also called the Geluk-pa, had been founded by Tsongkha-pa (1357-1419). Tracing his spiritual, doctrinal and liturgical inspiration back to Atīśa and his successors the Kadam-pas, Tsongkha-pa brought in strict discipline, and drew up two famous syntheses of Buddhism, the Lam-rim and the Ngag-rim. The school he founded was instantly successful. It gained the upper hand by virtue of a more centralized organization than that of the other sects, in which every monastery enjoyed a broad autonomy, its ties with other houses of the same school being strong only on the level of doctrine and theory. The other sects were therefore unable to oppose with united resistance the rise of the new sect. The spread of its monasteries bears witness to the interest it immediately aroused: Ganden was founded in 1409, Sera in 1419, Trashi-lhünpo in 1447 (cf. pls. 3, 46).

Meanwhile the pre-eminence of religious authority over the lay nobility was growing ever more pronounced due to the peculiar psychological set-up in which, with every human activity subordinated to the religious one, the monastic community reigned supreme through its power to mediate between present and future. The monasteries made the most of this state of affairs, and since religion particularly esteemed the merits procured by donations to the religious houses, the subjection of the lay to the monastic world was theoretically and morally justified. But even the 'yellow' sect had to seek out a secular champion, which it found in the Phagmotru-pas who, although they soon showed signs of collapse because of the conflicts between different branches of their own family—the abbots and the 'rulers'—and of the opposition of their dependants, represented nonetheless the highest authority in central Tibet.

For more than a century there was uninterrupted guerilla warfare that not only set Ü against Tsang but also implicated the principal fiefs, vacillating in their loyalties, who changed sides according to the fortunes of war. The nobility entered the fray as the tools of the monasteries and their claims. The opposing forces eventually pola-

13. Dancer wearing mask of a wrathful deity.

rized into two groups: one in central Tibet, headed by the Phagmotru-pas, and the other, in Tsang, gathered round the lords, of Samdruptsé, not far from Shigatsé. The former increasingly supported the 'yellow' sect, the latter backed non-'yellow' schools in general.

For a century it is very difficult to follow the complicated course of these struggles. The chronicles make them appear fortuitous by recording merely the simple facts and failing to explain the motives behind them, but they were actually due to the complex causes just mentioned. For much of this period Lhasa occupied a secondary position: it was a great religious centre, studded with temples attributed to the times of Songtsen-gampo, and it lived on its ancient glories. But in reality the seats of power were Tsetang and Neudong on the one side, Rinpung and Samdruptsé on the other.

In 1621 the breaking point was reached. Two successive heads of Rinpung in fact controlled Ü and the now waning Phagmotru: but the Rinpung-pas were allies of Tsang, where generals from Kham were in command with troops of their own. These lived in tented encampments and hence were called *garpa*, 'those of the camp'. The chiefs themselves usually went by this general name Garpa.

The kings of Tsang, whom Tibetan chronicles seek to leave in the shade, were about to get the upper hand. The Phagmotru-pas could not sustain the weight of the struggle on their own. The restless nobility sided now with one, now with the other of the contestants, seeking to turn the situation to its own advantage. The sects were directly implicated: the conflict between 'reds' and 'yellows' became so fierce that it was not allayed even when the Phagmotru-pas and their adversaries reached an agreement or called a truce. Indeed the warring princes went so far in the event of victory as to command the monks of the defeated region to change their hat. i.e. to change sect. As we should expect in a country so saturated with belief in magic, sometimes not only wars, but warlocks, were resorted to in the belief that one could worst the enemy by using spells to summon the aid of occult forces. Thus, for instance, a general's death in the war between Drigung and Phagmotru was attributed to the magical powers, *thu* (*spelt mthu*), of a famous exorcist. But there are also frequent records of Lamas who made use of their spiritual authority to try and soothe angry feelings and persuade the contending parties to lay down their arms.

At this very critical moment appeared one of Tibet's greatest figures, Lopsang-gyatso, the fifth Dalai Lama. He was born in 1617 on the eastern borders of Tsang (cf. pl. 5), of a family that had traditional ties with the Sakya-pas and also with the Nyingma-pas. As well as a scholar and thinker, he was a politician of the greatest acumen. He realized the gravity of the situation and the dangers that faced the Geluk-pas themselves. But the decision he took was pregnant with consequences: he called on the aid of the Khoshots, a branch of the Mongols among whom Lamaism had penetrated at the time of Sönam-gyatso (1543-88), the third Dalai Lama.

The Mongols had in fact appeared once more on the political horizon. After earlier Karma-pa approaches, the Geluk-pas, finding themselves continually threatened in Tsang, not knowing what forces they could rely on inside a country rent by internecine wars, sought the aid of the Mongols in the hope of renewing the understanding that had been established between the latter and Tibet during the Sakya-pa period. However, there was an appreciable difference between the old times and the new. Mongol unity was no longer what it had been, and the Khoshots found themselves opposed by a powerful China, which in Yüan times the Mongols had dominated. In 1578, Sönam-gyatso, abbot of Drêpung, had a meeting with Altan Khan of the Tümeds. His mission was successful; above all, the Mongol court showed itself sympathetic to Lamaism.

14. Tibetan thanka, showing the 'tree' of spiritual masters through whom teaching is transmitted. In the centre is Dorje-chhang holding a bell in his left hand and the *dorje* in his right hand.

From that moment Buddhism began to expand among the Mongols. Sönam-gyatso
had obtained an edict from Altan Khan abolishing animal sacrifices; on its side,
Lamaism closed its eyes to a number of practices and beliefs not entirely consonant
with its principles, but too rooted in popular custom to be suppressed. It accepted
these—as it had so often during its diffusion—and gave them a Buddhist colouring;
with the result that Genghis Khan and even some Shaman deities came to be included
in the Lamaist pantheon. The abbot Sönam-gyatso received the title of *Dalai* and
became the third Dalai Lama, thus *a posteriori* exalting to the same dignity Gedün-trup
(1391-1475) and Gedün-gyatso (1475-1542). But this meeting, and the consequent
prestige that the 'yellow' sect acquired with the Mongols, could not but have repercussions in Tibet. First and foremost, the Mongols sought to exploit the situation
politically, abetted by the selfsame Geluk-pas, who saw the guarantee of their own
success in closer ties with the Mongols. When Sönam-gyatso died, his reincarnation
was looked for among the Mongols: the fourth Dalai Lama, Yönten-gyatso (1589-
1617), was a great-grandson of Altan Khan. Duly recognized, he was installed upon
the abbot's throne of Drêpung. Thus the Geluk-pas had linked their destiny still
more with the Mongols. But the latter, as we have said, were no longer a single political unit: the Karma-pas and Tsang found an ally in Ligden Khan of the Chahars,
which was no great gain to them, however, since he was killed by Gushri Khan of
the Khoshots, before he could be any real help.

So Tibet implicated foreign powers in her own struggles and was accordingly involved in the rivalries that were breaking down Mongol unity, at a time when China
was beginning to watch with suspicion the restlessness of the Mongol tribes that might
threaten her frontiers.

The fifth Dalai Lama, Lopsang-gyatso (1617-82), had called in Gushri Khan to
put an end to the long conflict and get the better of his powerful adversaries, Tsang
and the Karma-pas. The king of Tsang was killed in battle in 1642. As Khubilai
had done earlier, Gushri Khan offered Tibet to the fifth Dalai Lama, but he imposed
a regent (*desi*) as his representative. However, Lopsang-gyatso soon changed the
situation in his favour and elected in 1679 as regent Sangyê-gyatso, his spiritual son.
And so begins the last period of Tibetan history, which coincides with the rule of the
Dalai Lamas and the reunification of Tibet.

His enemies were thus out of the way, and the country once more united—and
considerably enlarged for, after the peace of 1683, Tibet had conquered much of
Ngari (western Tibet: Gugé, Purang and Ruthok), taking away from the kings of
Ladakh much land which they had possessed since the time of Senggé-namgyel (died
1645). Lopsang-gyatso now set about reordering the state and its finances, which
long dissensions had bled white. Many convents of the rival sects were expropriated
and turned over to the 'yellow' sect, a new census was taken, penal laws were pro-
mulgated, trade prospered. Under his patronage cultural relations with India were
renewed. The Governor of Bengal, a son of Shah Jahan, sent a mission to Tibet in
1751-3. The translation of some Sanskrit grammatical texts was undertaken again,
and the Dalai Lama himself went to China.

The death of the fifth Dalai Lama, concealed for some time by the regent, led to
a critical situation. The choice of the new incarnation was not happy: the sixth Dalai
Lama, Tshangyang-gyatso (1682-1705), had profane rather than religious inclinations. He loved a carefree life, songs, and girls, and many love poems are attributed
to him. Moreover, this choice made by the regent came at a particularly difficult
moment: the Khoshot Mongols were confronted by powerful rivals, the Dzungars,

15. Detail from a Tibetan thanka,
the religious teacher Mar-pa
(Master of Mila-rêpa).

41

with their king, Galdan, who dominated the Ili region and were hostile to China. The Khoshot king, Lajang Khan, had allied himself with China to the detriment of his rival. The regent, Sanggyê-gyatso, left in sole charge of Tibet, unpopular and not so shrewd as the fifth Dalai Lama, made a mistake: he sided with the Dzungars. This made his position still more difficult because he now incurred the enmity of the Mongol tribes, who had supported the fifth Dalai Lama, and thus of their allies the Chinese.

China could not remain indifferent: rather than intervene directly, K'ang Hsi (1661-1722) for a time left Lajang Khan to act on his own account. Lajang invaded Tibet, killed the regent, burnt many monasteries and took away with him the sixth Dalai Lama, who died during the journey—not, it was rumoured, a natural death. The fact was in itself of exceptional gravity since the Dalai Lama's person is hedged with divinity: he represents the earthly incarnation of Chenrêsik, the compassionate Bodhisattva, patron of Tibet.

A crisis arose that brought faction into the heart of the very sect that the fifth Dalai Lama and the regent had laboriously steered to hegemony. This weakness deprived Tibet, at a delicate moment, of the sole authority that could rally the people. Lajang Khan went even further: he occupied Lhasa, ordered the assassination of Sanggyê-gyatso (1705) and proclaimed a new Dalai Lama who was put forward as the incarnation of Lopsang-gyatso. This alleged incarnation was a monk of twenty-five who was said to be Lajang's natural son. The political character of this choice and its peremptory imposition in violation of customary practice upset the Tibetans deeply and united them in opposition: if they had given in the very foundation of their faith would have collapsed. It was not merely a political question, but above all a religious reality: the Dalai Lama, for the reasons already given, cannot be selected without taking account of those unshakeable spiritual beliefs. The choice of the new Dalai Lama on the death of his predecessor is made with great shrewdness and care, though it does not rule out the possibility of favouring an apt candidate by discreet manoeuvring, provided no worldly concern is too apparent, and above all no offence is given to the holiness of the person whom everyone recognizes not as a human being but as a divine incarnation. For this reason Tibet rebelled against Lajang Khan's unfortunate choice, and turned to the Dzungars. Lajang Khan was killed in battle (1717), whilst the Tibetans discovered the reincarnation of Tshangyang-gyatso (1682-1705) at Lithang in a boy born shortly after his death.

China was prompt to act: she took the new incarnation into her own custody, but the Dzungars entered Tibet announcing that they would bring the Dalai Lama with them. The Tibetans, thinking they had been cheated when the Dzungars arrived without the Dalai Lama, rose in revolt; the Dzungars at first resisted the Chinese armies but were finally defeated in 1720. Having got rid of the two pretenders to the title, however nominal, of king of Tibet, K'ang Hsi had the seventh Dalai Lama, Kelsang-gyatso (1708-57), escorted by his troops to Lhasa. The Tibet-China road was controlled by Chinese soldiers; the Chinese garrison took up quarters at Lhasa; the walls of Lhasa were pulled down; and the province of Kham was incorporated in Szechuan. Though surrounded with the highest formal honour as head of the church, the Dalai Lama was no longer free. Effective power threatened to pass into the hands of lay and monastic ministers controlled by a Chinese delegate, who was vigilantly protected by his own garrison. Tibet was formally deprived of its autonomy, a situation that had never arisen before, even in the days of the Mongols. But the rule of the fifth Dalai Lama was still fresh in the minds of the Tibetans and their native spirit

16. A terracotta mask, representing a divinity in a fearful aspect.

of independence refused to accept the new situation. They were determined to restore the old independence. In 1727 the regent, *persona grata* to the Chinese, was killed through the intrigue of two *Kalöns* and with the probable connivance of the father and confidants of the Dalai Lama himself; the latter was brought to East Tibet (Ka-ta) on the pretext of an invasion to Peking, and remained confined there till 1734.

The Chinese troops, which had been withdrawn, returned. Pholanê Têji, right-hand man of the Chinese and one of the ablest figures of Tibet's political history, took charge of the situation. But this was henceforth under China's control. China would not have allowed a return to the *status quo*, and did not fail to profit from Tibet's political instability. The attempted insurrection of Pholanê Têji's son, who started a conspiracy against the Chinese after securing the recall of half of their garrison, came to nothing. He was killed by two Chinese delegates who defended Chinese supremacy with their own lives.

These insurrections and plots were fated to bring about what they had been intended to prevent. The office of regent was abolished in 1720. When the term 'regent' is used after this, it no longer refers to a layman, but to a monk who exercises the functions of head of state until the Dalai Lama comes of age.

The two highest ecclesiastic dignitaries of Tibet, whose rivalry, not to say outright opposition, became more and more pronounced during the last years of independence, offering the Chinese a pretext for intervention in Tibetan politics, resided in two different parts of the country: one at Lhasa—in the Potala, from the fifth Dalai Lama onwards—the other in the Trashi-lhünpo monastery in Tsang, close to Shigatsé. The name of this monastery accounts for the 'Tashi' or 'Teshoo Lama' of the travellers (cf. pl. 3): the more exact title is *Pan-chen* (pron. *penchen*), a Sanskrit-Tibetan hybrid term, signifying 'the great (*chen*) pandita', 'the great teacher', to indicate the vast theological and liturgical learning for which he is distinguished. Now the Panchen Lamas too are considered incarnations; that is, they embody on earth the divine presence of Tshepamé, the god of 'infinite life' (cf. pl. 84), whilst the Dalai Lama is the incarnation of Tibet's patron Chenrêsik. There exists a close link between these two beings: the first is one of the five Buddhas of the supreme pentad, the second is a Bodhisattva emanating from him. In paintings, in fact, he is represented with images of Tshepamé at the top of his head to denote the mystical connection between the two. The theory of the incarnation of the Panchen Lamas was instituted by the fifth Dalai Lama on the basis of a revealed tradition, to exalt the position of Lopsang-Chhökyi-gyentsen (1570-1662), whom it put fourth in the line, by starting the series of incarnations with Khê-trup. After the death of the fifth Dalai Lama and the events that followed, the peace he had succeeded in maintaining between Ü and Tsang began to weaken, so that, from force of circumstance, the Panchen Lama often found himself needing to act with complete independence. Besides this, the eighth to twelfth Dalai Lamas died very young and so had no time or opportunity to stand up against the long-lived and learned Panchen Lamas. All these facts often induced Trashi-lhünpo to follow an independent policy. This happened, for instance, after the Bhutanese incursions into Cooch Behar and the subsequent British military actions, which provoked a very restrained and moderate protest from the Panchen Lama to Warren Hastings. The latter seized the opportunity of dispatching to Trashi-lhünpo (1774-5) George Bogle, author of a delightful account of his adventures and a fascinating description of Tibet in those days. In this affair the Panchen Lama acted as a skilful intermediary. This was the first political contact between Tibet and Great Britain. At the same time Chinese diplomacy, faithful to its traditions, accentuated its tendency to

17. Detail from a Tibetan mandala thanka, representing the Vajradhātu-mandala.

45

divide the forces in the countries it controlled by setting one off against the other, so that there was less chance of their making a bid for independence. Thus circumstances combined to strengthen the antagonism between Trashi-lhünpo and Lhasa until a break took place in the time of the eighth Dalai Lama.

Bogle's mission is not the sole instance of the presence of Europeans in Tibet. Although Odorico da Pordenone (thirteenth century) mentions the country it seems certain that he did not set foot there; and even Marco Polo speaks of it only from hearsay. The hope of finding Christian communities surviving in the heart of Asia had indeed led Fr. Antonio d'Andrade to set out from Goa and cross the Himalayas in pursuit of his dream. He reached Tsaparang, capital of western Tibet, in 1624, and founded a mission, but its life was short, for the kingdom of Gugé was about to fall.

The attemps to renew the mission, made by Coresma and especially by Malpichi and De Azevedo, had no success; and after traversing, already late in the season, the road from Tsaparang to Leh and then from Leh across the Baralacha to Mandi and Lahore, it only remained for De Azevedo to report to his superiors the collapse of all their hopes. Almost at the same time two other Jesuits, Estavão Cacella and João Cabral, setting out in 1626 from Bengal, entered Tibet through Bhutan and reached Shigatsé, where they were received with favour by the king. The rigid organization of the monasteries, the dialectical skill of the monks, the theological subtleties of the teachers and the austerity of many rites of Tibetan Buddhism impressed them; they kept in touch with the Tsaparang mission through the irregular medium of the caravans, and twice returned to India, trying out new routes that were later to be followed by the Capuchins. But Cacella's death in 1632 put an end to this enterprise too.

In 1661 two other Jesuits, Grüber and D'Orville, entered Tibet and stayed in Lhasa for some weeks. Then in 1707 began the mission of the Capuchins among whom must be mentioned Domenico da Fano and Orazio della Penna, who left several interesting letters, and Beligatti, who wrote an important book on Tibetan customs. But in 1716, after a long journey beginning at Leh, there arrived in Lhasa Ippolito Desideri, author of one of the most interesting books on Tibet and certainly one of the most profound exponents of Lamaist thought. With him Tibetan philology was born. When he was recalled his mission was taken over by the Capuchins, whose officious zeal prevented them from winning the sympathies of the Tibetans; in 1745 the mission was closed.

Of the journey of a Dutchman, Samuel van der Putte, who went from India to China and back (1725-35), staying some time in Tibet, details are not known, for he wrote no account of his travels; unlike Huc and Gabet, who left a lively description of their journeyings. These few travellers, succeeding one another on the Roof of the World with various aims, may have helped to make Tibet better known in the West, but it cannot be said that Tibet itself gained any cultural advantages from their visits. Their stay was too short and their habits of mind, spiritual outlook and intellectual interests were too different for anything lasting to result from these encounters.

But to return to the course of events. The horizon, having cleared to the north, began to darken on the south. After the short-lived Bhutanese episode, a threat of greater dimensions loomed in Nepal. This country had been a good neighbour of Tibet, trading freely with it, and Nepalese teachers and craftsmen were welcomed in Tibet, but in 1769 it had been conquered by the Gurkhas, orthodox Hindus led by the able but unscrupulous Prithivi Narayan. The good relations with Tibet which had lasted for centuries, now deteriorated because of territorial and monetary considerations and, principally, because the wealth of the Tibetan monasteries tempted the new masters of Nepal. In 1788 Tibet was invaded and some frontier districts were occupied. The Tibetan and Chinese commanders, in agreement with a Tibetan minister, came to terms and, promising the payment of tribute, persuaded the Gurkhas to turn back. It was an arbitrary agreement which the Chinese delegates at Lhasa presented to the Emperor, in a report that twisted the facts, as a success. The Dalai Lama was against the agreement; the second instalment of the tribute was not paid. Immediately the Gurkhas entered Tibet a second time, with strong forces. Shigatsé was sacked, the monasteries that the Gurkhas encountered on their way suffered the same fate, and many precious examples of ancient Tibetan art were destroyed. The facts could no longer be kept hidden from the Chinese court. The Emperor was quick to intervene for two reasons: first, to re-establish his own prestige; secondly, because the second Gurkha expedition was not due solely to the euphoria after the military successes begun by Prithivi Narayan, but had in fact been pressed for by the sects hostile to the Geluk-pas (above all by the eighth 'black-hat' Karma-pa), and by certain centres in Tsang where, notwithstanding the policy of the fifth Dalai Lama and the vigorous steps he had taken, neither the old rancour nor the vain hope of recovering lost power were dead. The leaders of these dissident centres in Tsang, no longer able to count on their own forces, followed the fifth Dalai Lama's example and sought to engage foreign aid. China was faced, therefore, not only with an external threat, but also with a hotbed of resistance and discord in the interior. The imperial court organized a great military expedition which brought Chinese troops to the very heart of Nepal. When they had almost reached Kathmandu the Gurkhas sued for peace which was agreed on in 1792. The payment of a quinquennial sum was imposed on the Nepalese, according to the terms of a treaty that was carved on a stele at Lhasa —an ancient custom. These events had serious repercussions for Tibet: the power of the Chinese representatives at Lhasa was increased, and the Lhasa government became a shadow government carrying out the orders of Peking. China interfered still more in the choice of the various incarnations, so as to be able to keep a check on the internal situation and the moods of the monasteries. From the death of Jampel-gyatso in 1804 to that of the twelfth Dalai Lama in 1875, four Dalai Lamas succeeded one another. The longest-lived was the tenth, who died at the age of twenty-two. The country withdrew into ever-deeper isolation and fossilized under the leadership of the rigid monastic hierarchy: this was now subject to foreign supervision, but at the same time jealously guarded ancient tradition and was reluctant to admit change of any sort. The Chinese presence was felt as a burden, but not everywhere in equal proportion, at Trashi-lhünpo perhaps less than at Lhasa. Deprived now of the hope of showing or giving practical effect to their dislike of Chinese rule, the malcontents resorted to the old custom of the pretended discovery of concealed texts (*terma*) and circulated *lungten*, apocryphal prophesies attributed to Padmasambhava (eighth century), which were said to have been discovered by chance. These works traced the history of Tibet in prophetic form, and foretold that she would fall under the subjection of China. The torments of this subjection were listed, but it was predicted that in the end Tibet would cast off the yoke for ever and regain her lost liberty.

After this period of enforced stagnation came the thirteenth Dalai Lama, Thupten-gyatso (1876-1933), who is undoubtedly, with his predecessor Lopsang-gyatso, the fifth, the most considerable figure of the whole line.

Despite China's ultra-conservative policy at this time, Tibet slowly drifted into the stream of events which in a few years were to alter the face of Asia. The thirteenth Dalai Lama found himself caught up in the current. Energetic, and of a political shrewdness that grew with age and experience, he ruled Tibet at one of the gravest moments in her history, and saw the fulfilment, albeit briefly, of the prophecies mentioned above. Having come during his youth under the influence of a Buryat monk, Dorjé (Dordjieff), his initial leanings towards Russia were evident; he even accepted the Tsar's invitation to make an official visit.

It was a moment of the greatest tension between Russia and Britain, each intent on extending and consolidating its influence in Asia. Britain was anxious to protect the safety of her Indian possessions; Russia, which numbered among her subjects a large number of Lamaists, sought to include Tibet in her sphere of influence. The announcement of the Dalai Lama's visit to Russia, and the fear of a possible agreement between the head of Tibetan Buddhism and the Russian Emperor, led Britain to request explanations and to arrange to send a mission to Tibet to regulate trade relations with India. Since through continual temporizing no agreement had been reached, a British expeditionary force charged with escorting the mission commanded by Colonel Younghusband entered Tibet in 1904 and reached Lhasa in August of the same year. The foreigner trod the soil of the Holy City in spite of the protection of the gods and the lamas' exorcisms. The Dalai Lama fled to Urga. The road between India and Tibet was opened for the first time, the Sikkim-Tibet frontier was demarcated, and trade agencies were opened with Residents at Gyantsé, Yatung in the Chumbi valley and Gartok in western Tibet, on the understanding that Tibet was to be kept free of all foreign political influence. However, the agreement was signed only by the Tibetan authorities and not by the representative of the Chinese government. But London, to avoid damaging its relations with Russia, largely nullified the aims and results of Lord Curzon's policy and the Younghusband Mission, by declaring in the Anglo-Russian Convention of 1907 that the British would only negotiate with Tibet through China. What seemed most important at that moment was in fact the Central Asian policy of the two giants, and the creation of a buffer state between them.

The Dalai Lama's flight to Urga had surprised the Chinese court, which deposed him. But this measure angered the Tibetans who would not suffer foreign interference in a matter of divine authority. Whilst relations between Tibet and China thus grew more tense, the myth of Tibet's inaccessibility had also been exploded. The belt of mountains that protected it presented no obstacle to a well-equipped army and China no longer felt so safe on her western frontiers. The military steps taken to reestablish the influence over Tibet shaken by these events were inopportune; they provoked revolts (in 1905 and 1908) which were paid for dearly. Chinese repressive measures were extremely harsh, but did not succeed in quelling the discontent; in fact, they inflamed it. China was forced to recognize that she could not put down the Dalai Lamas. The thirteenth Dalai Lama was invited to Peking, where he was received with full honours, but not with all the solemn ceremony that the Sakya-pa hierarchs had once enjoyed. He was treated as a dependent ruler, though attended with special respect by reason of his religious dignity. In 1909, after the death of the Empress Tz'ŭ Hsi and her adopted son, at whose funerals he had presided in the previous year, the Dalai Lama returned to Lhasa. But in the intervening years the situation had changed a great deal. Tibet was coming more and more into the orbit of the conflicts sparked off by European policy in Asia. On one side were Russia and Britain, resolved to maintain the *status quo* from Afghanistan to Sinkiang and Tibet, and to profit from the weakness of the Ch'ing dynasty, now about to fall; on the other China, despite the clear signs of decay, refusing to renounce the prerogatives or position she had enjoyed in Central Asia for centuries. The Dalai Lama's return to Lhasa did not herald a

18. Gilt statuette of a lama in monastic robes; the lotuses at his side bear emblems of his spiritual status. The bell and the *dorje* are symbols of the two ways which, when they fuse, lead to salvation.

period of peace; soon after his arrival a revolt broke out in east Tibet and provoked a new intervention by China in 1910. The conflict between the Chinese court and the Dalai Lama was renewed. Thupten-gyatso fled once more before the advance of the Chinese troops but this time he did not seek refuge in Mongolia: pursued by the Chinese, and narrowly avoiding being taken prisoner, he took the road to the south and made for Kalimpong. Compared with a Russia whose symptoms of internal unrest were becoming obvious, or with an empire on the verge of collapse, Great Britain offered generous hospitality to the fugitive, who was determined at any cost, albeit with a certain amount of hesitation and vacillation, to carry out his own plan. From this moment, British prestige in Tibet grew: of the three contending powers, henceforth only Britain remained, and by maintaining a prudent detachment, she kept watch lest Tibet should be dragged into any of the storms that were gathering at her borders. She employed for this difficult task several excellent civil servants who showed great political ability and much sympathy for the Land of Snows. In 1912 Thupten-gyatso returned to Lhasa. The Ch'ing dynasty had fallen in 1911 and the Republic had been proclaimed. The Dalai Lama declared his independence and expelled the Chinese garrison. Tibet became autonomous once more, and the one country with which it kept up good-neighbourly relations was British India: Nepal alone was authorized to have its own ambassador in Lhasa. On the eastern margins the situation still remained fluid because of Chinese territorial claims and the warlike character of the people.

Republican China had officially declared Tibet a Chinese province, but could do nothing in this situation. She did not recognize Tibet's independence and did not renounce her own rights, but she took no action, aware that henceforth Britain was keeping an eye on Tibet and desired no change along the Himalayan frontiers. This state of affairs led to the Simla Conference of 1913 which divided Tibet into two parts —Inner Tibet (the far eastern provinces, bordering on China), and Outer Tibet— and sanctioned the *status quo* of Outer Tibet. The latter recognized China's nominal suzerainty, and China undertook not to interfere in her internal affairs. Since the Chinese, after endless evasions, refused to sign the agreement, the British declared officially that if China failed to ratify the Simla pacts, they would deal directly with the Tibetans in future. This in fact happened. Soon after, China wished to send a mission to Lhasa, but on one pretext or another Tibet parried the request. Only in 1934 was a delegation, laden with generous donations to the convents, admitted to the country to offer condolences on the death of the thirteenth Dalai Lama. But once there, it never went back: it had its residence not far from the bazaar, with a wireless transmitter and a large staff.

In the meantime, the tension between the Dalai Lama and the Panchen Lama had increased. The conflict between the two hierarchs, fomented by the Chinese, particu- larly in the time of the third and fourth Panchen Lamas, had led for various reasons to an increasingly pronounced administrative independence, which had, as we have seen, its precedents. The thirteenth Dalai Lama tried to put an end to this state of affairs, but met with much resistance from the sixth Panchen and, more particularly, from his retinue. The Chinese, exploiting the situation that had arisen in 1904 after the flight of the Dalai Lama, offered the Panchen Lama the post of regent, which, however he refused. This sharpened the conflicts between Lhasa and Trashi-lhünpo, which had come to a head after 1910, when the Dalai Lama took refuge in India and the Chinese renewed their pressure on the Panchen. After his return to Lhasa in 1913, the Dalai Lama asked Trashi-lhünpo to contribute to the upkeep of the army

19. Tibetan jewellery.
Left: ear pendants worn on the left ear only by lay state officials.
Right: ear pendants worn by ladies from Lhasa.
Centre: head ornament worn by officials and used for holding a knot of hair on top of the head.
Below right: chest ornament representing 'the wheel of the Law'.

711940
Cicero Public Library

but the request was refused. Then the situation grew still worse, and in 1923 the Panchen Lama, Gelek-namgyê, fled to China, where the greatest political profit was made from his request for asylum.

The thirteenth Dalai Lama died in 1933 and his reincarnation was officially discovered in 1935. Meanwhile, another incarnation, the abbot of Reting monastery, was appointed regent until the new Dalai Lama should reach an age to assume the responsibilities of government. This young and frivolous regent was dominated by an ambitious man, Lungshar, who for four months was the real master of Tibet. He was pro-Chinese and had a wild idea of making Tibet a republic ruled by the Assembly, which he meant to control, dismissing the Council of Ministers (Kashak). His aims were soon discovered, he was arrested, his eyes were put out, and he was cast into prison.

In the meantime, the Regent, Reting Rinpoché, inexperienced, mercenary and all too ready to listen to alluring offers, became increasingly unpopular. After the installation of the fourteenth Dalai Lama, which was achieved not without difficulty, in August 1939, he decided, in February 1941, to abdicate. In his place was elected the incarnate Lama of Taktra, an old man of 75 who represented orthodox views.

The retirement of the young Reting abbot so displeased his disciples and sympathizers that they conspired against his successor. But even in Tibet, it is hard to keep a secret. The plot was discovered and Reting, self-convicted before the Assembly of collusion with the Chinese, was shut up in prison and died there soon afterwards, almost certainly poisoned. But he was an incarnation, and an incarnation in Tibet is a saint; and saints, as is known, should be left alone. Not only his own supporters, but in particular the monks of the great foundation of Sera, north-east of Lhasa, which counted about six thousand inmates, habitually belligerent, revolted. Lhasa was in serious danger of being plundered either by the rebels or by the soldiers called by the regent, Taktra Rinpoché, to defend it. They were anxious days. The old abbot's firm hand got the better of the revolt, however, and the tension subsided for the time being. Meanwhile, outside her frontiers grave events had taken place and these Tibet could not ignore. The succession of the Panchen Lama was the cause of new friction between China and the Tibetan Government. Violating the principle that the final choice of the Panchen is a prerogative of the Dalai Lama (or, during the latter's minority, of the regent), the Chinese Central Executive Committee designated as the Panchen's reincarnation a boy born in Ch'ing Hai, chosen from among several who seemed to possess the necessary qualifications; it was decided to send him to Tibet under escort, taking advantage of the unsettled conditions there during Reting's regency. However, the official proclamation was made in 1949 on the eve of the Kuomintang's fall from power. The People's Republic of China henceforth had the successor to this high office under her control and could exploit him politically in her aggressive designs on Tibet.

In the recent past first Bhutan, then Nepal, and finally the Dogras who had thrust beyond Manasarowar under the command of Zarovar Singh, had faced Tibet with a problem which had been unknown since the time of the royal dynasty. Now the course of events dragged her ever more deeply into the complex and hard-fought politics of Asia. The situation had worsened during the Second World War, when a *rapprochement*, albeit momentary, between China and England in common defence against Japan had encouraged China to make pressing requests, always turned down by the Tibetan Assembly on some pretext or other, for internal roads in Tibet to be opened up. In 1947 India won her independence. In 1949 Chiang Kai-shek's China fell and Mao Tse-Tung's was born. In 1950 an army of the Chinese People's Republic crossed into Tibetan territory with the help of certain warlike Khampa tribes who, without being opposed to the Dalai Lama, could not brook the interference and financial trickery of the governors sent into eastern Tibet from Lhasa. The small Tibetan army was soon overrun. Chamdo was taken. Another Chinese army coming down from Khotan, across the Kun-lun, entered the cheerless and deserted region of north-western Tibet. The Nêchung oracle ordered that power should be assumed by the sixteen-year old Dalai Lama. India fruitlessly, and indeed feebly, protested against what she called an act of aggression, arousing the immediate reply from Peking that Tibet was an integral part of China, and the Tibetan question an internal matter. The protest which the Tibetan Government lodged with the United Nations in November 1950 went unheard. The Dalai Lama was then advised to leave Lhasa, because if he fell into the hands of the Chinese they would certainly make political capital from his spiritual authority. In December of the same year he made for the Indian border and took up residence at the monastery of Tungkar in Chumbi.

Meanwhile at Chamdo the first political meeting took place between Ngabö, ex-governor of Chamdo, who had been entrusted with the task of negotiating on behalf of Tibet, and the Chinese delegates. In 1951, a Tibetan delegation headed by Ngabö went to Peking. The Dalai Lama sent a cable to Mao Tse-tung promising his support for the pacification of Tibet and co-operation with China. In May 1951, the Sino-Tibetan Agreement on Measures for the Peaceful Liberation of Tibet was signed at Peking. It laid down the constitution of a regional government of Tibet and it affirmed that the Tibetan people had the right to exercise regional national autonomy under the leadership of the Central People's Government. The status and function of the Dalai and Panchen Lamas were confirmed and defined, and freedom of worship and noninterference with the country's traditions were promised; but the integration of the Tibetan army into that of China was agreed, as was the appointment of a Committee with military and administrative powers at Lhasa. In July 1952, the Dalai Lama received General Chang Ching-wa, Commissioner and Administrator of Civil and Military Affairs in Tibet, in the Chumbi Valley and, yielding to his pressure and that of some of his own advisers, he left Tungkar monastery, and returned to Lhasa. At the end of the year the Panchen Lama accompanied by a crowd of dignitaries, set out for Kumbum and took up his quarters in the monastery of Trashi-lhünpo.

Chinese soldiers were arriving in Tibet: three thousand were quartered in the capital and fifteen or twenty thousand in other parts of the country. A skilful job of organization began. The political power of the Panchen was built up to oppose that of the Dalai Lama. Though there was no interference in religious questions, efforts were made to end the financial activities of the monasteries. Certain traditions to which the Tibetans were very attached, such as placing Lhasa in the control of the monks during the New Year festival, were suppressed.

In 1954 both the Dalai and the Panchen Lamas were invited to China and in February 1955 celebrated the New Year festivities together there; on this occasion the Dalai Lama delivered a speech in which he thanked the Chinese Government for the benefits it had brought Tibet, and looked forward to an even better future. Meanwhile, the Chinese had begun putting a programme of modernization into effect: a big hospital was built at Lhasa and a large-scale health service was inaugurated, though a medical service had earlier been established at Lhasa, Gyantsé and Yatung with the help of the British. A branch of the People's Bank was opened to develop agricultural projects. But above all, arrangements were made to speed up the road system, from end to end of the country. The difficulties of the undertaking and the shortage of equipment were made up for by the employment of large gangs of labourers. China was soon joined to Lhasa by two roads, one to the south via Tachienlu and Chamdo, the other via Lanchou and Sining. On 25 December 1954, the first motor convoys reached Lhasa. Another road joined Lhasa with Shigatsé and yet another with Tsethang. The desert areas of west Tibet were joined with Sinkiang. A gigantic road network soon covered the country and replaced the slow rhythm of yak and mule-caravans with the swiftness of jeeps and lorries. Bridges spanned the rivers, tunnels bored through the mountains to avoid the high passes. A systematic investigation of the country's mineral wealth was undertaken and some mining began. Reviving old traditions of Chinese colonization in Central Asia, the soldiers stationed in Tibet taught the farmers more up-to-date and profitable means of cultivation. The impetus given to these tasks, together with the invitation of numerous Tibetans to China, the sending of young people to schools and universities, the foundation of modern schools in the towns and larger villages, the insistence on mass sports and other related projects were all designed to modify Tibet's economic and cultural structure; to train a new ruling class, nurtured on the ideological principles of the Chinese People's Republic along Chinese educational lines; and to destroy the social organization that had governed Tibet for centuries. The road network was not only a natural means of encouraging this social revolution but it was also a military necessity.

The reforms that were proposed or slowly carried out nonplussed the Tibetans. They are curious by nature and the Chinese themselves were fairly prudent and circumspect in the early years. Their cautious policy was further stressed when in 1956 the Dalai Lama and the Panchen, on the occasion of the anniversary of the Buddha's *Parinirvāna*, travelled to New Delhi, although the Chinese certainly made some attempt to prevent their going or get them sent back. Chou En-lai at once joined them there. The Dalai Lama seized the opportunity of making known to Nehru his resentment at the claims of the Chinese and his doubts about the future, but the Chinese declared that they would keep faith with the 1951 agreements, guaranteeing Tibetan regional autonomy and removing the hesitation that the Dalai Lama seems at first to have felt about his return to Lhasa.

The following year Mao Tse-tung himself declared that Tibet was not yet ripe for the reforms envisaged and that they must be postponed for some years. Some of the soldiers stationed in Tibet were recalled, as well as some of the officials in charge of the programme of reform.

The Dalai Lama therefore went back to Lhasa, but he found the situation quite as black as before: the disturbances in the eastern provinces, which a mission he had himself sent there in 1956 had sought in vain to settle, had grown fiercer. In a region where people are impulsive, independent and quick to fight, and where foreign agents were quite possibly operating, the clashes multiplied. Reprisals on both sides grew harsher. The monks, too, took an active part in the revolt, although the Chinese had begun to restore some of the monasteries they had bombarded. A guerilla conflict sprang up which gradually spread towards Lhasa. Here too the situation was tense: the Tibetans disliked the 'Preparatory Committee for the Autonomous Region of Tibet' which they saw as a scheme to limit the Dalai Lama's authority. The shortage of food and the increased cost of living, which they attributed to the presence of Chinese troops, added to their discontent and stiffened their opposition, which had already been encouraged by the presence of Khampa and Amdo guerillas and secret outside help.

The Chinese took the drastic step of expelling a large part of the male population

20. Pilgrims walking round a *chhörten* in the courtyard of a monastery.

21. *Chhörten* in the Yarlung Valley; in the background, ' *oṁ maṇi-padme hūṁ* ' cut in the hillside.

20

21

from the city, thus adding to the number of the insurgents, who succeeded in inflicting considerable losses on Chinese troops in the immediate neighbourhood of Lhasa. The Chinese garrison at Tsethang on the right bank of the Tangpo was routed, bridges were blown up, and guerilla attacks made communications as difficult as before. The Chinese tried to make the Dalai Lama responsible for putting an end to this state of affairs by asking him to send his soldiers against the rebels. The Dalai Lama clearly could not accept this proposal without prejudicing his position and damaging his religious prestige, which was recognized by the guerillas themselves; it was against the Chinese, not him, they had rebelled. Aware of his importance to their schemes, the Chinese tried to persuade him to go to China where they hoped to be able to make use of him for their own ends. They did not succeed. The situation had become explosive. The Dalai Lama took shelter in the Norbu-lingka and all the attempts of the Chinese Commander in Lhasa to lure him out were in vain. An emissary sent to treat with him was discovered and killed by the crowd outside. The members of his suite urged him to flee Tibet. Their uncertainty and his own, and the absence of any unanimous decision in the sudden grave emergency, are demonstrated by some letters that the Dalai Lama sent at this time to the Chinese authorities. They were subsequently pubblished by the Chinese and they make the perplexity of the Tibetan government all too clear. In the end, those in favour of flight prevailed. On the night of March 17 the Dalai Lama, quite unnoticed, left the Norbu-lingka with a following of a hundred and, ably protected by them, arrived at Tezpur in Assam on April 18.

News of the flight did not break for two days: but as soon as the Chinese were acquainted with it retaliation was swift. The Tibetan government was dissolved and a sort of military junta set up, composed of Chinese and pro-Chinese Tibetans. Of subsequent events it is hard to say much. In the official reports that seep out of China and in the accounts given by the Tibetan refugees who flocked in increasing numbers into India (there are now more than sixty thousand there) one does not always meet with objective assessments. It is known that the Chinese resorted to every available means to speed up and extend the process of ideological indoctrination, to undermine the religious feeling of the masses, which represented the most serious obstacle to their propaganda and reforms, and to change fundamentally the country's social and economic order. Though the reforms have been carried out fairly slowly and with some changes of plan—but more forcibly and ruthlessly after 1959—priority was certainly given to the drive against landed property and the nobility thriving on it, and against the power of the monasteries. On a likely estimate, 30% of the landed property belonged to the state, 40% to the monasteries, and the rest to the nobility. Usually, the relation between the landlord and his dependants was fairly humane. Caste did not exist in Tibet, and in religion all found that equality which poverty or social custom denied them. Monastery life was open to all, and even if the love of all living creatures and the spirit of sacrifice for the suffering, inculcated by Buddhism, remained generally theoretical, a fundamental humanity governed social relations throughout the country.

There is no doubt that in order to dislocate Tibetan society the Chinese at once put in hand the redistribution of property. The holdings of families that had opposed them and taken part in the various rebel movements were certainly confiscated. Public trials of individual landowners were also instigated. The property of non-hostile families was likewise confiscated and distributed among the peasants, but on the promise of compensation to be paid over ten years. The same thing happened to the monasteries which, to start with, were promised a minimum subsistence for the remaining monks. But later it seems the monks were forced to earn their own living, to

22. The outside of a box to be worn as a pendant, containing relics, etc., showing the eight auspicious emblems (clockwise from the small ring: conch, love-knot, umbrella, wheel, standard, fishes, vase and lotus).

take an active part in the new life of the country either as teachers, or in public works, or in the fields, so that the monastic community has been reduced enormously. The Chinese empire had adopted this policy several times during the periods of persecution against Buddhism, a religion the Confucians did not care for because of its indifference to social life.

The peasants among whom the land was distributed were told that the crops would be wholly theirs to dispose of. When the time came, two-thirds of the harvest were requisitioned for the benefit of the community. Mutual aid groups were also organized between a number of peasant families—the first step towards the Chinese-type co-operative system.

This campaign to reshape the country from its roots was conducted in accordance with the usual Chinese classification of the three 'antis' and the two 'reductions', that is to say, anti-revolt, anti-*corvée*, anti-slavery, and the reduction of profits and interest. The land was distributed so that each member of a family of peasants received a quarter of a hectare. As regards livestock, here again that owned by rebels was confiscated, but though the landlord-herdsman relationship has been abolished, there has been no redistribution of livestock.

Even from one of the latest reports of the Second Secretary of the Executive Committee of the Chinese Communist Party in Tibet, summarized in the *Peking Review* of 25 December 1964, it appears that both active and passive resistance to the reforms imposed by China still continues in Tibet and that, consequently, the class struggle will be complicated and long drawn out, sometimes even bitter. Its object is to 'deepen the struggle against the serf-owning feudal class, and curb capitalism and any spontaneous capitalist tendency'. In any case, at the end of 1964 the Communist Party had 5,800 cadres of Tibetan nationality, one thousand of whom were acting as heads or deputy-heads of districts. The mutual aid groups in the villages were fully developed, agricultural production had risen, irrigation had been extended, and the number of sheep and cattle increased. Factories have gone up all over the place, producers of household and agricultural equipment, mills, cement works. However—and this is a great danger—the infiltration or, rather, the plantation of Chinese in Tibet (in 1952 Mao Tse-tung planned to send 50,000 Chinese families there) has continued on the pretext of training Tibetan workers and technicians and has been increasing. More than a hundred and fifty clinics are said to have been opened in different centres, staffed by Chinese with Tibetan assistants. The *Tibetan Daily* (published in Tibetan) had a circulation of 5,400 copies at the end of 1964, according to the same source. It would also seem that the Chinese are trying to compel mixed marriages between Chinese and Tibetans with the object of speeding up the process of assimilation.

The most important recent occurrence is without doubt the removal of the Panchen Lama from the Vice-presidency of the Committee for the Autonomy of Tibet. This manoeuvre, which was announced by Chou En-lai in December 1964, was the result of the Panchen Lama's refusal to assume the Presidency of the Committee, left vacant after the Dalai Lama's flight to India. The post of chairman of the Tibet Autonomous Region was taken over by a Tibetan Nyabö Nawang Jigmé who had, from the beginning of the occupation, co-operated with the Chinese. Other more recent reports seem to confirm that after the Chinese Premier's public reproof, the Panchen was put under house arrest, but some rumours suggest that he has been secretly removed to China. It appears too that the military are requisitioning labour, and that the wheat and barley reserves, stored by the Tibetans according to traditional custom to cope with emergencies and famines, have been confiscated. Such measures increase the general hardship, aggravated by the fact that the war against religion and the monastic community has been harshly intensified. The verdict of the International Commission of Jurists was a strong condemnation of the methods adopted by the Chinese.

It seems that Tibet did not escape the turmoil caused by the conflict between the Red Guards and their opponents—the pro-Maoists and the anti-Maoists—and that it was at least for some time under control of the anti-Mao group, whose leader was general Chang Kuo-hua. During the riots it appears also that the Jokhang Temple in Lhasa, was sacked and that the old image which was worshipped there was damaged, some parts of it being smuggled to India. Also other monasteries, like Sera and Drêpung, have suffered a similar fate.

The extent of these measures, and the harshness with which they have been applied in the different regions in proportion to the resistance met with, should of course be ascertained in an objective manner. As far as practical life is concerned, I feel sure that Tibet is being organized on lines more in accordance with modern needs. Obviously there is much advantage in this, if not for the present generation, which will have to face many sacrifices and privations, then at least for the future. The trouble is that this change has been imposed suddenly and violently, and, with a few exceptions, against the inclination of the Tibetans themselves, and, what is more, by a foreign power which forced Tibet to accept its methods willy-nilly. It must be remembered that Tibet's situation was completely different from that of other Asiatic countries, where nationalism, struggling against colonialism, or mass movements trying to achieve political reform and independence, have spontaneously forged ahead, sometimes almost too hastily, on the path of progress. In Tibet nothing had changed; the West had not set foot there. Suddenly Red China put forward her claims on Tibet with a thoroughness and peremptoriness never experienced before: the take-over by the heirs of the Celestial Empire with its policy of expansion was perfectly organized. The relationship between the Dalai Lama, or the Panchen Lama, and the Chinese authorities was no longer that of priest to patron, but of civil servant to sovereign. The driving force behind many modern Asiatic states, and none so much as in China, is what Gianbattista Vico called 'national arrogance', the revival of a hegemony as it was in the periods of greatest expansion, even if it had nearly always been transitory.

Until recently, Tibetan history had developed in isolation, due partly to geographical factors, partly to the social and spiritual situation of her people: an isolation penetrated only intermittently by ideas from the surrounding countries and all these ideas, from the time when Buddhism was first introduced, religious or marked by religion. Further, such influences nearly always involved individuals, not masses—and individuals who had a peculiar spiritual interest. All this served to reinforce a conservative tendency and an atmosphere of orthodoxy fearful of any change. Politically, Tibet contained the elements of disruption: groups of noble families at loggerheads with each other. The unification under the royal dynasty lasted less than three centuries. In the period that followed the fall of that dynasty local autonomies revived, but these were quickly opposed and overcome by the power of the monasteries, which was at once economic and spiritual. The great monastic communities replaced the lay nobility, made it serve their purposes and involved it in their struggles. Whilst in theory all sects were supposed to have an identical aim—the salvation of living creatures— the reality was that those sects gave a new form to the old individualism, which later expressed itself (ignoring to some extent the provinces east and west of Tibet proper), in the fundamental antagonism between Ü and Tsang. The country's energies were drained by the long struggles for hegemony. The inclination to restore the ancient unity was evinced first by the Sakya-pas, then by the Phagmotru-pas, but when they failed, that ambition passed to the Geluk-pas who, with the foreigner's aid, united the country under their rule in a mild kind of theocracy.

The country's subjection to the priestly class, however, did not encourage its possibilities for development. Religion saw perfection in the past rather than in the future, and considered the present a decline. It could not further the spirit of progress because every change signified departure from the forms sanctioned by tradition. The sufferings of this life were explained as the inevitable consequences of *karma* that each had brought about: sacrifice in the present ensured a better fate in the future. The outcome was a society that tended to live on itself and in itself, that poured out its resources on rich temples or in religious donations.

Deep religiousness, capable of mystical raptures, but pervaded too by a magical *Angst*, and expressed in varying symbols—genial or grotesque, tranquil or obscene, often hard to understand in their apparent strangeness—precisely on account of these contradictions cannot long, I fear, withstand the new ideas forced upon it by foreign domination. The encounter between Marxist rationalism and the Tibetan's ingenuous blend of myth, fantasy and magic brings two entirely different conceptions face to face: an inflexible abstract scheme, all figures and duties, on the one hand, and on the other the fundamental anarchy of invisible presences that control us but which we can dominate, if we know their secret. Facts on the one side; imagination on the other. The life of man confined within time and space, in the service of a community which seeks economic and social betterment at the cost of individual frreedom, with the new ideology; affirmation of the personality through its dialogue with the transcendent world of the divine, belittling of the real in comparison with the invisible, transcendence overriding time and space, with the Tibetan spiritual tradition.

Millennia of religious experience, supported by the innate archetypes of the Tibetan spirit, are hard to root out; but the very complications of a great deal of Lamaism, the bizarreness of some of its symbols, cannot long, I think, resist the disenchanted cold-bloodedness of the new principles.

The Buddhism of the Little Vehicle with its ordered simplicity, which would have been even more robust had it not been overlaid with monkish experience, would have more chance of adjustment to the spirit of modernity; indeed, for the Little Vehicle (*Hīnayāna*), the Buddha is not a god, but a teacher. His teachings do not conflict with the progress of science, his moral injunctions encourage men to live with full sincerity and awareness. Ethical principles necessary to social life and only repaid in a future existence, active love towards one's neighbour, and the habit of cool reasoning, make the co-existence of Hīnayāna Buddhism with the most advanced social theories not at all impossible—I would say not even difficult. The structure of Lamaism, however, is pervaded by too much imagination, fear and magic, requires a dramatic framework, insists too much on ritual and the intervention of supernatural beings; and then it easily degenerates into liturgical formalism, which is not entirely redeemed by the mystical serenity of the chosen few. The excessive demands of the Great Vehicle (*Mahāyāna*), the way it magnifies the sacrifices of the *changchupsempa* (bodhisattva) or potential Buddha beyond all human imagination or endurance, and offers as a pattern examples whose exaggeration turns them into fairy-tales instead of human possibilities—these empty the ethical content of Lamaism as well. When this formalism breaks up it will be hard to find anything to substitute for it.

Today Tibet has been forcibly laid open to a different, indeed, contradictory,

23. A corner of the golden roof of the Jokhang Temple in Lhasa, with the Potala Palace in the distance.

24

25

statement of the problems: the present is preferred to the next world, the ideal of *homo oeconomicus* to that of the holy man, labour to meditation. With the supremacy of the clergy and nobility abolished, the demands of collective living have the upper hand, work is organized, technology progresses. The interests of the community predominate over those of the individual. The various regions of Tibet are brought within easy reach of one another. A new situation has been born. These are the facts: their assessment is another matter. One can argue *ad nauseam* about the legitimacy of the Chinese occupation, the juridical value of the suzerainty China claims over Tibet, or the autonomy enjoyed by Tibet in the past. The fact remains that Tibet is today under the Chinese, whether she likes it or not.

But the Tibetan people have little in common with China, neither language, nor traditions, nor outlook, nor psychological make-up. Tibet has learnt much from the Chinese—certain aspects of their ceremonial, their craftsmanship, some of their artistic styles, for example; but Tibetan culture is spiritually a creation of Buddhism, and hence of India. Buddhism throve in an extremely favourable soil, deeply sensitive to religious problems. Confucianism, with the exception of a few ancient and rare instances, did not take root in Tibet, whilst Buddhism has often been felt in China, (despite the success it enjoyed there) as something foreign to the Chinese spirit. India's great logical edifice, the solemn structures of Diṅnāga and Dharmakīrti and their commentators—found a wonderful response in the Tibetans, but with China the literature of logic remained almost unknown, for the Chinese only translated one elementary textbook. The complications of gnosis and of Tantric esotericism have had far less success in China, with its strictness in morals and manners, than in Tibet.

Without setting up as a prophet of the future course of events, which are obviously bound up with the development of international affairs, it seems to me undeniable that Tibetan culture as I saw it, still thriving and intact, and as it is described in the books of those who, like me, were fortunate enough to enter the forbidden land, is on its deathbed. It might survive for some time in the small communities of scholars, lamas and teachers in centres founded in India and elsewhere expressly for that purpose, but it will not be quite the same. Even in India many forms of the ancient religious feeling have become attenuated in recent years. But even more serious will be the repercussions felt by these surviving representatives of the Tibetan spiritual culture, forced to live in countries which are not theirs, exiled from the surroundings where their predecessors were trained, faced with new ways of life and new methods of inquiry. The historical and philological fields will gain by this, but the spiritual heritage of a people who lived for centuries anchored to their profound convictions, to their fantasies, longings and griefs, will of necessity change its form if not its content. The Tibetan people, by nature industrious, curious, of kindly disposition, but dignified and independent, will end by adapting themselves to the undeniable but troublesome advantages, achieved after heavy sacrifices, of a new economic organization.

A new generation formed from an élite trained outside their own country according to methods and ideologies foreign to the world of their fathers, will not, I think, find much difficulty in settling down with the beliefs implanted in them, practising and spreading them, training future generations in the same way of thinking and living. Whatever happens, tomorrow's Tibet will no longer be the Tibet of yesterday. But it is also possible that the new education and a certain innate spirit of independence will one day restore the Tibetans to an awareness of what is unique and special in their culture; so that they may assert their sense of nationality to more practical effect —signs of which process are increasingly clear wherever we look.

24. Monastic roof ornaments in the Jokhang Temple in Lhasa, showing the Wheel of the Law (with Sanskrit inscriptions on its spokes) flanked by gazelles.

25. Thigh-bone trumpet bound with wire.

Religion

TIBETAN BUDDHISM is like a tree with many branches. These ramifications, starting from a single origin, have come about through the special stress each group has laid on particular aspects of liturgy and doctrine. Speaking in a general way, we can distinguish two principal schools in Tibet, which are called 'red' and 'yellow' after the colour of the hats they wear on ceremonial occasions. By 'red' we denote all the non-reformed schools from the Nyingma-pas to the Kagyü-pas, whilst 'yellow' refers to the followers of the reformed school founded by Tsongkha-pa (1357-1419). This was the sect that rose to power with the coming of the Dalai Lamas and won the real political control of the country. It called for a greater purity of discipline and reasserted the importance of the main monastic rules of Indian Buddhism, imposing ecclesiastic celibacy and forbidding the use of alcohol; it stressed the study of Buddhist dogmatic texts, and of dialectics in particular, in the education of its monks, who were schooled in debates on formal logic from the time they were young novices; and it made a through reappraisal of religious practices based on those gnostic or magical texts, the Tantras, considerably reducing the authorized Tantras themselves in number.

The Geluk-pa, or 'yellow' school, represents the conclusion of a slow process of revision begun in the thirteenth century during the Sakya-pa supremacy, when there was a move back to the wellsprings of Buddhist doctrine and experience, and when it was first sought to sift genuine from apocryphal tradition, under the guidance of Indian and Nepalese teachers. The task was completed by the famous writer Pu-tön (*Bu ston*), of the monastery of Shalu in Tsang (born 1290). He compiled the catalogue of the two great collections, the *Kangyur* and the *Tengyur*, that contain the philosophical and liturgical literary heritage of Indian Buddhism. The first comprises over a hundred volumes of texts regarded as the revelation of the Buddha himself; the second, in over two hundred volumes, contains the works of the commentators, expounders and annotators, as well as treatises on subsidiary disciplines such as medicine, veterinary science, palmistry, Sanskrit grammar and prosody, and even poems like the *Cloud Messenger* (*Meghadūta*) of Kālidāsa that have nothing to do with Buddhism. The two compilations, a total (in the Dergé edition) of 317 volumes containing 4,567 works, define the literary tradition generally available to the Lamaist schools. But the Dzokchen, who go back to the ubiquitous Padmasambhava, add a collection of their own, the *Nyingma-gyümbum* (*rñin ma rgyud 'bum*), which contains a great number of Tantras—manuals of mysticism and magic from divers sources—that other schools do not accept as genuine. It seems established that many are of dubious authenticity

The corpus as a whole has appeared in several different editions, of which the best known are those of Narthang, a large monastery in Tsang not far from Trashi-lhünpo, and of Dergé, in Kham. The great task of re-examining the tradition became necessary because Buddhism, lacking authentic spiritual guidance after Langdarma's persecution, had assumed unorthodox forms. Due to the Tibetan's inborn love of magic, it

26. Detail from a Tibetan thanka, showing Kālika, one of the sixteen sthaviras or arhats.

27. Detail from a Tibetan thanka, showing the poet and mystic Mila-répa.

26

27

28

29

was the magical texts and the arbitrary interpretations of ritual practices that were the most popular.

The true rebirth of Buddhism began in the eleventh century, when Rinchen-sangpo (958-1055) had revived Buddhism in West Tibet after being sent to Kashmir by the king of that region, and Dīpankara Atīśa, one of the greatest teachers of Indian Buddhism, arrived in Tibet in 1042, having been invited to their kingdom by the same dynasty. The religion was propagated anew, but by teachers and ascetics of such diverse intellectual and mystical attitudes that it ran the risk of splitting into separate trends. Retreats, where little groups of disciples gathered round a master, proliferated in Tibet. Schools sprang up everywhere, each concentrating on particular experiences, interpretations, or texts, and passed on directly from master to disciple. But as soon as the great monasteries were founded these groups had a focal point and their amalgamation produced increasingly well-defined sects. The schools that were gradually formed in this way, went on gaining in individuality and definition. One group became the *Nyingma-pa* or 'Ancients' who trace their origins to the teaching of 'Guru-rinpoché' (i.e. Padmasambhava), consecrator of the monastery of Samyê (eighth century A.D.); they particularly favour magical rites and the deeper practices of yoga, convinced that the divine light hidden in man can reveal itself to the adept, in its saving purity, through appropriate yoga exercises and meditations. This is the essence of the *dzokchen* teaching. Another school, stemming from Marpa (1012-97), the teacher of Mila-rêpa (1040-1123), carries on from the Haṭhayoga schools of the Indian Siddhas. They concentrate on accelerating the process of transcending the temporal e istence, as it appears in its manifold forms, less with the aid of the scriptures than by mastering psycho-physical activities and functions through conscious breath-control and the rapt state of ecstasy. This school is generally called the Kagyü-pa and, as with the Nyingma-pa, its hat is red. Because of the particular fondness that one or other teacher showed for one method or another, it falls into several subgroups: the Karma-pa, founded by Tüsum-khyenpa (1110-93), the Drigung-pa emanating from the ascetic Drigung Rinpoché (1143-1216), the Shang-pa descended from Shang Rinpoché (1123-93), the Druk-pa, and so on.

The teaching of Rinchen-sangpo and of Atīśa, including the arcane Tantric element, insists on progressive meditation, employing two complementary methods: illuminating analysis and a deliberate stilling of the mind—known to the Indians as *vipaśyanā* and *sámatha*. The conjunction of these gradually silences the discursive process that we call reason and sets free a luminous motionless purity identified with Buddhahood. This school led to the Kadam-pas, in turn re-formed into the 'yellow-hatted' sect, the Geluk-pas, by Tsongkha-pa, though teachers of other sects also contributed to his spiritual training. Between the Kagyü-pas and the Kadam-pas stand the Sakya-pas.

Lamaism cannot therefore be seen as a single religious current: it is divided into many trends, although they all set out from the same premises, have sprung from the same concern with salvation. The Tibetans recognize this plurality of schools, but rightly insist on the fundamental unity of inspiration and aims: different methods are used to reach the same end — salvation by rebirth in some paradise, or final escape from rebirth with the attainment of nirvana.

All are variations on the essential principles of Buddhism, caused by the inescapable influence that the continually evolving historical and intellectual scene exercises on all religions.

Despite polemical debate among the schools on points of doctrine and liturgy,

28. A page of an illuminated manuscript of the Prajñāpāramitā (Perfection of Wisdom), one of the most popular religious books, thirteenth-fourteenth century.

29. Statuette of Chenrêsik, the god of mercy.

RELIGION all Tibetans accept the same Law, that of the Buddha, and so describe themselves as *nangpa:* they are all 'inside' the Law. Other people are *chhipa*, those 'outside' it, who do not accept the Buddha's teaching.

Tibetan religion has been dubbed 'Lamaism' because of the great importance lamas have in it, but *lama* only means 'teacher', 'master', and not every monk is a master in the sense of the spiritual guide of those bent on salvation.

Most of the monks content themselves with the humbler function of making the liturgical and magical operations and formulae in which they are experts available to the laymen. Outwardly deployed in a powerful monastic organization, Lamaism finds expression in complicated rites and rigid formalism; yet it has inspired spiritual movements of great interest, and produced outstanding mystics and thinkers. Small wonder that it has been subject to the most divergent assessments. Some travellers have seen in it nothing but magic; others supposed that Buddhism's purest spiritual traditions lived on, thanks to the country's isolation, in the monasteries and, still more, among the hermits of Tibet, preserving ancient wisdom lost elsewhere. Both opinions are, of course, mistaken. Here, as in all religious institutions, there is adaptation to the needs of the common man, with his simplicity and his fear of the many forces he imagines to be at work around him. This aspect is the legacy of older and cruder religious forms, but alongside it appear such profundities of thought, longings for spiritual renewal, and mystical fervours, that no overall judgment can be sustained.

What redeems a religion from the corruption into which it is plunged by history is not the masses, the number of its adherents, but the sincerity of belief, the spiritual and intellectual heights it is able to command when ancient revelation is renewed by the power of faith. Naturally the Tibetan world did not strike Western minds as edifying at first sight; neither was the Indian scene, crowded with ascetics sincere or otherwise, and pulsing in an extravagant religious orgy. Of Tibetan religion, a further unflattering impression was given by the throngs of itinerant monks, the excessive number of clerics, the complicated ritualism, the daily recourse to exorcists to ward off calamities or cure illness, the commercial interests of the monasteries and their wealth. This impression might be strengthened by visiting the shrines, with their countless images and bizarre or monstrous statues, utterly different from our conception of divine beings. Yet monastic life was a hard apprenticeship that demanded years of sacrifice; life's best years tamed with an iron discipline, in a monotonous rhythm of liturgical ceremonies and study; learning thousands of pages of essential books by heart; and, for the better minds, meditation or the exhaustive study of dogmatics.

This was all achieved through a schooling under watchful masters; a shrewd dose of psychology; and tests and examinations arranged so judiciously, with rites of such magnificence, that it was almost with anguish that the neophyte approached the crucial moment—the confirmation of a metamorphosis of mind and soul by the granting of a rank in the hierarchy. When talking with such people, I have often observed how vividly they recalled their excitement at that decisive moment in their life, and how moved they were as they retraced the stages of their spiritual journey. That emotion was proof of a sincerity every human being must bow to, for these people had clearly succeeded in attaining the hardest goal of all: the total rooting out of Man from the man, with no turning back or regret.

Buddhism has always been very tolerant. From 1624 to 1636, while west Tibet was still an independent kingdom, it allowed European missionaries, like Antonio d'Andrade, to practise and preach their own religion there. A little later, in the eighteenth century,

30. Nê-nying gönpa Monastery near Gyantsé.

68

31

32

central Tibet was so hospitable to the Jesuits that Father Ippolito Desideri of Pistoia, who reached Lhasa in 1716, was able to debate theology with the Tibetan monks and made a thorough study of the *Lam-rim chenmo* of Tsongkha-pa, of which he wrote a confutation in Tibetan. This remarkable enounter between the thought of Aquinas and of Tsongkha-pa on the Roof of the World was soon cut short, not through any fault of the Tibetans, but due to the fanaticism of the Capuchin Fathers who supplanted the Jesuits and went as far as burning in public the sacred books of Buddhism—an ill-advised action, for in Tibet the book is deeply sacred, representing the third, verbal, body of the Buddha, the other two being the physical one (images) and the spiritual (the shrine or the *mandala*).

Buddhism was preceded in Tibet by another religion, *Bon* (pronounced *p'ön*), which we might loosely call a kind of Shamanism, as the official state religion. Its chief priests, called *shen*, ensured the fortune of the state with traditional rites, and played a very great part in important funeral ceremonies, as may be gathered from certain ancient rituals concerning royal funerals, which required a great number of participants and the sacrifice of many victims, even of human beings. They had also worked out cosmogonies and genealogies which had to be recited on special occasions, particularly at the beginning of the year in order to ensure the continuity of the cosmic order. A reformer, or rather systematizer, of this school was Miwo Shenrap (eighth century?) a native of West Tibet. Under his influence Bon absorbed some of the rites of neighbouring countries, particularly Kashmir and Gilgit, and was probably influenced by popular forms of Shivaism.

Bon not only still survives in some parts of Tibet, especially in the eastern provinces, but has also influenced the folk religion. The latter, however, is by no means a sort of Bon combined with Buddhism: it is an ancient religion which varies considerably from place to place, and it primarily governs the relations between the human and demonic worlds. Buddhism has not eliminated either Bon or this popular religion, but has tried to absorb them. Where it has not wholly suceeded in doing so it has fitted them into its own pattern, so that the three currents, Buddhism, folk religion and Bon are found side by side, and indeed often within one another. This further complicates matters, but is easy to explain. The people cling to their ancestral beliefs and put particular trust in the rites that give them control over the supernatural beings and powers around them. They cannot, however, easily grasp the involved theology and gnostic sublimities of which Buddhism is made up, even in the Tantric schools, which are less close to the Buddha's teaching. Buddhism reached Tibet at a time when it was on the wane in India. From the doctrinal point of view, it had already completed its glorious career. The creators had been succeeded by annotators or dialecticians putting up a magnificent, but vain, fight against Hinduism. The Tantric schools then made their mark. They set out from the assumption that the divine Buddha-essence is within man, and co-essential with him; and they either mapped out the complicated roads that lead to reintegration with Buddhahood (when the illusory appearances of this world would vanish), or degenerated into dreams of magic and miracles. The ideas and theories that Lamaism inherited from India might seem to be contradicted by the improbable number of images of deities which make its pantheon one of the richest in any religion. But it is precisely in this that the essential principle, whether of Buddhism or of Hinduism, appears—that the revelation of the doctrine takes place by degrees, and that truth is twofold: a relative truth, accessible to the ordinary run of men, and the absolute truth, when the veil of ignorance has been finally torn away. The images represent, in symbols, the forces striving together

31. A village temple.

32. A *chhörten* ' with many doors (*gomang chhörten*).

71

in ourselves and the cosmos; they are intended in the first place to develop devotion and faith with the aid, punitive or compassionate, of these beings. Little by little, through repeated devotional exercises and encouragement to good works, and through a dread of the grievous consequences of evil, we learn to distrust impulsive instinct, and are slowly purified. Then light dawns, and those same images, which before seemed to stand for actual divinities, appear as the symbols of complex patterns of redemption they really are. Lamaism, like the Mahāyāna and Tantric Buddhism whose Tibetan version it is, teaches that all is empty; that which we think real is mere illusion, bred of ignorance. Reintegration in Buddhahood can only come about when one recognizes the fallacious reasoning of ignorance, for to recognize is to eliminate. *Nirvāna*—alone—which Tibetans call *Nyangenlê-dê*, 'that beyond pain and evil' — is truth, and this side of it lie only error and misery; hence the need is to restore that essential state.

Figs 2 & 3. Drawings of costumes worn at a festival in a monastery.

But how? Not just by understanding the mechanism of our psycho-physical life and acting accordingly, pursuing the analysis that ends by abandoning all logical constructs for the pure light of intuition; but also by showing compassionate love (*nyingje*) for all beings who are still ignorant of their real condition, and therefore doomed to suffering. The two activities are mutually indispensable, and combine to produce an irreversible state which words can only hint at as 'Enlightenment', 'the Buddha-nature', 'the Mother of all the Buddhas'. This state of total oneness is not achieved through the intellectual or the practical activity alone, but through both together. The need to translate these exalted conceptions into visual symbols has led to the representations of paired images so frequent in Tibetan art (*yab yum* = Father-Mother). They must not be taken literally as an erotic obsession: the male symbolizes 'Means' or active compassion, and the female stands for Higher Knowledge. Similar assumptions inspired the ecstasies of Tibetan ascetics who, like the Indian yogins in whose steps they followed, reached that state after prolonged exercises.

For Tibetans, the Buddha Śākyamuni is no longer the teacher who was born at Lumbinī and died at Kuśinagara, but truth made manifest in the body or, according to other schools, an illusory form projected by that same Being in order to save living creatures. No longer is the 'Deer-park' sermon, at Sarnath, the only preaching of the Law (cf. pl. I): it is the first and the most apt for human comprehension, but there are many others, each of which is a 'vehicle', revealed to disciples in a particular place or paradise. The preaching goes on for ever, whether by Śākyamuni or by the other Buddhas peopling the myriads of worlds that star the universe. With faith it is possible to attain levels of ecstatic absorption at which one takes part in this continuous revelation.

But all this is so difficult, so lofty and remote, that easier paths are shown to encourage the faithful. What qualifications, after all, does Lamaism require, to count oneself a Buddhist? Hardly any, really. Enough that one has faith in the triple refuge, the 'three Gems', which are regarded as man's sole protection: the Buddha, the Law revealed by Him, and the Community, the ensemble of people who have espoused the religious life. This is quite enough, for endless complications arise when people begin to argue about what the Buddha is, or the exact meaning of his words: the maze of doctrinal interpretation is best left to the divines. The layman who contents himself with those three principles can clearly be considered one of the *nangpas*. He can also go a step further: as a follower of the 'Great Vehicle', the *Mahāyāna*, he can vow to attain supreme enlightenment, Buddhahood, and to conform to the rules of life that guarantee its realization. However, no man should seek to pass into nirvana: there are too many suffering people in the world, too many creatures caught up since the beginning of time, through their ignorance, in the fearful round (*saṁsāra*) of births and deaths. It would be the height of selfishness to think only of his own salvation, and long, like the followers of the 'Little Vehicle' (*Hīnayāna*), to dissolve forever in nirvana. Instead, he should become a *changchup-sempa*, a bodhisattva, one who has attained enlightenment but refuses nirvana and remains among the living with the sole aim of being an example and teacher to suffering creatures. The bodhisattva assumes a visible body and, to the world in which he is to accomplish his mission, gives the impression of being born, studying, preaching, and dying; whereas, in fact, he is beyond all that because he is beyond life and death, omniscient, untouched by anything. And so we have the *trülkus* or incarnations Tibet abounds in, sometimes erroneously called 'Living Buddhas'.

Fig 3

The Bodhisattva Vow is a serious business. Taking it should mean setting out on a trail that winds across the millennia, the one the Buddha himself trod, with its sacrifices, heroic acts of self-denial and countless sufferings serenely accepted for the sake of others. But the acknowledged immensity of the task and the numberless lifetimes it must take, make the Vow much less of a commitment: it ends up as another profession of faith, and in practice loses much of its substance.

But there was still another way. One of the countless paradises in which the Buddhas, themselves countless, preach from time immemorial, has for various reasons acquired special popularity. This is the blessed paradise of the west, where the Buddha of Boundless Life, or of Boundless Light, (cf. pl. 84) carries out his mission. The delights of this paradise have been described with a wealth of imagination in books famous all over the Buddhist world, from India to Japan, from China to Tibet. And it is to this region that the conscious principle of the dying or dead man can be transferred—if he has not achieved reintegration with the luminous and unmoving Consciousness, the One—through the recitation of a famous book, of ancient origin, which I shall discuss later.

It is this conscious principle within the individual that makes him morally accountable, for it is loaded with all his past experiences; and these direct him to a new form of existence, which is determined by their charge of *karma* (*i.e.* the accumulation of actions performed). The conscious principle is thus not easily distinguishable from the idea of the 'soul' that other religions speak of. The similarity is understandable, as the concept of the soul was not foreign to the ancient Tibetans: they called it *sok* (spelt *srog*) or *la* (*bla*). They even believed a person had several souls which might not only reside in his body but could also shelter in a tree or rock, on whose safety the person's life would depend.

So we come back to our earlier point. Lamaism is late Buddhism, set against a background of beliefs it has not eliminated, but lived with in perfect accord. Their survival, it might be claimed, governs the whole outlook of the common people. The presence of temple or monastery does nothing to lessen their certainty that guarding the country, the earth, the air, and every locality, there are *sadak*, *yül-lha* and *lu*— 'lords, of the ground', 'gods of the region', and serpents. In the mountains there are *nyen*, and *tsen* are nearly everywhere. The Tibetan has to reckon with all these beings, since if they are not propitiated and are offended they are sure to cause disaster. This religious situation is shot with a certain ambiguity: on the one side the fear of capricious spirits that was inherited by Lamaism from the country's original religion and, on the other, the conviction that man possesses the means to control those dark vengeful forces demanding propitiation. Magic ritual, acts of piety,

RELIGION liberality towards monasteries and teachers, exorcism, liturgical technique, all come to his aid. And the human victim he was at the outset, at the mercy of a thousand invisible forces, is able to become their master.

This distinctive attitude might seem to put the Tibetan in continual expectation of the miraculous. From our point of view one might speak of miracles, since we imagine nature governed by her own precise laws; only a divine intervention can, according to some, halt or change her course. But to the Tibetan things appear differently: nothing can resist the will and the thaumaturgic power of man, or at least of certain particularly able and expert men. No limits are set to these faculties, with the infinite horizons they open up. I have often met monks or laymen in Tibet who left one in no doubt about the wonder-working power of their teachers. They were convinced, for example, that the latter could fly through the air from one monastery to another. But the wiser lamas were rather evasive on this question, whilst affirming that to a holy man nothing is impossible, inasmuch as his body has become a body of diamond, like the Buddha's, and hence beyond common experience. They added however that one must beware of assuming certain powers that derive from the practice of yoga to be signs of sanctity, when they are merely signs or means of purification and must not become ends in themselves.

The thing to talk of in Lamaism, then, would be marvels, not miracles. Indeed, we could say that the miracle for Tibetan religion would be the constant and unchanging course of things, like a congealing of the cosmos, to halt the running fire of infinite possibility. Here we see Asia's age-old experience in yoga and magic ennobled by contact with the Buddhist anthroposophy that had placed man above everything, gradually even easing the rigidity of karma itself. For unlike early Buddhism, where man has no choice but to reap what he has sown, the fruit of his own actions, the Great Vehicle (*Mahāyāna*) and the magico-gnostic Vehicle (*Vajrayāna*) assert that karma can be modified, halted, channelled along other paths, or dissolved altogether.

The visitor is amazed by the number of deities—portrayed in paintings and frescoes, or in bronze, copper and other metals—with which Tibet's shrines are crammed. The significance of these images is accessible only to the initiated: the layman sees them with mingled awe and apprehension, and understands them vaguely at best. Even if the images stand in his chapel and his Lama has told him what secret 'heart' syllables he must recite to propitiate the forces they represent, he may still be unable to follow the intricacies of the rites and meditations that centre on them. It is enough for him to utter the sounds expressing their inmost identity, and to make his usual daily offering; these acts will earn for him the spiritual elevation and purification that results from any contact with the divine. But it is with other deities, more within his understanding, that the layman feels most at home. The first of these is Shakya-thuppa (Skt. Sākyamuni), the historical Buddha, who may be represented preaching; meditating; touching the ground with one hand to call Earth to witness that he has attained enlightenment, that timeless instant that transforms the whole perspective (cf. pl. 97); or in the gesture of protection, to symbolize the defeat of evil; or bestowing the highest of all gifts, the Law. Much significance attaches to the varying position of the hands. This not only serves to identify the deity, but must also, in the course of ritual, accompany the spoken sounds that contain the spiritual essence of the gods; to pronounce those syllables without the appropriate gesture would be like posting a letter without an address. Such *chhagya*, as they are called, are very numerous and each of them has its own name; they are a sign-language designed to attune the officiant to the deity he is addressing, and they enliven the ceremonial during the liturgy.

33. Wayside *chhörten*.

74

34

Next to Shakya-thuppa come the five supreme Buddhas, the *ri-nga*, in whom the five postures just referred to take independent life, though in much more abstract form. They symbolize the first five embodiments of the universal Light-cum-Consciousness, in its process of being enveloped in individualized consciousness, and hence are guides to reintegration in that same Luminous Consciousness, which is Buddhahood. The five-pointed headdress often worn when performing rites is also called a *ri-nga*, because each of its five panels carries the figure of one of the five Buddhas; the officiant himself is thus reintegrated in the One. The names of the *ri-nga* are Ö-pamé, Namparnangdzè, Rinchen-jungden, Mi-trhukpa and Tön-yö-truppa. They are represented regally robed and crowned, each with his hands in the appropriate gesture.

Three particularly popular deities, who always go together are the Bodhisattvas Chenrêsik, Jampêyang and Chhanadorje. The white-coloured Chenrêsik (Tibetan for Avalokiteśvara) is the supreme embodiment of Compassion, whose essence is expressed in the famous six-syllable formula *Oṁ maṇi-padme hūṁ*. This was originally the invocation of a deity, called Maṇipadmā, but afterwards took on deeper implications. For liberation results from the conjunction of Means (compassion) and Higher Knowledge (the void); *mani*, 'jewel', is equated with the dorje (male), symbol of Means, and *padme*, 'lotus', with the bell (female), standing for Emptiness. Together they suggest the esoteric union to which I earlier alluded. Chenrêsik is the great protector of Tibet as well as of individuals: he mediates between the mundane and the supramundane, and frees from all physical and spiritual dangers, whilst his formula is recited thousands of times a day. He is even recorded to have descended into the hells to let the sinners out.

Chenrêsik is represented with four arms: the hands of two of them are joined, whilst in the other pair he holds a rosary and a lotus flower (cf. pl. 101). But this most common form is sometimes replaced by another in which he has eleven heads (cf. pl. 34). The second head from the top is dark blue and angry-looking, to show how violently, when necessary, the compassion with which this deity is co-essential can oppose the powers of evil. Nothing escapes him: his eye ranges over the universe and rays of pity stream down, from that mindful glance, on all who suffer. His hands are quick to rescue anyone about to be seized by hostile forces. Thus (and by indirect assimilation to certain Indian deities) is born the wondrous image of Chenrêsik *Chentong-chhaktong*, the 'thousand-eyed and thousand-armed'. Arms radiate from the body, enclosing it like a scallop shell, and an eye opens on the palm of every hand, a miracle of creative fantasy to show anew the inexhaustible mystery of the divine. Chenrêsik may be rendered in other ways still: as Chhanapèma (Skt. Padmapāṇi), standing upright with a long-stemmed lotus in his left hand (cf. pl. 53), or as Jikten-wangchuk (Skt. Lokeśvara), gracefully enthroned with one leg resting on the ground and the other folded back, while his right hand toys with a lotus flower.

Jampêyang (Mañjuśrī in Sanskrit) is red, and the symbol of saving Knowledge. He holds book and sword, for that Knowledge is contained in the book, and severs the fetters of ignorance like a sword. Chhanadorje (or Vajrapāṇi) is dark blue; he represents the militant side of Jampêyang, coming out to do battle when spiritual foes close in about us. His right hand brandishes a *dorje* in the air, and his left threatens, its little finger and forefinger outstretched and the others tucked in. Images of these three deities are everywhere: vases of red, white and deep blue flowers are often seen at the windows of the houses, as emblems of the sacred presence.

A female Bodhisattva whose compassionate aid is a source of great popularity is Drölma (Skt. Tārā) (cf. pl. 98), whose principal forms are white and green. She is

34. Eleven-headed and eight-armed form of Chenrêsik (Avalokiteśvara).

all the more venerated because the two wives of Songtsen-gampo, the King who, traditionally, introduced Buddhism in Tibet, are regarded as incarnating those two manifestations of the goddess, the white and the green. But she has many aspects: some litanies, recited when in danger or special need, list twenty-one. Drölma is usually represented with her right hand in the attitude of giving, the left holding a lotus flower breast-high.

Another very popular deity is Tshe-pamé, the Buddha of 'Boundless Life', whose colour is red. His hands rest palm uppermost in his lap to support the vase holding the Water of Immortality (cf. pl. 84). In the absence of this vase, leaving only the arrangement of the hands, in his kingly robes and diadem, he becomes Ö-pamé, the Buddha of 'Boundless Light'. The two are aspects of the same personality, who reigns in the western paradise: this is where all Tibetans aspire to be reborn, to enjoy the never-ending bliss of hearing him preach the highest secrets of the Law.

The foregoing are the deities that most often appear in private chapels. There are often also paintings depicting the 'wheel of existence', which illustrates the inevitability with which the cycle of births and deaths is enacted and re-begun due to our ignorance of what we are and of the world's unreality. Or they give warning of fates that await us if we do not heed the advice contained in the 'Book of the Dead', when it is read to us on our death-bed.

The great teachers, Indian and Tibetan, are not forgotten either, preference naturally being given to the sect to which the family feels most devotion. Followers of the 'yellow' sect venerate Tsongkha-pa; the Sakya-pas turn particularly to Sakya Penchen and in general to the most celebrated masters of the school; and so on for the other sects.

But whatever the school, the household shrine is hardly ever without an image of Padmasambhava, the Guru-rinpoché. He is the great teacher of the 'Ancients' (Nyingma-pa), but everyone regards him as one of the most authoritative manifestations of the Law on the strength of the miracles recounted in his many extremely popular biographies, his thaumaturgic power, his (erroneous) reputation as the strongest propagator of Buddhism in Tibet, and his effective defeat of the power of Bon, opposing the new religion. All alike pay him homage. The preference Tibetans may show for a particular school does not imply a narrow exclusiveness. The doctrinal animosity that has often flared up between the leading lights of the various sects has made little impression on the lay mind: every teacher, every Lama is sacred because of his spiritual experience and contact with the divine world.

Some of these teachers live on in Tibet in the marks, real or supposed, they left whilst there in person. One is often shown the more than lifesize imprint of Guru-rinpoché's hand or foot, drawn or scratched on the rock. Other teachers receive similar treatment, and a kind of sacred topography has taken shape—a tangle of itineraries in pursuit of evidence testifying to the sacred presence. The Tibetans follow the example of the *tīrthayātrās*, the meritorious pilgrimages prescribed by India's religious tradition, in considering it a duty to visit places made specially holy by some legend, presence or relic. Such pilgrimages converge not only on Lhasa, but on famous monasteries like Ganden, Trashi-lhünpo, Sakya, Mindrölling and Kumbum. These are all centres of attraction for the adherents of their respective sects. Finally, there are the mountains, particularly Kailāśa and Amnye-machen at the country's western and eastern confines.

Buddhism has taken over earlier traditions here. Tibet's original faith centred on the mountain-cult, and very often this meant an ancestor-mountain, which was identi-

35. Window in the Tibetan Institute of Gangtok.

36. Silver, partially gilt, Tibetan ritual ewer. In the centre is a phoenix, symbol of long life, reflecting Chinese influence.

36

37

38

39

40

41

fied with the founder of the family to whom a particular region belonged, or had been that ancestor's landing-place when he first came down from the sky. The ambiguous but predominantly evil *tenmas*, goddesses inherited by Buddhism from the old religion, also inhabited mountains—or were the mountain itself. The first king of Tibet descended from the sky to a mountain; and it was on a mountain near Tsethang that the country's patron, Chenrêsik, manifested himself in the form of a monkey. These mountains belong to a sacred geography, which matters more than the earthly kind.

Buddhism has assimilated this world, not turned from it. The Guru-rinpoché legend primarily concerns the transformation of the ancient deities into defenders of the new faith; it tells how, after fierce struggles, the miraculous power of the Guru forcibly converts them into stern guardians of the Buddhist Law.

Another characteristic of Tibetan Buddhism is its love of ritual. This again results from the interaction of lofty speculation and the common understanding, as well as from an irrepressible interest in magic. The layman's task is to support the monastic community with his liberality. All that remains, when that is done, is to genuflect before the images of the gods or light the altar lamps. But in moments of danger exorcism is resorted to. First of all the sacred texts are read. Since they represent the Buddha's verbal body, they release great powers, and one of the greatest merits is to write the scriptures of the Law, or to have them read or written. The monasteries abound with copies of the collections containing the Buddha's revelation, and the more the work costs, the greater is the resulting merit. The pages of these collections are often coloured with indigo, with the characters written in gold and silver. That the monks responsible for reciting them often do not understand their contents at all is of no consequence.

Lamaism believes in communication between the worlds of gods and men: it allows the possibility of supernatural forces taking possession of a person in order to reveal what is to be done in perilous times, or what the future holds. This is the function of what are known as the *chhökyong*, of whom the one at Nêchung, a monastery not far from Lhasa, is recognized as particularly authoritative.

The Nêchung Chhökyong is the state oracle, consulted both at the beginning of the year and at moments of national crisis or anxiety. Before the expectant onlookers, he comes out dressed in his special robes, propped up by solicitous acolytes, and convulsed by tremors of increasing violence, till it seems he must lose his balance at any moment. In a hoarse, unnatural voice, and ambiguous phrases, he reveals what may happen or what measures can be taken to avoid impending danger. Then he falls to the ground exhausted, and is presently led back to his quarters. The chhökyongs are not as a rule monks, but laymen: their training starts as soon as the signs of possession appear in them.

I must emphasize my point that all this formalism and the general tendency to confound religious practices with magic, are offset by the many great thinkers and mystics Tibetan Buddhism has produced. By the terms 'thinkers' and 'mystics' I wish to suggest Lamaism's two principal currents, in its highest expression. On one side are the 'scholars', men who hand on and enrich the theoretic heritage of Indian Buddhism; this they interpret, summarize, and expound in penetrating and subtle dissertations. They are the authors of a vast literature, which is Tibet's unique contribution to the understanding of Buddhist teachings. On the other side are the mystics. And always, bridging the gap between the two, we have liturgy: the basic prerequisite of every believer, as purification and propaedeutic if nothing more. The

37. Detail of two lions from the throne of a deity.

38. Dorje-Shakpa (Vajrapāśa), one of the four fierce 'gatekeepers' of the mandalas.

39. A Chinese tent used by high-ranking monks or officials during the summer holidays.

40. A peasant woman from Western Tibet.

41. A nomad.

contrast between the two currents lies in the idea that liberation cannot be attained solely by *knowing* the Buddha's word and the sacred scriptures. To be freed is to *experience*. Even those who belong to the 'philosophical' schools must, at least in theory, be contemplatives as well, since they must themselves embody the truth of which they speak.

This is a convenient place to mention another pursuit open to monks—logic— on which first the Sakya-pas and later more especially the Geluk-pas laid stress. This interest was inherited from some of the Indian schools, and was based on the premise that a concept verified by formal logical inference is effectively valid in itself, so that even logic becomes a means to salvation. Proficiency in logic was tested and increased, after long apprenticeship, by public debates held in certain gardens and places set apart for the purpose in the monastery grounds which were called *chhötra*, or 'Dharma schools'. The debates were attended and judged by the abbot or other notables. As these contests had questions of doctrinal interpretation and the meaning of texts as their subject-matter, they served also to clarify the teaching. There were two contestants: the challenger, who stood, and the defender, who sat before him. The debate proceeded with syllogisms, examples, quotations, in a rapid fire of question and answer that testified to the disputants' acquaintance with formal logic, but seldom to their originality or invention. Because they were staged in such a theatrical way these debates attracted laymen too, entertaining them hugely, even though they could understand precious little of what was said.

The most coveted title was that of *Geshé*, or Doctor of Divinity. The Geshés were divided into a lower and a higher category and, in the Kagyü-pa and Nyingma-pa schools teaching took two forms: the *shè-tra*, based on the scriptures, and the *trup* on mystical experiences. Their highest title was *Trupla*, 'Master of Mystic Powers'.

The monastic organization has always differentiated clearly between liturgic, speculative, and mystical functions, on the one hand, and those primarily concerned with discipline and administration on the other.

I shall now deal briefly with another very important aspect of Lamaism: its techniques of yoga. These derive largely from India, but in part also from pre-Buddhist shaman practices. *Tummo*, or voluntary hyperpyrexia, is an example. Its practitioners are easily recognized by the thin, off-white cotton garment they wear; hence their title of *rêpa*, 'the cotton-clad'. The absence of the heavy woollen robe normally used in Tibet marks them as masters of the art of tummo.

The theoretical basis of the technique is simple. Conscious thought is carried along by the life-breath through two lateral channels, on the right and left of the body, communicating with the cosmic breath at the nostrils. It has to be forced into the median channel running up the spine, and there burn with a fire in which the illusion of individuality disappears, the ego vanishes in the whole. It is the tummo that produces this burning.

Practical procedures vary with the schools, but a combination of mental and physical exercises is required in every case.

The physical drill has three aspects: sitting in a particular way, special movements of the body, and breath-control. It is necessary to sit cross-legged with the calves and the thighs resting on the feet, the big toes level with the knees; the hands are then passed into the cavity between the legs to embrace the haunches. The stomach is moved from right to left three times, then another three from left to right, and vigorously rotated. Then the body is shaken 'like a wild horse', and one gives a sudden leap —springs sharply into the air keeping the legs crossed—and lets oneself fall

42. A thanka representing a much-worshipped goddess of the Tibetan Pantheon, Nampargyelma. This is an example of one of the *serthang*, 'golden thankas', so called because the images are drawn on a gold background.

43. Extensive detail from a carpet showing two stylized dragons, reflecting Chinese influence.

back at once. Control of breathing involves inhaling deeply, then contracting the diaphragm hard so as to hold the breath for a long time.

The psychological training that goes with the physical exercises amounts to a process of auto-suggestion. Once in the proper posture, the student must seven times visualize himself transformed into the Buddha Heruka and made huge enough to fill the whole of space; his body is luminous; as he breathes in and out, the whole cycle of fierce and tranquil deities enters and leaves his pores, visibly portraying for the purposes of meditation the play of forces that go to build up the world. In the meditation's second phase, this emanation-reabsorption procedure is applied to letters symbolizing the same deities in sound. They are imagined placed to the right and left of the spinal column and bright red in colour. The third phase is to concentrate on the syllabic letter *haṁ* envisaged _____ _____ head just where one of the three channels we spoke of earlier emer _____ _____ with flames that surge into the body with every br _____ _____ ble of each foot and another on each pa _____ _____ gining a further sun in the perinaeum, a _____ _____ indled by chafing the suns of hands an _____ _____ to pervade the whole person and after _____ _____ While this is going on twenty of the si _____

After repeating these exercis _____ _____ bitterest cold, naked or clothed in a si _____ _____ the right to wear a cotton garment, is gr _____ _____ e coldest time of the year. Students wh _____ _____ e ice and plunge into the water of a fr _____ _____ length of cotton dipped in the water _____ _____ ndidate is the one who dries most pie _____

Tummo is practised in all monasteries o _____ _____ ne of them, as in Pêpung in Kham, the rêpas give an annual public displa _____ skill. A few days before the New Year, when the weather is particularly cold, they leave the monastery naked or wrapped only in pieces of cotton dipped in icy water, and all perform the ritual circuit of the sacred area together. Their imperviousness to the icy winds rouses the admiration of the crowd that has come to watch. Not all do well at the test, however, as the technique demands years of practice.

Tummo is described in a treatise ascribed to Nāropa, one of the greatest yogins of Buddhist India, and teacher of Marpa, who in his turn was to be Mila-rêpa's guru. The book is known as the *Six Laws of Nāropa* since, besides tummo, it deals with dreams, the intermediate state between death and rebirth, the 'subtle' or illusory body, the transference of consciousness to another form of existence, and the manifestation of light. It is a short work, but of the greatest interest for the study of psychophysical phenomena, which were closely investigated by Indian and Tibetan teachers.

The various yogic methods practised by Lamaism are meant to divert sense and perception from the outward to the inward, regardless of whether the meditator begins by concentrating on a statue, lamp, or *mandala* (one of the paintings and diagrams that reproduce mystical systems in the symbolism of colour, line and shape). There is a succession of stages to attain, of which the first reduces all sensory activity to mere physiological function, so that sensation does not lead to perception. In the second stage of absolute concentration, all distinction between subject and object, I and not-I, dissolves. In the third, breathing regains its primal value as cosmic energy. In this way, the meditator becomes part of the great harmony of the universe, the source of

44. Detail from a Tibetan thanka, showing the retinue of eight riders of the god of Wealth, Namthösê.

creation, which reveals itself to us in the form of brightness. And indeed through the mist that appears in the fourth stage, there begin to dart brighter and brighter flashes of light. These settle into small flickering dots, like fireflies, which grow by degrees almost to the size of a lamp flame. Finally they explode into a vast steady brightness, like the cloudless sky. In the fifth stage this brilliance pervades the whole of space, and in the sixth and last the meditator too is absorbed in it. This meditation with its culminating burst of light is more especially a Dzokchen-pa practice.

The schools that concentrate on yoga are not much given to the study of doctrinal theory; they represent the 'rapid path', from existentiality in space and time to realization of Buddhahood, and bring the adept to a state of perfect blessedness. The life of a hermit is more suitable for this exercise than life in the monasteries.

I visited many hermitages during my travels. Sometimes they are rock-hewn cells, known as *tshamkhang* or meditation houses, under the aegis of some monastery, which are sited behind and, as a rule, uphill from the monastery itself. They are reached by steep rough paths up ledges in the mountainside, and contain one or two rooms where the monk lives alone for a set time. He may stay for the seasonal retreat prescribed by monastic rules, or longer. His cell may have a porch, also cut in the rock, with a little wall in front on which the occupant can grow flowers. The view over the mountains and valleys beyond, in all its interplay of light and shade, induces the receptive calm required for meditation. There are also whole communities of contemplatives, reminiscent of the ancient hermit-cities of Christian Egypt. Their tiny dwellings, each to house one monk, were purposely built some distance apart and quite far from centres of population. But some go even further; they are incarcerated in a cave, the entrance of which is walled up, harder to reach from inhabited places, vowing to stay there either for a certain number of years, or until their death. I have sometimes spoken with such 'walled-up' hermits, through the little window that is cut in their wall, and the conversation undeniably gave one the impression of confronting beings of no common order. Like Indian ascetics, and certain hermits of the Thebaid, they have no desire to preach to others, believing that the truth, once found by them, shines on all alike.

As well as these solitary mystics and recluses there are the itinerant mystics, who correspond, in a way, to the Indian sādhus. Like the latter they are divided into two groups: those who follow this way of life to impress and exploit the credulity of the people, and the minority who are true ascetics. Nearly all belong to the Kagyü-pa and Dzokchen schools. Perhaps these gifted and restless minds retain a race-memory of the ancient nomadic life. This way of life survived, under religious stimulus, in the pilgrims one met on all the routes of Tibet. Many of them went down to India, to Bodhgayā, Sarnāth, and all the traditional places connected with the life of the Buddha; they travelled alone or in small groups, careless of the world, possessed by a divine discontent that kept them continually on the move.

Reminders of the sacred world stand along the tracks to the great religious centres, in the distinctive structures known as 'mani-walls'. These are parapets of varying breadth, low enough to allow any passer-by to see their upper surface easily; stones carved with the formula '*Oṁ maṇi-padme hūṁ*' rest on top of them. Sometimes instead of this prayer entire books are found carved on blocks of stone, especially the *Dorjechöpa*, the Tibetan translation of the *Vajracchedika-sūtra* which sums up the teachings of the 'Perfection of Knowledge'. In this famous book the Buddha is supposed to have condensed the essential teachings of the doctrine of the illusoriness of things. The wayfarer keeps these monuments respectfully on his right, because to go past them

45. View of Gyantsé, the third most important Tibetan city.

46. In the Monastery of Trashi-lhünpo.

45

46

47   48

in this way is equivalent to reciting the prayer carved on the stone for as many times as it is repeated there.

The pilgrim's devotion sometimes takes strange forms: that, for instance, of the *kyangchhak* or long prostration, where a person vows to prostrate himself all the way to the holy places, whatever the condition of the road, touching the ground with his forehead in the posture called the 'eight-limbed obeisance'. Each time, before standing up, he marks the spot where his head rested, to put his feet there for the following prostration. These movements he interrupts only for sleep and food. To protect their hands these pilgrims strap on small hardwood boards. The prostration is performed in several stages: the pilgrim first of all places his hands together at his chest, throat and the crown of his head, and back again, reversing the movements to return his hands to chest level; then he kneels and places his forehead to the ground. The three points where the joined hands pause correspond to the three planes of our essential nature: physical, verbal and spiritual. (Authors of works on ritual complicate matters by associating physical actions with particular points of doctrine. For example, something as commonplace as lighting a match—or using a flint—can be transformed into a good thought and beneficial karma, if its performer interprets it as the lighting of the fire of gnosis which destroys the darkness of error. Even walking can serve as meditation if one thinks that one leg is Means, the other Knowledge.)

Any description of Tibetan Buddhism must deal with the monasteries and monastic organization. The existence of so large a religious community was one of the most conspicuous characteristics of Tibetan society—not only the vast number of monasteries and temples throughout the country, but also all the monks who lived by touring the villages, and were less tied to conventual life.

The sincerity of these religious feelings—save in those clear cases where human nature was to blame—cannot be doubted. But the prestige and privileges of monastic life certainly exercised their attraction. It guaranteed a livelihood; but more important than this, it was a position of great dignity. The community, guardian of the Buddha's teachings, gained still greater importance in Tibetan Buddhism because the Lama, the teacher, is man's indispensable guide, without whose help there is no hope of salvation. The Tibetan who had embraced the monastic vows, even if he could not always claim to be a teacher, shared some of the glory of being a part of the community. Moreover, save in the case of certain sects and of the contemplatives who chose isolation, monastic life was not, on the whole, too uncomfortable. The discipline was, of course, severe: study, religious offices, the recitation of texts, took up much of the day and night. The educational system was rigid, but at least even the poorest were cared for. In fact, so long as he belonged to no infamous trade (the butcher's for instance), and was not irremediably debarred by the physical or moral disabilities listed in Buddhism's earliest disciplinary rules, anyone could be admitted to the monastic order. In some cases the monks might even go back home to work on the land, with their superiors's permission, and could freely own property.

Huge monasteries, dominating the landscape, demonstrate the supremacy the monastic community enjoyed. Some were positive cities, growing over the centuries: the more recent buildings had spread around the ancient nucleus, nearly always bound up with the memory of a famous historical figure. Such a case was Yerpa, associated with Atiśa and Padmasambhava, its chapels, seminaries and colleges climbing the precipitous mountainside, which grows increasingly sheer as though to keep the hermits' cells inviolate. Drêpung and Sera, not far from Lhasa, Ganden further east, and Kumbum in Amdo, each housed several thousand monks.

47. Outdoor merry-making of south-west Szechwan Tibetans during a religious festival.

48. An exterior view of the Jokhang Temple in Lhasa.

It was inevitable that the monasteries should acquire power, if only because they alone provided the education necessary to train an *élite* capable of leading a country. The studies of the novices who were not content with the rank of the officiating monks, but hoped to make some progress in the ecclesiastical 'career', so to speak, were anything but simple.   Mechanically reading from the scriptures was not enough in their case; they were also required to understand their meaning with all the abstruseness of dogmatics, gnosis, logic and metaphysics. They had to master a difficult literature, translated or recast in Tibetan but originally written in India, bristling with the subtleties of Indian thought. The outcome of this study was a tempering of intellect and the powers of argument, a keen eye for detail, the ability to put problems in the right light, clearness of judgment: all virtues that have just as much place in the outside world as in ecclesiastic life.

Although theoretically the organization of Tibetan monasteries is modelled on rules laid down by the Buddha, it is at a considerable remove from them in practice. Their pattern is not the ancient code of monastic discipline, so much as the system followed by Indian religious colleges when the Great Vehicle was at its height, and by Central Asiatic and even Chinese monasteries. The spiritual head of the community is the abbot or *khenpo*. Venerated for his real or presumed wisdom, sometimes he may be an incarnation; he is hardly ever concerned in the functioning of the monastery, and then only at really critical points; administration is in the hands of the *chipa* or *nyerpa*. Discipline is entrusted to the *gekö* who see to it that the rules are not broken and that everyone attends during religious services; in the great monastic cities they make the rounds by night as well, in the company of lictors who beat the ground with heavy iron staves and by their din warn delinquents to shelter in dark corners or to return to their quarters. These cities contain row upon row of dwellings, each inhabited by a monk with his pupil or pupils; though actually the latter are quite often so taken up with dancing attendance on their master that they fail to profit from their education and are content to be his servants. When the moment comes for him to recite the sacred texts, the student must sit with his back to his master, ready for reproofs, which may not be confined to words, for every error or failure of memory. First the texts used in the daily office and then, if the pupil is able, the standard doctrinal works, must be learnt by heart in their entirety, before anything else can be done.

In nearly all monasteries there are *trülkus*, or incarnate Lamas. All schools of Tibetan Buddhism have them, and among the Nyingma-pa they rank with the abbot.

Each monastery owned a great deal of property in land, villages, pasturage, and livestock. They amassed great riches, not only in the revenue from their estates, but also by trading with the village people or with the Drokpa nomads. The monasteries needed a huge amount of butter and barley, both for the support of the community and for liturgical ceremonies: the large monasteries consumed many tons of butter a year for the votive lamps, some of them gigantic, kept burning upon the altars, and the tea repeatedly served to all the monks during ceremonies. Monastic real estate either belonged to the foundation as a whole, as in the case of the 'chapter' or *tshokchen* in which the whole body of monks assembled daily, and where solemn ceremonies were performed on great feast days; or else it belonged to the individual colleges into which each monastery was divided. Every college had also freehold lands of its own. The villages that belonged to the monasteries and colleges were in fact benefices managed by trustworthy individuals who were answerable to the chipa.

Another considerable source of income for the monasteries was loan interest, which amounted each year to a fifth of the sum lent. Individual lamas could also amass

49. A cremation ceremony.

50. Tibetan monastery
     near Darjeeling.

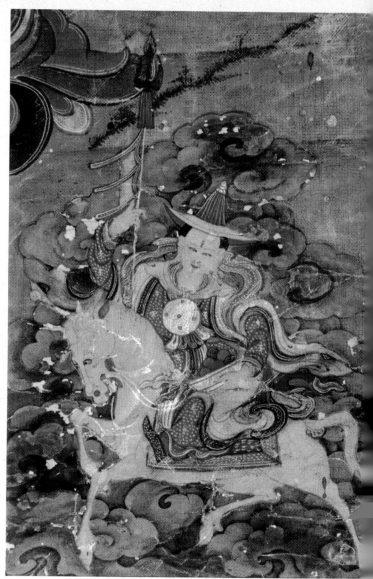

51

52

great wealth through trade and moneylending. In theory this wealth was inherited by the favourite disciple: but part of the property might already have passed to the Lama's relations. This was another reason why so many parents did their utmost to place sons in the monasteries.

In the case of great land-owning families, as a rule, the consent of the *Dzongpön* or prefect, representing the government, was required before a boy could become a monk; such permission was customarily granted as long as at least two brothers remained to look after their property and serve the state if necessary. In the case of smaller estates, permission was granted if only one remained. This rule held for tax-paying families. If for some reason the monasteries had places to spare, it was the duty of all families to supply novices. This duty was called *tr'a-trhê*, 'monk-tax'.

Obviously this does not mean that all monks were rich: many were poor, even destitute, and these acted as servants, herdsmen and cooks, or went out to beg. Alms were, in fact, another source of monastic income, together with gifts both in cash and in kind, nearly always made with the object of ensuring regular religious services for the dead or for the future benefit of the donor. These financial concerns have considerably blurred the spiritual purity of religious life, and have had their share in leading Lamaism, as a whole, a long way from the teachings of the Buddha.

The administration of justice among its monks was the monastery's responsibility. If a monk committed murder, an enquiry was first held in the monastery itself; if he was found guilty, his name was struck from the monastery register and he was handed over to the lay authorities for trial and sentence.

The state hardly ever interfered in a monastery's affairs, provided it was not hostile to the government: where an investigation became necessary, it was carried out by the Dzongpön; but since there were always two Dzongpön, one layman and one monk, the enquiry was naturally entrusted to the latter.

Every village had its modest shrine, the *lha khang* or 'god-house'. The monk in charge had the same duties as the parson in our villages: he performed the daily rites, helped the sick and dying, and lived on the offerings of the public. In some regions where the population had declined, monasteries famous in the country's political and religious history, like Toling and Tsaparang in West Tibet, or Chasa in Central Tibet, were almost abandoned to their ruin.

However one may regard them, the monasteries were the most impressive proof of the place religion occupied in Tibet. They were built mostly with funds from the donors, known as *jinda'*, who became their supporters, contributing themselves and inviting others to subscribe. When the monasteries or temples needed repair, the abbots themselves would launch a subscription. Monks were sent from house to house with a paper describing what was needed, signed by the abbot or some other authoritative person. In the blank space below the subscribers signed and set down the amount they intended to give.

51. Detail from a Tibetan thanka, showing a religious teacher, wearing the cap of an Indian pandita.

52. Detail from a Tibetan thanka, showing a 'Guardian of the Faith'.

Art

NATURE HAS ENDOWED the Tibetans with considerable aesthetic sensibility which, even in ancient times, judging by the few objects that have come down to us, found its chief expression in detailed decoration. The decorative sense dominates the development of Tibetan art; the object, whether sacred or profane, is seen as a useful excuse for spontaneous ornamental ingenuity. It is, however, a sacred art first and foremost, and its *raison d'être* is to reproduce the images, subjects and tenets of religion. It is not the offspring of untrammelled inspiration, but a carefully worked out method of representing divine visions and aiding contemplation.

Art provides a further instance of Tibet's dependence on the centres of civilization that were instrumental in her conversion to Buddhism. This dependence was modified by indigenous influences, however; in all likelihood works of art reached Tibet before the royal dynasty became established, and chroniclers speak of Bonpo paintings in the time of Songtsen-gampo. Buddhism, like Hinduism, cannot be imagined without the visual representation of its religious ideals. It inspires wonderful art as well as dizzying metaphysics: an art to recount its Founder's and his followers' deeds, and depict the glory of paradises whose presiding deities are contemplated by choirs of the elect. It also expresses doctrinal principles in symbols and traces in line and colour the complicated patterns by means of which our space-time world evolved from the primaeval luminous consciousness. Hence Buddhism came to Tibet not merely as a body of doctrine, but with a highly developed art whose business was to teach the same things in visible form.

Influences in art followed the path of political expansion and of cultural and religious penetration: Central Asia, China, Nepal and Kashmir. With the missionaries, artists arrived in Tibet, either of their own accord or summoned by the king or the nascent Buddhist community. Generally we are accustomed in an artistic tradition to distinguish manners or styles, which allow us to assign a work to a period, school or artist. For reasons I shall give later, this is almost impossible in Tibetan art. In the oldest period, however, Nepal, Central Asia and China exercised a clear influence on the beginnings of Tibetan religious art. The fact is attested by literary tradition, suggested by the historical situation, and proved by a number of works which have come down to us.

Some chroniclers, not unconvincingly, put the presence of Nepalese artists as early as the reign of Songtsen-gampo (seventh century A.D.). One of them was an expert in stone-work (*bal po'i rdo bzo pa*); others are indiscriminately termed *lha bzo pa*, 'makers of (images of) deities'. The architects who built temples in the border regions were also foreigners—*Minyak, Hor, Thogar,* and Nepalese.

King Trhitsuk-detsen threatened to declare war on the king of Li (Khotan) if he did not send him a famous artist. The latter went to Tibet, and worked there in company with other artists and craftsmen whom the same king summoned from various parts. In the temple of Iwang, near Samada on the road to Gyantsé, according to the descriptions I discovered accompanying them, some of the murals were executed ART in the style of Li (*li lugs*), i.e. Khotan, and others in that of India. Moreover, the presence of Khotanese artists thus vouched for in the time of Rêpachen (ninth century) is explained both by Tibet's political expansion into Central Asia, and by the insecurity there, which forced many Buddhists to flee.

The monastery of Ngari-Tratsang, which I visited in 1948, contained a magnificent gilt bronze stupa of T'ang dynasty Chinese workmanship. In Chhöding monastery I found an embroidered silk thanka similar to those discovered by Sir Aurel Stein in Central Asia, with the various figures on it identified by their names written in Chinese characters. There was of course the possibility of decorative motifs being introduced into Tibet from other countries in the course of trade. One cannot doubt that Sassanid textile designs inspired the ornamentation on the robes of the gigantic Bodhisattva images in the temple of Chasa, south of the Tsangpo. The Lhakhang Chhenmo at Sakya held a whole gallery of bronze and other metal statues from various parts of India and from the Pāla and Sena dynasties in particular—a collection that would be the envy of any museum, as would that of Narthang. Splendid Kashmiri bronzes were preserved in the war-devastated temple at Toling in West Tibet, whilst at Samyê, in Ü, there were others from the Pāla kingdom and from Central Asia.

Groups of religious subjects exist which retain the form in which they were first brought to Tibet. The cycle of the god of wealth, Namthösê, for example, follows the original Central Asiatic version, and the group of sixteen or eighteen Arhats is still recognizably Chinese.

Many of the West Tibetan temples, such as those at Tsaparang, which was the capital of the region for some centuries, those at Toling and other shrines of the same period, preserve murals and paintings on cloth in the style of Kashmir. The presence of Kashmiri artists in West Tibet is affirmed by literary sources: these state that when Rinchen-sangpo (founder of Toling) returned from Kashmir, he brought back not only manuscripts and teachers to help in the translations of sacred texts, but also artists, some of whose names are recorded, to build and decorate the shrines their royal patrons were erecting throughout the country.

There is proof of this at Mang-nang, a small temple I visited on my 1933 journey, once the home of a translator (*lotsawa*) who took his name from it. Here frescoes of Buddhas and Bodhisattvas, ascetics and celestial nymphs (apsarases), the work of eleventh century Kashmiri artists, clearly demonstrate the kinship of the Kashmiri art of that time with Indian classical painting. Other frescoes in the temple, though executed in the same style, present a certain formal rigidity that suggests their attribution to native apprentices. Supple figures predominate, in canvasses as well as murals, with the body softly flexed to one side and with long slender legs, save where the canons of iconography have led to a certain stiffening of the central images in the separate pictorial groups. The commonest colours are red, white and turquoise, and gilding is used extensively. Further evidence of Kashmiri influence at work in West Tibet is provided by the wooden pillars flanking the doors of Tabo in Spiti, which was put up at Rinchen-sangpo's command; reliefs on their successive panels represent leading episodes from the life of the Buddha.

The statues of Kashmiri provenance met with in other monasteries may, of course, have been moved to Tibet in later times, when anti-Buddhist persecutions began in Kashmir. This could perhaps be true of the very beautiful gilt-bronze images that are venerated at Sakya, particularly those of Jamyang Ösê-barwa, and others in the Utsé-nyingpa.

When the first dynasty of West Tibet, which claimed descent from the Lhasa kings, was succeeded by another that enlarged its sway to cover much of western Nepal as well, Nepalese influence joined that of Kashmir.

Because of her prolonged relations with Tibet, Nepal was destined to leave a lasting imprint on Tibetan art. The manuscripts, often illuminated, which the abbots of the great monasteries, particularly the Sakya-pas, had copied, and the welcome extended to Nepalese artists, who enjoyed great fame in Tibet, gave rise to the Nepalese style; and this long dominated the development of Tibetan painting, especially that of Ü and Tsang. Indeed, the renown of Nepalese artists was such that even the Mongol emperors asked for their work to embellish the temples and palaces they were building. One such artist (of whom the Chinese chronicles also tell us) was the seventeen-year old Aniko who, with twenty-four colleagues, went to China on Phakpa's advice.

One gathers from biographies of the more famous founder abbots that Nepalese craftsmen were often brought in to paint the newly-built walls in fresco; in some cases the actual names of the artists are recorded, as in the case of those who decorated the Lhakhang built by the founder of the Ngor sect, Künga-sangpo (1382-1444).

The custom of patronizing well-known Nepalese artists never lapsed. Tāranātha and the fifth Dalai Lama kept it up: the latter's biography cites several by name (under the year 1659). Since sacred objects must not be a source of gain, they were not paid for in cash; but all expenses were met, and the artists received substantial gifts.

During the Sakya-pa period the renewed influence of Chinese painting on Tibet was considerable. Mountains, which had been drawn almost cone-shaped in the Indian manner, for instance, began to take on the appearance of crags in the Dolomites.

The great monastery of Shalu was decorated by Mongol and Chinese artists, we are told by Pu-tön, and this is borne out by the multicoloured ceramic ornamentation that covered its roofs and colonnades; at the pagoda-type roof corners, the mouths of sea-monsters (*makara*) in deep blue majolica, served as dripstones.

It is attested by the fifth Dalai Lama that this was also true of Tshê monastery; and we come across the same influence in some frescoes at Narthang, where the figures are represented in fashionable Chinese dress.

The further spread of Chinese influence came primarily by way of the artistic centres of Kham, where proximity has always made it strong; these have therefore represented a special, easily recognizable school, which can be classed simply as a branch of Chinese provincial art. Chinese artistic penetration, particularly in painting, was intensified in the eighteenth century through the agency of the larger monastic centres.

But obviously geographical neighbourhood did not always determine which style would prevail. When the monasteries arose, the dominant influence in their art depended on the cultural contacts each of them had with this or that region, however far off. In this way they arrived at their own artistic language, which became standard. Their printing departments housed wood-blocks for the illustration of certain religious cycles, alongside those for books: at Narthang and Trashi-lhünpo were sets of line-prints of the Arhats, the Panchen Lamas, the Dalai Lamas, the life of the Buddha, and so on. When brought back by pilgrims to their own villages these xylographic prints became the models for local artists, who took good care not to depart from them.

53. Detail from a Tibetan thanka, showing Avalokiteśvara as Padmapāṇi—Lotus-in-hand—surrounded by a chorus of sixteen *changchupsempas*.

54. Detail from a Tibetan thanka, representing listeners to the Buddha's teaching.

Since we know the dates at which some of these blocks were carved they make a fairly precise chronological *terminus post quem* for the countless repetitions deriving from them. We read for instance that the blocks depicting the sixteen Arhats (*nêten* in Tibetan) were cut by order of Pholanê and his sons, *i.e.* between 1728 and 1747; others which represent the various episodes of the Buddha's last and previous lives,

53

54

55

56

based on a famous narrative by a Kashmiri poet, were due to the munificence of
Gyurmé-tsheten, killed in 1750, the elder son of Pholanê.

Altogether, painting reflects the character of Tibetan culture and its dependence on that of other countries; a dependence that is never mere copying, for the different inspirations that meet in it are so well blended that Tibetan art is distinctive.

The enormous demand for religious paintings and sculptures, whether for adoration in temples, or to supply the needs of daily worship in private chapels, has laden the country with an astonishing abundance of works of art. This is in some ways a negative factor, making as it does for the repetitive stagnation of art, the tired permutation of themes and patterns. Another negative factor is the very nature of the art itself. It curtailed the scope of the artist's imagination, through its need to be inspired by religious themes, depicting deities, devotees or paradises or representing theories of salvation in image and colour symbolism, according to precise rules. The shape the artist gave to his particular vision did not obey an aesthetic urge but a liturgical and iconographic command. Here too Tibetans followed the teachers of India. To paint or sculpt was to evoke a divine presence which had to be recognized in precise and stable forms. Otherwise painting and sculpture would have no ritual value — would not speak the language they were meant to; and therefore effective communication between man and the divine plane they represented would be impossible.

A further handicap was that the figure itself had to be constructed in accordance with patterns laid down by iconography. We are justified in speaking of its 'construction' because the figure was developed in terms of the ratios between and combinations of certain standard measures. This 'iconometry', as I shall call it, is described by both Indian authors and their Tibetan successors. But it is worth recording that one such work is attributed to the Buddha himself, and treated as revelation to stress the inviolability of the iconometric rules. The scheme is based on a vertical and a horizontal line, crossing at right angles, which act as a skeleton to build the figure on. The measuring unit is the middle finger, which corresponds to the 118th, 116th, 120th or 124th part of the height of the image; with very large figures this finger measure is replaced by another, the *tala*, equal to twelve or twelve-and-a-half finger breadths.

In the case of sculpture it was not uncommon for the patron's own finger to be adopted as the unit, so that something of himself was reproduced in the resulting image. These standardized proportions hold for all the sacred figures, including, in pictorial compositions, the large central figure, in its static ritual pose, which gives the painting its significance. Towards this focal point flock the adoring choirs, while other divine beings (variations of the main figure) are ranged around, equally motionless and absorbed; or a series of a scenes from traditional stories may be shown. The consequence is a rigidity and coldness that leave these images scant individuality. All the artist concerns himself with representing is either the deity's contemplative concentration or his fury; but whilst in the latter case one finds convincing, lively examples, in the former one rarely gets away from the conventional pattern.

So the artist, governed by laws of iconography he cannot escape from without committing sacrilege, exercises his skill in the arabesque, in the insistence on detail, the jewels, the decoration of the garments. This is the general rule both for sculpture and for the figures that occupy the central position in paintings and thus represent their ideal centre—*tsowo* in Tibetan. Painting does allow the artist greater freedom than sculpture, however. The painter's inventive faculty can find more expression in the rhythmic structure of the whole, the balance of the composition, and the enchantment of clouds, birds in flight, solitary trees—none of which are subjects imposed by

55. Detail from a Tibetan thanka, showing a man carrying away a cub from its parents—a popular story.

56. Tibetan currency note for 100 *srang* (in use up to 1959).

ART iconography, but which spring from the artist's imagination, as eloquent as the resulting colour scheme is vivid. This happens above all in portrayals of the life of the Buddha, and of the great teachers of Tibetan Buddhism. Whilst the deity enthroned at the centre of the painting on cloth (thanka), or mural fresco, is fixed in a hieratic and expressionless composure, tales of life on earth or scenes of paradise unfold about him in separate episodes. In this way, the Tibet of everyday life breaks into the sacredness of the painting and lends it warmth.

The artist transposes the landscapes of his own countryside into the painting (cf. pl. 54)—the sun-dried white houses, the monasteries and temples with their golden cupolas and roofs, their throngs of chanting monks; or horses at full gallop whilst preposterous curly clouds sail across an azure sky. Familiar scenes are shown against houses and palaces that lie open like the backcloth of the Japanese theatre, in such a way that the people inside are surprised in their everyday activities or in conversation. For background there are waves of mountains, sometimes shown awkward and triangular like big tents planted on the green expanse of the plains, sometimes drawn in the Chinese style, with improbable crags and sharp peaks, on which rest tired, transparent clouds. The joyful narrative flows on, bathed in an unvarying southern light, the pictorial reflection of Tibet's pellucid sky. This art was not acquainted with perspective. Even when the influence of Chinese painting breaks up the accumulation of figures and flat masses of colour, the Chinese model is not heeded; its aerial perspective crystallizes into a translucent void, where shapes are suspended in unreal stillness and the narrative turns into a fairy tale or takes on the weightlessness of a dream. This at least gives the paintings a gaiety and a homely air—as though the artist, once he had finished the construction of the central image according to the precepts of iconometry, let the innate joyfulness of his character, or love for the countryside he knew, guide his hand.

Indian esotericism taught that the fearsome divinities are simply the belligerent aspect of good forces, taking on that shape to conquer their evil counterparts which continually lie in wait for us. This interpretation received a response in the substratum of magic and terror that lies in the Tibetan's subconscious. Art found a fertile field of inspiration here, and hence liked to dwell on this theme. Alongside the meditating Buddhas, the teachers rapt, motionless and absorbed, in detached contemplation, is the seething throng of misshapen forms—chhökyongs, ḍākinīs, sungmas (cf. pl. 63).

Heads and arms sprout from their bodies like jungle creepers from a moist tree-trunk; their faces have a terrifying look; their mouths leer, displaying ferocious fangs; and the pupils seem to start from their horribly dilated eyes as though propelled by inward fury. The arms grasp weapons, bodies lean over to spring up in wrath or toss in warlike dances, trampling the corpses of slain and conquered demons. Shapes lose all composure: swollen bellies overflow on wide-set, brawny legs; the dance, devoid of all lightness, gives the feeling of a brute mass whose moving makes the world quake. Often these wrathful divinities are coupled; male is matched by female, frequently in sexual embrace, and thus united they dance in a frenzied outburst of exultant fury.

There is no doubt that the Tibetans reached the summit of their art in the portrayal of this demonic world. But are such images really terrifying? They certainly appeared so in the atmosphere of the gönkhang, the dark, lonely recess cut off from the rest of the monastery or temple, where they were kept and evoked or propitiated. All around in the gloom hung the skins of animals, keeping guard, together with weapons, armour and the mummified remains of enemies or brigands. The deity's image was hidden by dusty robes, from under which the implements he brandished stuck out. The lama murmured his recitations in a deep, guttural voice, to the accompaniment of a great one-legged drum which he beat rhythmically with a curved stick. The sight of the monks' own reluctance to enter these gönkhang, the mysterious fittings, the darkness, the appearance of the deities invoked—everything inclined the visitor's mind to anxious expectancy: an air of fear was breathed in those places, which the Tibetans felt all the more, coming to it with the spiritual training produced by centuries of experience at the back of their minds.

But viewed objectively, with the detachment needed when judging any work of art, the fearsome softens into the grotesque. The leer, the bulging eyes, the convulsed movements are unconvincing. The fury is stylized and superficial: it is weakened by its own exaggeration and lack of proportion, and also through the recollection that many of these images represent transient forms of kindly beings. The initial bewilderment subsides; the terrible becomes merely monstrous. It does not frighten, but interests—with the interest always to be found in attempts to express the weird and unfamiliar, and in the shape given to the fantasies of a wild imagination or one that enjoys its nightmares. Yet in these very representations Tibetan art finds, as it does in the depiction of everyday life, a power of expression normally limited or indeed suppressed by the static nature of its iconographies. Iconometry laid down precise rules for these figures too, of course, but the need for motion in them, and the dropping of ordinary conventions in order to enter a fantasy world that dissolves the harmonies of the human form, allowed the artist greater liberty. He could give an expression wholly his own to an iconography which he himself had to experience as visions and then translated into graphic form. This does not mean that Tibetan art thereby took any new path. Once again it followed the precepts of India, where every representation presupposes a vision: that is, before being portrayed the image must be visualized by the artist, either within or in front of himself, by a process of evocation. The image is not produced as a lifeless object, but must contain within itself the ritual power with which it is associated. It has to be quickened by investing it with 'life'. This is brought about in various ways. The formula *oṁ āh hūṁ* is written on the reverse of the painted figure, its syllables corresponding to the physical, verbal and spiritual plane of which every human or divine being is composed: or certain formulae that sum up the arcane essence of the deity in a sequence of speech-sounds are inserted in the body of the image. A special ceremony may be performed in the course of which the deity's eyes are opened. These ceremonies are termed *rabnê*.

The main charm of the paintings is in their colouring. Naturally the colour of a deity is itself laid down by rite and dogma, and this cannot be departed from: yet in spite of this limitation the Tibetans have given proof of remarkable skill in combining colours. The uniformity of the older paintings in which one or two colours, red and dark blue, predominate is gradually superceded by an exuberant palette, evidently as a result of greater familiarity with Chinese painting. The new liveliness is often further lit by large patches of gold—for gold is completely multivalent, being the synthesis of all substances—and the sudden blazing contrasts produced by alternating reds, blues and greens are most effective. They are solid colours with hardly any shading: bold splashes that meet without half-tones, a brilliant mosaic so gay that even those who cannot interpret the secret meanings of the paintings can yet enjoy them. But as well as colour one should also note the use of outline. In space, the line serves to set a limit to the design, and acquires a magical value by fixing the ecstatic moment's evocation in a composition of which it forms a basic part. The figure is not an illusory image of light and shade, but a pattern picking out the essential shapes. Hence the significance of the diagrams (*mandala*) in which the psycho-physical world is brought under control for the mystic by the use of circles, squares and angles.

Public and private collections, in Europe and America, abound in Tibetan paintings on cloth—'*thankas*' or 'banners'—whose decorativeness, bold colouring and air of naïve astonishment, eplain the interest they give rise to in the West. This is to judge them on externals, of course. The real point is their content, the endless variety of religious themes, the search to express a profoundly complicated mystical world through these figures' symbolic attributes. Hence Tibetan painting can be examined at two distinct levels. One way of appreciating it, the purely visual, is accessible to all: it pleases the eye with this vividness and decorative harmony, without regard to the content. The other is reserved for the student, not merely of Lamaism, but of Buddhism as a whole—the student of religious experience who has the ability to translate it into a language that can be understood only by those who know the subject-matter which the paintings set out to express.

It is plain that we cannot speak of 'schools' in Tibetan art, or only in a very general way. When we discuss schools, as I have tried to do in my book *Tibetan Painted Scrolls*, we are referring to groupings that can be suggested on the basis of shared characteristics, but which have neither a strictly chronological nor a geographical basis. When certain paintings are said to be in the Nepalese style, it means that they reproduce the Nepalese artists' forms of expression in a manner that may be more, or less, tried and conventional. But the forms in question can last for centuries: sometimes in retreat, sometimes more in evidence. The same can be said for the Chinese style. Moreover, as has been pointed out, certain schools which grew up under the patronage of the more famous monasteries enjoyed such prestige that their artistic language spread throughout Tibet. Anyhow, as I think Tibetan painting is valuable in its own right, it is more appropriate to follow these groupings, imprecise as they may seem, than to stick to the usual system of classifying thankas according to the religious subjects they treat. This would be tantamount to denying them any artistic value. By limiting the distinguishing criterion to one of religious content, Tibetan art would be reduced to mere iconography, just as would happen if Western religious art were to be discussed by subject-matter—'The Holy Family', 'The Madonna' and so forth.

In the course of these pages we have often spoken of 'thankas'. What are thankas? They are paintings of sacred and ceremonial subjects, which are hung up in temples or private chapels, or carefully rolled up to be carried over the shoulder when travelling, for the divinity lodged in the painting saves the bearer from the perils of his journey.

The paintings are done on cotton, more rarely on canvas: hence their name of 'cotton-drawings' (*rê-tri, rê-rimo*). The piece of cotton used is generally oblong, but may also be square. It is cut to the desired size and kept at a suitable tension on a frame. It is then saturated with a mixture of lime and vegetable gum. When the material is dry any remaining porousness is eliminated by repeatedly passing across it a spatula or some other well polished object, such as a piece of conch-shell. The outlines of the figures and the subjects to be represented are sketched in charcoal or Indian ink on the surface thus obtained; frequently this first cartoon is gone over again in Indian ink. Drawing always begins with the central figure which, as mentioned above, represents the focal point of the composition. Next, the various colours are applied with a brush, thinning out or strengthening the shade with lime and glue blended in suitable proportions, the latter giving the paintings greater toughness. The colours that used to be employed were mineral or organic: arsenic for yellow, indigo or lapis lazuli for blue, cochineal for red. Gold was widely used either for the details

57. Sakya: the main altar of the Great Temple, showing large images of deities.

of garments or the emblems of the deities represented. Highly valued were the paintings on a gold background, which were known as *serthang*, 'golden thankas'.

The completed painting is finally enclosed in a cloth surround. In earlier times this meant simply two pieces of cotton above and below, the ends glued or sewn around two wooden staves, the one at the top to hang it by, and the heavier one underneath to keep it well stretched out. Later it became usual to frame the thankas completely in precious stuffs or Chinese brocades. Two strips of silk or brocade in contrasting colours—yellow, red or blue—were sewn round the picture; these are termed the 'red, yellow (etc.) rainbow', according to the colour of the material. Then the painting was framed all round with a broader band of silk or brocade, taking care to make the upper portion shorter than the lower, and those at the sides narrower still. A panel of silk brocade in another colour, and of yet more costly quality, was often inserted in the middle of the lower part for greater relief. It was called the 'door of the thanka', *thanggo*.

At the end of the staves were fastened knobs of bronze, brass, silver, etc. A piece of thin silk or other material, as large as the thanka, was stitched on at the height of the upper stave: it covers the painting and protects it when rolled up. Two ribbons, also coloured, sewn above it at equal distances from the edge, serve to keep the thanka firmly rolled.

Mural paintings are similarly executed. In their case a layer of impasto is first spread over the wall and a lime and gum mixture applied; the line-drawing is sketched out on the prepared surface and then painting is begun.

The pictorial displays that cover the temple walls follow a sacred, ritual logic inspired by the devotional or mystical vision to be induced in the particular religious building. The great pictures succeed one another in the order required by the texts describing them. Their aim is not decorative: it is to bring the place to life, esoterically, by transferring the temple to a non-human dimension, and imbuing it with the sacred character it must have in order to fulfil its task. These sequences of temple frescoes are chiefly addressed to the initiate, who can understand their secrets. To the layman they serve for edification: he can read their general significance in the inscriptions that often accompany them.

We come next to the plastic arts. The metals used for statues are bronze, brass, copper, silver, and even gold. As in the case of painting, the Tibetans took an interest in various styles introduced from other countries. The writers who dealt with sculpture listed a number of principal styles. The Indian was subdivided into the styles of central, southern, western, northern and eastern India—as can be seen, the scheme is too closely modelled on that of the five cardinal points (including the centre) to be taken literally. In respect of the Chinese style, an early and a recent manner were distinguished, in appreciable agreement with the facts. To the above they added the Uighur, Khotanese and Central Asian styles. The classification is one which, as we have just said, roughly corresponds with the actual cultural and artistic influences that operated on Tibet. But when it comes to establishing what are the characteristics that distinguish one style from another, vague generalizations ensue. However, these writers correctly recognized that, in order to assign a given statue to any school, attention must chiefly be paid to certain details, such as the drawing of the eyes or the drapery. It is evident that the likelihood of an exact stylistic attribution being made will depend primarily on the statue's antiquity. The formal characteristics are more plainly recognizable in the earliest period, when outside influences were direct and continuous, whereas they become much harder to define, or disappear altogether, in the *koinē*,

58. General view of Likhir Monastery, Ladakh.

59. Yuru Monastery, Ladakh.

that increasingly sets the pattern of all Tibetan art as we approach modern times. Moreover these influences must be determined separately for each case, after close comparison with the characteristics of various artistic periods in the countries to which Tibet has been culturally subject.

In Tibet, by contrast with China and India, sculpture in stone was not very popular —at least in recent periods, for we have seen that expert stone-carvers are recorded in the older historical works. A few examples of their work are known, such as the lion figures discovered by Richardson near the tombs of the kings in Yarlung, which were evidently inspired by similar statues on Chinese funerary monuments of the T'ang period. To the same period and influence we owe the stone tortoise in Chinese style, perhaps a pillar-base, preserved at Samyê. We also know of groups of stone deities such as the five buddhas of Trhadru. On the other hand, the rock-face at such danger-spots as suspension bridges and roads liable to landslides was frequently carved with the more popular deities to protect travellers, and these show considerable skill in bas-relief (cf. pl. 62). The custom was probably introduced from countries with similar geographical features where such carvings marked the route of pilgrims bound for the sacred places—Swat, for example. Some sculptures in Ladakh date back to the first kings of the local dynasty, and are of gigantic proportions. Carving in relief is also employed on the 'mani walls', to alternate the protective deity's actual image with his formulae carved on the stone. These figures are generally in very low relief, sometimes simply graffiti, carved by local people and with no pretensions to art.

Statues were, naturally, made of other materials, especially wood. Choice and costly sandalwood was imported for this purpose from India. There are records of sandalwood statues being specially ordered from India or Nepal down to fairly recent times, an example being the statue of Lokésvara which was brought from Nepal to the newly-built Potala. Other statues, called *dzaku*, were made of terra-cotta; others again—particularly in western Tibet, using a technique widespread in Kashmir—of papiermâché. I saw many of these still standing in the temple, unfortunately laid waste during the Dogra invasion, at Kyunglung in West Tibet. Statues are as a rule gilded, except for the wooden ones which more often have coloured drapery and ornaments or are left to the slow action of time, which clothes them in a venerable black patina. A heat-process is used for gilding the metal statues. Images in more costly materials are also known, like the coral Tshepamé, the mother-of-pearl Chen-rêsik, and the turquoise Drölma which were kept in the Chakpori, probably having been imported from India or China.

Once the raw materials of sculpture have been discussed we come up against the same restrictions we noted in the case of painting: iconography is in command, with its set forms. It leaves the craftsman less freedom than ever, in fact. His handiwork is a monotonous repetition of types, divided only into calm and wrathful deities. The latter are the livelier product of Tibetan sculpture on account of the shifting play of forms and the rhythm of their dances; in spite of the limitations imposed, stagnation is replaced by a dash and dynamism that seem to vent their inward fury.

This is not the case with the tranquil figures. A meditative stillness grips them yet fails, with rare exceptions, to impart the spiritual lightness and the indescribable completeness of certain statues of the Buddha from India and China. The face, constructed mechanically to the prescribed measurements, is frozen in an unconcerned smile from which there shines no secret such as it should contain (cf. pls. 98, 101). Only when this part is completed can the artist really begin to carve on his own: the robes with their embroideries, and the emblems of the figures represented, are a pretext for his skill. Since his inspiration fails to reveal the spirit, he lets himself go on detail. But this art is occasionally redeemed, as with painting, by portraiture. Once again, the everyday life driven out by formalism finds its way back through the portrayal of teachers, ascetics or monastery founders—in other words, of reality. Such images were similarly contructed, but with greater freedom. One frequently marvels at the close observation displayed, the care to portray the subject exactly as he was, after a shrewd study of the features with the aim of making the subject's inner personality immediately apparent, as in the case of the images of certain monks, wrapped in robes that hide them like cocoons from which only their shaven or mitre-crowned heads emerge.

To make or commission a statue is a pious work. The larger the statue, the greater the merit accruing to both parties: the patron for spending more on it, the sculptor for working more. This belief occurred quite early on in Buddhism and has travelled everywhere with it. Tibet abounds in gigantic statues, so much so that special many-storied shrines have been built to hold them, allowing the visitor to perform the ritual circuit in successive stages. The different floors have balustrades opening on to the statue so that every part of it can be seen. Its huge bulk towers upwards, wrapped in the robes appropriate to its dignity and significance, the draperies suggesting the illusion that it is really alive. Only the face, diademed when iconography requires it, is left uncovered, gleaming with the splendour of gilt that must be renewed annually according to ritual.

Tibetan art is essentially anonymous, and it is unusual for works of painting or sculpture to be signed. To paint or sculpt is an act of worship, and as such implies the negation of the person who performs it. In temple frescoes, however, when the visions of a religious experience or the glories of some paradise are depicted, the name of the painter appears alongside that of the lama who suggested the layout. The two are recorded to perpetuate an act of piety, not a specimen of their talent; and the aim that unites them with the donor or donors is not that of producing a work to admire, but of making truth accessible and performing a meritorious action. One may on occasion read allusions to the proficiency of the artist (his skill in 'putting the colours together') in these commemorative inscriptions, but what counts is the merit accumulated as a result. Painting is an act of faith, a source of good, dedicated to the welfare of all beings. 'Through the merits thus procured' runs the customary formula, 'may the donor with his kin obtain the state of Buddhahood'.

This explains why repeated journeys through Tibet have yielded me no more than three score names of painters, nearly always in the explanatory or dedicatory inscriptions appended to the cycles painted on the walls of temples or in *kumbum* shrines. But some have their names recorded in literary sources as particularly gifted artists, examples being Töndrup-gyatso, commended by the fifth Dalai Lama as 'supreme painter', and Chhöying-gyatso of Tshang, summoned to decorate the Potala by the same Dalai Lama. Menthanpa, along with his son, is mentioned in numerous works.

The starting point of Tibetan architecture is the Transhimalayan house, which Chinese chroniclers noted of old. These massive, rectangular houses are an imposing display of strength. They are made of stone, or big, oblong, sun-baked bricks, on a foundation of rocks. Tapering slightly upwards, flat-roofed, the buildings have a certain rude dignity. Poor houses have one storey, rich ones two or more, with well-proportioned windows in the second-storey walls, set in brightly painted wooden frames. Each window has a lintel similarly decorated, the ornamentation following the idiom of the wood-carving on the entablatures. They are 'glazed' with paper or

ART cloth for protection against wind and sun. A band of dark red runs below the flat roof whose edges are surrounded by a raised portion acting as a balcony. Such houses have a stern appearance for all their simplicity, but they do not repel like the grimly guarded *qala* of Afghanistan and eastern Iran, with their flanking towers and peeping arrow-slits covering every approach, to protect the family or tribe from enemy attack.

The same quality of line, made more impressive by their monumental scale, is found in sacred buildings. There is a distinct cleavage in monastic architecture between masonry — simple, silent, jealously protecting the sacredness of what it encloses — and ornament, gay and garrulous by contrast. A colonnaded entrance-hall dominates the temple façade. The ridge and corners of its roof are adorned with monsters and dragons, a disc flanked by two gazelles — representing the Wheel of the Law, symbol of everlasting revelation (cf. pl. 24) — the eight auspicious signs, and so forth. The glitter of the gilded roofs, the massive red building itself, the happy choice of site, combine to yield a shining spectacle which stands out boldly against the glorious backdrop of the landscape. But the love of withdrawal (*gönpa*, monastery, really means 'lonely place, hermitage, wilderness'), meditation, and the supremely lyrical language of nature, are also in evidence.

Although the architecture of the great monasteries now follows a set plan, varying only in size, it is the end product of a process of evolution. In the earliest period, and far from the centres of political power, the *lha khang* were of modest proportions. Their plan is rectangular, with a covered verandah or portico in front. The statue of the deity to whom the temple is dedicated rests upon a quadrangular base situated at the far end of the inner chamber, and often surrounded by a passageway for the ritual right-handed circumambulation. The temples founded by Rinchen-sangpo in western Tibet and the few left in other parts of the country from the oldest period (Chasa for example) follow this model, as do the lha khang in the villages. The case is otherwise with temples specially distinguished for any reason. Let us consider two instances differing in date and region: Samyê, built *c.* 775, and Toling in western Tibet, around 1020. We know from reliable sources that certain buildings in both these monasteries were designed on the model of Odantapuri (Paharpur), one of India's most famous shrines. But in the case of Samyê, as though to show the variety of cultural influences acting on Tibet during that brief period, our sources relate that Mutik-tsenpo erected a palace of three stories, each in a different style, not counting the ground floor. The first floor was designed in the manner of Li (Khotan), the second in the Chinese and the third in the Indian fashion. Even in modern Samyê the statues of the deities on each floor were said to be in a different style—Tibetan, Chinese, Khotanese and Indian.

The lha khang of Toling was built, on the same Odantapuri pattern, for initiations. It consists of a ground floor and three upper floors, progressively reduced in size, with wooden decorations on the outside in the form of pillars, and with capitals and entablatures that evidently take the place of a verandah. The Thrülnang at Lhasa, a no less famous temple, ascribed to the time of Songtsen-gampo, is said to be a copy of Vikramaśīla, another great Indian temple. The model for Drêpung, built in 1416, is stated to have been the temple of Dhanyaktaka in South India. The major temples sometimes have quite a lot more stories than those so far mentioned though we are not told what they were modelled on. The temple of Ushando built by King Rêpachen (815 - 838) had nine stories, like certain noble palaces and the much later Potala. However, the type with lavishly gilded pagoda-roofs that later became common was due to Chinese influence. Tibetan writers call them *gya-phuk*, 'Chinese domes'.

60. Courtyard of the Great Temple, Sakya.

112

In the course of time a mingling of architectural elements took place, especially with regard to ornament—conspicuously absent in the simple primitive type of lha khang—which develops with a great variety of patterns in later architecture. The building is generally approached through an entrance lobby, with or without columns before it. Carved or painted figures of the 'protectors of the four cardinal points' keep watch at either side of the doorway. They are depicted in the Chinese manner, with body armour, a look of disdain, and enormous muscles.

The interiors are variations on a single theme: a great hall, divided into aisles along its length by rows of high pillars on either side. The number of aisles is not fixed, but depends on the size of the building. This hall is called the *dükhang* or assembly hall, since the monks sit here during ceremonies. At its far end the image of the divinity to whom the temple is dedicated and after whom it is named, known as the *tsowo*, is enthroned on the altar surrounded by minor deities (cf. pl. 57). The capitals surmounting the pillars are carved, and coloured red, blue and gold. Upon these rest beams supporting the ceiling, in the centre of which an opening, its breadth proportionate to the size of the hall, lets through rays of light that cannot quite dispel the darkness within. In other buildings the roof is covered, in which case the light filters through lateral apertures running between the roof of the aisles and the raised roof over the centre of the hall.

In some temples, in place of the paintings that usually cover the walls, there are other images arranged on altars to left and right. One is reminded of a Catholic church by the succession of altars and statues, standing out against a background of frescoes reproducing particular cycles in a many-coloured curtain across the wall. One of the most striking examples is the shrine at Tsaparang now known as the 'white temple', Lhakhang-karpo (built in the sixteenth century).

Before and on both sides of the main altar, and along the rows of pillars, are ranged the cushions on which the monks sit during the temple services. The abbot's throne is at the centre.

Around the principal lha khang which forms its heart, lies the monastic city with its proliferation of other lha khang—since every college has its own. The individual dükhang of each college is subject to the *tshokkhang* or chapter, where joint assemblies of all monks living in the gönpa, or its colleges and training-schools, are held.

The mansions of the nobility follow the pattern of ordinary dwellings. They differ only in size. Floors are added; power is expressed as height. This is especially the case with castles and palaces. The palace of the kings of Ladakh, built by Senggenamgyel (*c*. 1600-45) in the seventeenth century, is an outstanding monument in the grandeur of its nine stories (cf. pl. 9). The Potala, begun by the fifth Dalai Lama and finished in 1694, is the last and most gigantic example of this tradition of architectural audacity and technical skill. Like a new mountain built over the one it stands upon, and imitating its solidity and boldness rather than imposing premeditated rhythms of its own, details of the craggy truncated pyramid are swamped in the hugeness of its impassable walls, with their stairways that seem to reproduce the zigzag patterns of mountain ledges (cf. pls. 4, 12).

Military architecture is closely allied to that of the nobles' palaces. When clan rivalry and the ensuing wars made life insecure, the mansion was perforce converted into a castle, bristling with defensive structures. Round or square towers, perimeter walls and buttresses give the buildings a very impressive character. Their great sun-dried bricks, though of such apparently flimsy material, are actually very tough, and these castles have weathered the elements with the tenacity of stone.

61. The *mantra* 'oṁ maṇi-padme hūṁ' carved on rocks near Satsukul, Ladakh.

62. Rock sculpture near Mulbek, Ladakh.

Most of the ancient strongholds are now ruins. The few that survive, thanks to traditional prestige as relics of the past, have not come down to us in their ancient form. The Yarlung Photrang, where according to legend the first omens of Buddhism's coming triumphs in Tibet were miraculously vouchsafed to King Lha Thothori, is a case in point. The palace has been completely rebuilt, but its foundations are probably ancient, though how far back they go one cannot say. Ruined towers are all that are left of the palace in Yarlung attributed to Songtsen-gampo (seventh century).

One remarkable type of building demands special notice—the *chhörten*, whose name means literally 'receptacle of worship'. Here again Tibet has drawn its inspiration from India, where the same structure is called *stūpa*. The original function of these buildings, which was to contain relics of the Buddha or great teachers, was combined with a ritual significance, and these became linked in the course of time with a symbolism making the monument a means of salvation. The stūpa reached Tibet in its maturity: the old structure, as it appears in monuments ascribed to King Aśoka, consisting of a base and a hemispherical dome surmounted by a central axis bearing a number of 'umbrellas', had evolved into much more complex types differing considerably from one another.

Certain architectural features apply to chhörtens in general. They rest upon steps leading up to a square-shaped base, technically known as the 'throne', over which are four more steps of decreasing breadth. These support the bulbous structure known as the 'pot', and from an intervening portion above this rise the 'wheels' culminating in the image of the crescent moon and sun. The number of umbrellas or wheels on the ancient prototype has increased to nine or thirteen. A wealth of literature grew up around these buildings, setting forth their measurements, describing them, and extolling the spiritual merit procured by their construction. It rapidly became, in Tibet, a work of the highest benefit to one's spiritual well-being to build a chhörten, and a great deal of money was spent on doing so. The first recorded chhörten were built by the various ministers at Samyê (eighth century A.D.), in the sacred area marked off by the temple precinct, which symbolizes the universe. Each coloured differently, they represented the four major and four minor continents held by Buddhist cosmography to occupy the cardinal and intermediate points of the compass. Others are situated near monasteries, outside towns, and along pathways (cf. pls. 21, 32, 33, 73). Here their purpose is twofold: as well as a source of merit for whoever makes the ritual circumambulation around them, they are also landmarks the traveller can see from a long way off. Relics of various kinds are deposited inside them, the most common being bone-fragments or ashes of saints, collected after cremation and placed in a vase, following the Indian custom; or objects that belonged to the person concerned, a few pieces of his clothing for instance. In other cases the hollow of the edifice is filled with *tsha-tsha*. These are made of clay kneaded with water and stamped with a bronze or copper mould whilst still fresh. Sometimes they bear sacred inscriptions: the epitome of the *Perfection of Wisdom* in the single verse 'Of all things that have a cause the Buddha, the great ascetic, the truthful one, has revealed the cause and the stopping'; or the syllables into which the secret essence of a deity is condensed. Alternatively they may be images of these deities, or be moulded into the shape of a chhörten. In some instances the tsha-tsha themselves become relics, for when a person of saintly repute died, the ashes of his body were piously gathered up, to be mixed later with the earth and water required to fashion them.

But chhörtens can shelter any sacred object, whether put there when they are built, or inserted later on through special openings—particularly books. There are chhörtens specially built to hold books—incomplete, crumpled or illegible. At Sakya monastery, if what they told me at the time of my visit is correct, a large chhörten close to the main temple contained the entire collection of the Buddhist scriptures in Uighur, probably lodged there when no one was left who could read it. A deep-rooted sense of awe reinforced the religious teaching that forbade the destruction of objects having anything sacred about them. The chhörten therefore became a natural repository through whose small windows any traveller or visitor could deposit leaves of books, thankas, statues—whatever sacred or ceremonial articles could not be deconsecrated but which the passage of time had made unsuitable for use. When meeting them along their routes, members of caravans would always keep them to their right, reciting, as they passed round them, the formula '*om mani-padme hūm*'. The very animals are so used to the custom that they never take the wrong side even on their own.

Since their architectural development had to take into account the canons laid down by scripture and usage, chhörtens adhere, with greater or less perfection of workmanship, to established models. They differ very much in size, however. There are huge ones, called *kumbum* ('hundred-thousand images'), whose base is subdivided into successive stories capacious enough to contain numerous chapels. Starting from the entrance to the building, these chapels are reached in such a way that the visitor's path always keeps the core of the structure, magically identified with the world axis, to his right. Individual chapels are dedicated to particular cycles of gods. The wall-frescoes portraying them represent symbolically the widely varying paths of our redemption from error and our subsequent climb to purification, or the living awareness of reality. Gradually one passes from the symbols of the simpler experiences to the more complex, ascending from one level to the next, till finally, on the topmost floor, representations of the most soteriological cycles are displayed upon the walls, encircling the image of the deity to whom the whole dazzling procession has gradually led up. The deities at the top usually express the ultimate pinnacles of initiatory revelation, with god and goddess united to symbolize the synthesis of supreme knowledge and true compassion, in the luminous unity of Being. By the time he gains the summit, the visitor will have made a pilgrimage into the mystery of Being, and trod the long path from the manifold to the One. The chhörten, which enclosed him throughout his ascent, has led him back to his origin. From this point he descends once more, retracing his steps from the One to the many, from total identity to duality. In this way he is shown the interrelationship of Being and appearance, the Eternal and the temporal. Even for the slow of understanding there is purification in merely seeing the tales these chapels tell, for to approach a holy place is like being struck by a sudden gleam of light.

This is the meaning behind the building of these superb psychocosmograms, wherein the very breathing of the universe is portrayed. They have come a long way from their beginnings in the Babylonian ziggurat, to find a haven on the Roof of the World. Here, in the highest chapel of the building, the god-and-goddess images perhaps echo the sacred new year nuptials of Mesopotamia, celebrated by the royal couple on the summit and axis of the world-mountain, to renew the course of time.

There are many of these monuments in Tibet. Among the best known is the one at Gyantsé, built by Rapten-künsang-phapa (1389-1442). One of the oldest is that founded by the *lotsawa* of Throphu early in the thirteenth century, in a valley between Jonang and Shigatsé. Others equally important, for the fresco cycles they contain, were erected at Gyan near Lhapse-dzong in the fourteenth and fifteenth centuries; at Narthang in the second half of the fourteenth century by Nyaktak Sangpo-pel;

and at Jonang by Sherap-gyentsen in the fourteenth century, with later modifications by Tāranātha. In central Tibet the chhörten of Champaling in Tra, built in the late fifteenth century by Thumi Lhündrup-trashi, deserves mention. As already explained these buildings are a good deal more important for the paintings in them than for their architecture, which is essentially repetitive. Since individual dates of construction are known, these monuments mirror the history of Tibetan painting over several centuries, though lamentable gaps have resulted from restoration work.

It is to be hoped that the Chinese authorities, who have shown some regard for the protection of ancient monuments, will take steps without delay to save what is left, if there is still time.

The chhörten is sometimes transformed into an arch over a road or across the approach to a bridge. The base is hollowed out, and only the dome and umbrellas remain. Their original purpose comes to the fore when chhörtens are intended to hold the remains of great men. This is the case at Trashi-lhünpo and in the Potala, where the deceased Panchen and Dalai Lamas, respectively, are enclosed in huge silver and gold chhörtens, decorated with a richness rivalling the costliness of the metals. Devotion is displayed in waste, which seems to confirm the law of expenditure that Georges Bataille regards as an essential factor in human society. Being unable to consume what she produced, Tibet lavished her surplus on the fleeting embodiments of the divine with bountiful extravagance. But all this opulence and the invariability of architectural forms made it hard for the artist to put any strong feeling into his work. Grandeur of scale, perfection of detail, are his sole concerns—a triumph of the artisan and the goldsmith. It is an expressionless rigidity that envelops these chhörten-tombs.

It must be apparent from what has been said that its exuberance of ornamentation imparts a faintly baroque flavour to Tibetan art. I refer to the liking for fullness, well-rounded lines, and weighty, bombastic language to say simple things; the urge to fill up empty spaces; the intricate entwining of the same rhythms and decorative forms over and over again—all of which is characteristic of Tibetan craftsmanship. And at first sight, indeed, Tibetan art might well seem to be little more than a craft. But this would be a mistaken generalization. For in spite of its repetitiveness of theme, the restrictiveness of some of its rules, and its imitation of foreign models, Tibetan art gives worthy expression to a special vision of things, faithfully interpreting the national taste in language the Tibetan people could readily understand. We cannot judge this art by our own standards, particularly those now fashionable, which cannot be universally applied. In Tibet, more than anywhere else, it was content, in its intensity, that determined form. The latter had to express its implications in exactly the right manner, so that its spiritual values were not distorted or misunderstood. What Tibetan art really tries to do is to show us a divine world, evoked so vividly it becomes luminous. This art's approach to man is that of a translucent meditation or the earthly counterpart of a transcendental reality, presented now with the ingenuousness of marvelling faith, now with theological complexity. We are bound to recognize that in the best of its output it has succeeded in saying what it set out to. Craftsmanship naturally played a leading part, due to the limitations we have discussed, and also because of Tibetan technical ability, which was turned primarily to metal-working. Chinese historians were the first to observe this, noting the Tibetans' skill in fashioning and ornamenting arms and armour, and equally in wood-carving.

63. Detail from a Tibetan thanka, showing a fierce deity (Mahākāla), holding a *dorje* and a skull overflowing with blood, and a serene victim; note portraiture, animals etc.

To the Tibetan, objects were never merely functional, but provided an excuse for indulging his taste for ornamentation as well. From earliest times, certain motifs spread through contact with the Chinese world and the art of the steppes. These

were chiefly limited to belt-buttons, shields and the decorations on sword-buckles, hilts and scabbards. They showed animals facing one another in combat, dragons (cf. pl. 43), waves and trailing banks of clouds. Subjects from Indian good-luck symbolism were later added: the eight auspicious emblems (cf. pl. 22) or, with a more specifically Buddhist symbolism but the same meaning, the seven gems (elephant, wheel, umbrella, etc.) belonging to the universal ruler and hence to the Buddha, sovereign of all sovereigns, supreme king of the Law. Alternatively there were the three Gems, denoting the Buddhist trinity: the Law, the Buddha and the Community. Finally, to this already complex wealth of motifs China contributed her symbols of longevity, prosperity, and good omen: the phoenix, the fish and the immortal old man.

These motifs of differing origin and the baroque exuberance of workmanship are underlined by a certain heaviness of design and the concern not to leave any space unfilled. Even the shape of Tibetan utensils and furniture is overblown. The bulging teapots, rather short-necked, with their high domed lids, have none of the lightness of the Persian or Chinese ones. Neither the decorations in cast or wrought silver round the neck, nor the gem symbol that surmounts the cover, are enough to turn the teapot's weight to grace. The spout often emerges from a silver casing shaped like the head of a sea monster (makara) of Indian inspiration, sometimes married fancifully with the Chinese dragon. The handle is not exempt from this decorative prodigality either, and assumes the forms of a dragon with well-marked scales. Tea is sipped from cups made of jade, agate, or silver, or steel inlaid with silver or gold. They fit into the recessed top of a stand or pedestal whose design simulates the out-spread petals of a lotus-flower, with a cylindrical base whose diameter decreases slightly towards the top (cf. pl. 95). To prevent the tea from getting cold, they are protected by a cover consisting of a flat-rimmed dome with a jade, coral or turquoise bead fastened on its crest. These stands offer the Tibetan goldsmiths endless ways of showing off their expertise: the auspicious signs and symbols mentioned above, floral whorls, and tendrils—the whole decorative heritage of craftsmen expert at their work but of limited invention.

Similar tendencies are encountered in furniture, such as the table one squats at when taking tea. It is open on the side facing the person seated at it, but the other three sides are hinged on wooden pins set into the outside of the table-top, and so it can easily be folded up and carried wherever it is needed. The three sides are deco-rated with inlaid figures of dragons and phoenixes, or flower patterns painted with vivid colours and sparkling gilt. The altars which lamas keep before them for their ritual implements, or for cups of tea served during the services, are also of this type —a flourish of brilliant polychrome in which red and gold predominate. The same goes for cupboards and bookshelves, delicate lattice works, whose wide panels are painted with religious subjects. The rich Tibetan's house is a gay palette of vivid colours, juxtaposing bright shades with sparkling splashes of silver and luminous gold, with rich hangings of Chinese brocades for background.

What is true of the teapot also applies to the butter-lamp, a religious utensil always required in temples and private chapels. The shape is that of a chalice—either hemis-pherical or slightly flared out as though to symbolize a blossoming flower—resting upon a high stand which incorporates the symbolism of the bumpa. The latter is the vase that holds the water of immortality, a form of ritual and decoration that has travelled from Mesopotamia to India and many other parts of Asia.

So there was always this combination of symbolism and concern for ornament, displaying a love of fine things and good living. We have obviously been speaking

64. Polychrome terracotta image of the Buddha in his 'earth-touching' pose.

121

here of the furnishings of rich houses. Amongst the poor the nobler metals yield to copper and often even wood. Yet the craftsman's loving care always shows through, producing pleasant alternations of light and shade by applying brass or copper ornamentation to the wooden teapot that will soon be darkened by use.

Equal care is devoted to the decoration of the purely structural part of the house. The pillars supporting the verandah or dividing up the rooms are surmounted by capitals and beams containing various features, each with its own name and symbolism, even if the latter is not always clear or present in the craftsman's own mind. In poorer houses the surfaces are smoothed with the adze, but in those of the well-to-do the capital terminates in whorls folded over like flowers under a weight, while the decorative repertoire is displayed in all its variety on the open surfaces, enclosed in panels, or in a lively sequence.

Fig 4. Brass Citipati Skeletons dancing *c.* 19th century.

Daily life

WHAT WAS THE PATTERN of life like in Tibet? That led by the laymen was not much different from the life of any other society. The religious communities had their own traditional rules for living, and the rest of the people of Tibet can be divided into three main groups: the nobility, who were the greater landowners, the small landowners dependent on the nobility, and the peasants. The merchants did not form a separate section of society since anyone could take part in trade and it was not the privilege of one class. A large number of nobles, and even of monks, made profitable use of their natural inclinations by engaging in intensive commercial activity. This was not limited to the sale or exchange of agricultural products and of animals but included an import and export trade. Although Tibetan economy has been primarily a closed one, there has always been trade with the merchants of China, Nepal, India and Mongolia. Exports were limited to the principal resources of Tibet: wool, which for the most part went to India in caravans, rock-salt, which was sent to Nepal and Kashmir, borax, and carpets. Although there are many deposits of gold in Tibet, it was not exported as it was reserved for religious purposes, and mining was strictly controlled because it was held that gold was a guarantee of the fertility and fruitfulness of the soil. Imports consisted mainly of materials, the Chinese silk and damasks necessary for the robes of the dignitaries and monks, and much-prized articles made by Chinese, or on occasion Indian craftsmen, woollen cloth, cotton, hats from Europe and Japan, and aluminium goods.

Trade was therefore a subsidiary activity for the nobility and monks. The main branches of trade were monopolized by the great monasteries and a few families who had their own agents in the foreign countries or big cities where their interests lay. Business was wholesale; goods were collected together in warehouses, and from there found their way into the countless lanes of the local bazaars, or were set out on the street itself, especially during religious festivals. It was by the accumulation of riches, and the prestige derived from this, that some families, which did not belong to the nobility by right of long-standing tradition, attained high rank, and brought a new life to the old, feudal, landed aristocracy. The latter has, however, always formed the nucleus of Tibetan society; from the great landowners were drawn the officials, both lay and ecclesiastical, who staffed the administration. Since the institution of the Dalai Lama as head of state, the administration has been organized as a parallel system, with the responsibilities of office divided between religious and civil magistrates or officials.

In several provinces at least, the land was divided into that belonging to the big landowners or *chhuda'* and that belonging to the small landowners (*nyamchung*). The latter, although they possessed a modest strip of land of their own, were subordinate to the first group and were obliged to give service to the chhuda. Each family among the small landowners had to provide at least one man to work on the overlord's estate, or to serve him for certain periods to be determined as the need arose. This service was really a corvée (*ula'*) in exchange for which the labourer would receive his food for each day's work, and, in some cases, a modest sum of money. If the help of other members of the same family was needed, they were in theory free to give or refuse it, but if they consented they were paid (*mila*). In hard years seed would be lent by the overlord, and would have to be paid back with interest at agreed rates; money was also lent on the same basis, especially for marriages and funerals. If the debtor was unable to pay back whatever had been lent to him, with the interest owing, he became a serf (*yola*), bound by his debt to the service of his overlord, as opposed to the free peasant who was only obliged to serve him as described above.

A survey of the property and of the harvest took place every autumn when the wheat, butter, barley and cattle were weighed and counted. A tenth of the harvest went to the government as tax, then the seed to be sowed the next year was put aside and the rest of the crop, except that needed for individual sustenance, was stored in the *kangchu'* to be used in case of famine, or for loans or unforeseen emergencies. A part might be used to sow new land, and some would be for religious offerings. This was normal practice on estates owned by the laity and the monasteries alike.

Irrigation (*yura*) was often organized collectively, especially in western Tibet and in Kham, where greater equality was practised. In other provinces the main irrigation canal was sometimes in the hands of the family owning the land with the natural supply of water, but other families would use it in turn, first asking permission and offering the owner the usual gifts of butter, tsampa, and the inevitable ceremonial scarf.

How was the ordinary Tibetan's day spent? I do not intend to use as an example a very rich family, nor a very poor one; let us look at an average household, moderately comfortable, with its own piece of land and its own flock. Life for them was simple. The power of the Central government was weak, if not completely ineffective, because of poor communications, and it had control only over the payment of the customary proportion of the harvest. Each family was a more or less autonomous unit, although three authorities had to be recognized: the Lord of the Manor, the two prefects (*dzongpön*) in each district, one drawn from the laity, the other from the priesthood, and finally the local religious community. Life went on according to the rhythm of the season, and was governed by the needs of land cultivation and the rearing of animals. Even a family of modest means would possess the necessary beasts for working the land, as well as horses or mules for riding and transport.

All this was true for the agricultural community; the Drokpa and the Horpa were nomads who lived in tents, moving from pasture to pasture according to the season. They possessed no land, only cattle and sheep, goats, yaks and *dzo*; thousands of animals which migrated up on to the high plateau in summer and came down into the valleys as winter approached. While the Horpa were usually owners of the animals themselves, the Drokpa were herdsmen or shepherds, and the beasts in their care belonged to noble families or to the monasteries. Every year, in a specified month, they would deliver the agreed proportion of animals to their owners, and would account for any missing by showing the skins of the dead animals.

While considering Tibetan architecture we looked at a typical house from the outside. Now let us go in and see what the interior is like. Even a family of modest means has a two-storied house, built round an inner courtyard, sheltered from the wind and trapping all the sunlight possible. The horses, sheep and other animals are kept in buildings in front of the house, in the space within the surrounding wall and near the gate, which usually faces east. A large part of the house is used for storing supplies:

65. Brooch inlaid with turquoise and coral. In the centre is a representation of a *khyung* (mythical bird), a Tibetan adaptation of the *garuda* of Indian tradition.

66. Silver and gilt container (*gau*) used when travelling. Inside are sacred formulae, printed or hand-written. The decoration shows Central Asian influences.

65

66

67

68

hay, wood and grass are all kept on the ground floor. The centre of the house is the kitchen (the *chakhang* or *thapkhang*) which is often actually called the 'home' (*khyim*). This is the scene of family life; next to the kitchen are the bedrooms, the chapel and the storeroom where the family possessions are kept: clothes and other objects of value; or the *gakhang*, which means literally 'saddle-room', used for the storage of the horses' equipment, such as saddles, harness, and rugs to put under the saddles. There is also a storeroom for meat and one for grain, and a verandah (*nyira*) where the family can take advantage of the winter sunshine. Along one of the walls outside the house there is the '*thogra*' where the grain is threshed. There are of course variations in the lay-out of houses depending on the wealth of the families, but the general plan is the same all over Tibet. The upper floor is reached by means of a proper staircase or else by tree-trunks with footholds cut into them. The roof is flat and at the front corners of the house and in the middle there is a *pökhang*, the seat of the 'male god' (*pholha*), surmounted by branches, usually taken from a juniper tree. Coloured cords curve from branch to branch, and *lungta*, pieces of cloth or paper with magic formulae printed on them, hang from the cords. In the courtyard, or just in front of the house, stands a high pole with large lungta tied to it.

These ritual additions defend the house against harmful forces and evoke beneficial powers which bring the family success and prosperity. So the house is a real castle, guarded by the divine presences installed there at the moment of its construction. A man's protecting pholha or *dralha* is born with him and watches over him, disposing of his enemies, both human and demonic. In this way he is assured of a long life and the continuation of his family. Every morning the man of the house invokes his protecting god and placates him by burning juniper leaves and branches. The woman's god is the *molha* or *phulha*, whose dwelling is not on the roof of the house, like the god protecting the man, but in the kitchen, at the top of the pillar supporting the roof. He is offered branches cut from a juniper tree or from some other plant of good omen, intertwined with different coloured strands of wool or pieces of cloth in five colours. The phulha is offended if anything falls in the fire while food is being prepared and smoke is produced, but is easily placated if a little salt is thrown on the fire. The phulha's irritation is easily aroused. He will not tolerate the presence of exorcists, who are always assumed to be accompanied by capricious and rather malevolent divinities necessary for the performance of their miracles. And his anger is clearly shown. If the flocks are restless when they return from their pastures at sunset, if deformed animals are born or if the children cry in the night, it means that the phulha has been in some way offended, and a lama has to be called to perform the necessary expiation ceremony. When a bride leaves her family, the members are careful to propitiate the god, for fear that he might become vexed, or follow the bride to her new home depriving the rest of the family of his presence. As soon as she arrives at the bridegroom's house, she must pay homage to the phulha installed there; it can happen that she is not at all well received by him, and signs of ill-omen will necessitate the intervention of the lama. As well as these two gods, the home is protected by other divinities: the god of the door, the god of the hearth, the god of the storeroom and many more, so that the security of the Tibetan's house is assured. But he is on his guard, since these divinities, although protective, are all extremely sensitive and become angered if anything is not to their liking.

It remains to be added that in many houses there is a guest-room (*drönkhanh*) used also as a sitting-room. All over the East a guest is welcomed with warmth and generosity, the more so in Tibet since the inhabited parts of the country are separated by

67. Figure of a female divinity, the 'goddess of the white umbrella', from Lhasa.

68. Conch-shell trumpet in a typically Tibetan mounting: silver flange inlaid with turquoises and pastes, used for summoning monastic assemblies.

great stretches of wilderness. Meetings start by each party exchanging a *khata*, a silk scarf, usually as fine as gauze. The traveller keeps a supply in the ample folds of his robe, and on arrival he will extract a khata swiftly and hold it on his upturned hands so that the two ends hang down, each the same length. It is accepted in the same way, and normally the exchange is made simultaneously. The khata can also be placed round the neck of an honoured visitor or guest, who bows his head to receive it. The ends of the scarf must hang level with one another over his chest. Every gift is accompanied by a khata. When a party arrives in a village, as soon as the visitors begin to pitch their tents the village chief, or the *dzongpön*, the prefect himself when there is one, brings suitable gifts or sends them with servants if the new arrival is a man of importance. The gifts may consist of the flesh of sheep or yaks, tsampa, or similar things, and scarves are always exchanged in greeting when the gifts are presented. The same ceremony takes place when pilgrimages are made to temples, the khata being hung round the necks of the images. In this way the monasteries have an inexhaustable supply. Even letters are never delivered without being first rolled in a scarf, sometimes with a dried flower attached.

The quality of the furnishings depends on the wealth of the family. Broad, flat cushions take the place of beds and are covered by rugs woven in a number of places in Tibet, from Lhasa to Gyantsé, and from Lhokha to Kham, and based on Chinese patterns. They have a dark blue or yellow background, with pictures of dragons (cf. pl. 43) and flowers in bright colours and the full range of Chinese decoration, stylized and a little heavier. In front of these 'divans', where during the day the family squats to eat, or to drink tea, are the little tables whose carvings, inlaid work and painted decoration were discussed in chapter IV.

The Tibetan is an early riser, like every man whose daily life is still governed by the slow and eternal rhythm of nature. He rises at dawn, and the woman lights the fire, the first sign of life stirring again in a new day. In recent years matches imported from India have been widely used, but formerly, and always in poorer houses or more isolated parts, the tinderbox, that indispensable possession of every traveller, was employed. The flint was kept in a case made of copper or brass, and protected by a leather cover, often decorated with designs of animals fighting and other subjects reminiscent of the art of the Steppes (cf. pl. 102).

So the new day began with the lighting of the fire, and before starting on its ordinary tasks the family would manifest anew man's links with the world of which he is a part. In the family chapel the altar lamps would be lit, homage paid to the tutelary gods and prayers recited. Then, to placate the *Tsen*, the *Nyen*, and the *Lu*, who could be malevolent, the head of the house would offer *sang*, burning juniper branches or other aromatic plants used in exorcism or purification ceremonies. In this way the success of the work about to be undertaken was assured, provided that the day was favourable from an astrological point of view. The head of the house understands this, and he knows both his own astrological chart and those of his relations, so he is careful not to disregard any warnings. Astrology is part of normal experience, and there is no need to consult books or an astrologer.

The interpretation is very complicated. As well as the general indications applying to everyone, individual horoscopes must be taken into account, especially in doubtful cases. In general, it is recognized that Saturday, Sunday and Tuesday are always bad for travelling, Monday is doubtful, favourable for those travelling south, but unfavourable for other directions; Thursday is unfavourable for the west, and Friday for the south and the west.

Concerning business transactions, Tuesday, Thursday and Friday are good, Monday and Sunday could be favourable, and Tuesday and Saturday are to be avoided. For marriages, Monday, Thursday and Friday are favourable, and Sunday, Tuesday and Saturday unfavourable.

After prayers the family would breakfast on tea and tsampa, flour made from roast barley, which had already been prepared by the women or the servants. Tea is the staple food of the Tibetan, tea being a rather misleading word, since it is prepared very differently from tea as we know it. It is first pounded in a mortar, then put into an urn and left to boil for some time. It is transferred to long cylindrical vessels of wood, together with butter, a pinch of salt and a little soda, and then the mixture is whisked with a wooden implement. This is a long stick, with two wooden discs at the end, a small one underneath and a larger one, about the same size as the inside of the vessel, set slightly above it. The great whisk is pushed up and down energetically like a piston so that the ingredients are well amalgamated and the tea is ready to pour into the pot (cf. pl. 80). The members of the family sit on the ground or cross-legged on cushions each in front of his own table, on which his cup waits to be filled, and the tea is swirled rapidly round in the teapot to make sure it is properly mixed before being poured out. On being served, each person sprinkles a few drops in the direction of the four points of the compass as a symbolical offering to all beings whom ideally they would have liked to invite to the meal. In a poor household the cups would be made of clay or pottery, whilst the rich would have cups of agate, jadeite imported from China, or even silver. Before the tea is drunk, in deep and noisy gulps, more butter is thrown in, each person serving himself with his hands from a receptacle made of leather or skin, taking care that the butter remains at one side of the cup so that it does not dissolve immediately. Then a handful of tsampa is added to the tea left in the cup and mixed into a brown ball with the fingers of the right hand.

The other meals are taken at about eleven in the morning and before sunset. It cannot be said that Tibetans live on nothing but tea and tsampa, although these are the commonest foods and the poor eat little else. Mutton or yak meat, boiled in copper pans or even in the tea-urn, is especially popular.

Tibetans are very fond of noodles, first brought from China, like other delicacies savoured by the rich. Meat balls wrapped in noodle dough (*momo*) are much appreciated, but the dough is made without egg. Cheese (*chhura*) is also eaten, but it is very hard and is dipped in tea to soften it. The diet is further varied by sour milk, vegetables, *droma* roots (*potentilla anserina*) and dried apricots.

After breakfast work begins; one of the servants leads the sheep and cattle out of their pens to graze, guiding them with cries. In order to round up straying animals he uses a sling made out of a strip of woollen material with a stone in the middle, sending it in the direction of the straying animal with great accuracy.

The head of the household, his wife or a servant, depending on the wealth of the family, visits the field to see that the irrigation canal is working properly, repairs the banks if this is necessary, or carries out other work in the field according to the season. The most important time of year, for this agricultural society, is the time of ploughing. A specially favourable day is chosen for the start of ploughing, and the yaks wear bows of red wool for the occasion—red is considered to be a lucky colour. The plough consists of a wooden pole attached to a blade of wood or metal, a very simple implement, with an edge that scarcely scrapes the ground. Whoever is in charge of the ploughing walks up and down with the slow, labouring yak, singing, always in the same rhythm, at the top of his voice.

As ploughing is considered work of a sacramental nature, the lamas conduct special rites a few days before the work is begun. In some areas, one field is chosen to be ploughed before all the others. It is strictly forbidden to begin work before the necessary ceremonies have taken place, infringement of this rule being likely to bring down the wrath of hostile gods on the heads of all, to the destruction of the harvest. The possibility of hail must be faced, so before the period when the corn is ripening precautions are taken and exorcists specializing in the necessary rites are called in. Lamas from the nearby monastery walk round the fields in procession, chanting, and carrying holy books (usually the *Bum*, or 'Perfection of Wisdom', cf. pl. 28). It is believed that hail is not the result of weather conditions, but of evil forces or the displeasure of some sorcerer. This is illustrated in the story of Mila-rêpa (cf. pl. 27), who studied the art of magic in order to ruin the crops of relatives, at whose hands he and his mother had suffered. He invokes the powers governing the elements, and when the storm-clouds collect he directs them to the right fields by pointing his finger at them.

Then I went to Khyorpo in the land of Yarlung, to the house of the master who was to instruct me in the art of causing hail to fall, and I gave him the letter from my Guru, with the ceremonial scarf and a gift of three ounces of gold. I then explained my reasons for coming and he enquired if I had already been successful in the field of magic. I told him that I had already killed thirty-five men by using my powers. He was satisfied and taught me the magic words and gave me other instructions. I practised in an ancient cell set aside for such purposes and after a week, clouds collected inside it, with thunder and flashes of lightning. The lama himself agreed that I was now capable of guiding hail with my finger...

Then I went up to the top of a hill overlooking the valley and I recited the magic words and performed the rites I had learnt. But no cloud appeared, not even as big as a little bird. I called on the gods whose help I needed, swearing that I was no teller of falsehoods and that I had indeed been wronged by the people of my village; I threw myself to the ground and wept. After some time, an enormous black cloud gathered in the sky above, and a moment later there was not an ear of corn left standing in the valley.

Ceremonies to ensure that the harvest will be good are conducted by the village lama or by the lama who concerns himself with the families involved. These rites are called *losang*, or 'purification in order to be granted a good harvest'.

Women share in the work of the fields. At the time when the ground is manured, they carry on their backs baskets filled with the dung that has accumulated in the stalls during the winter; they also do the weeding, singing appropriate songs learned in their childhood, as they bend over their work.

When the corn is ripe, men and women reap side by side, gathering armfuls of corn with their left hands and cutting it with a sickle, but in the drier areas it is necessary to tear the stalks out of the ground. The first sheaves to be collected are piled up in the middle of the field and a branch of juniper, with different coloured strands of wool tied to it, is placed on top, as an offering to the *lu*, or underground gods.

The reaping over and the straw put aside for the winter, the owner of the lands stands in front of the corn and shares it out among the peasants. Then come the harvest festivities, horse-races, archery competitions, and the firing of guns by day and singing and dancing by night, sometimes for a period of three days. But in a bad year, instead of waiting for the propitiation ceremonies which take place on the last day of the year, the villagers resort to the *lolü*, a complicated redemption ceremony, intending to placate the angry gods and to direct their malice elsewhere.

69. Monk's room at Likhir, Ladakh.

Corn is threshed according to the resources and customs of the district. One method is to spread the wheat or barley on a smooth threshing-floor around a pole with horses, or else dzo, harnessed to it. The animals tramp round, freeing the grain from the ear as they do so. In other parts, the young men line up facing the young women, with the heap of corn between them. The instrument used by each one is a heavy piece of wood, attached at one end to a cord, which is held in the right hand. Each group in turn swings the wooden implement down violently on to the corn, with precisely timed movements; and as they work they sing.

The women also take part in the winnowing; handfuls of grain are put into a wicker basket, which they shake so that the wind carries away the chaff. The grain is spread on the roof until it is dry and then it is stored in sacks.

So the Tibetan comes to the end of his year's work, and to ensure that he will have the blessing of the gods in future years, he performs acts of charity. The poor are allowed to glean and they are given alms, as are the wandering lamas who go from village to village with their little drums and bells reciting blessings.

The women work mainly in the house, when their help is not required in the seasonal work on the land. The lady of the household will supervise craftsmen who are called in to perform special tasks. Tailors, for example, rarely work in a shop, but go from house to house as their services are required, and stay in one place until the garments requested are finished. In addition to payment, nearly always in kind, they are given their daily food. The preparation and weaving of wool is carried out by servants in rich families, but in families less well-off it is the man who spins the wool as he takes his beasts to pasture, or while he is on the road with a caravan, or sitting at home in the winter. The women wash and comb the wool, and weave it on simple looms (cf. pl. 7). The finished pieces are no more than ten or twelve inches wide, and vary in length from two to three yards. They are light grey in colour and are dyed, by the women, with vegetable dyes. Sometimes designs in the form of a Greek cross are printed in the middle of white circles on a dark red or yellow background. Some of the most important centres of production of this kind of material are to be found in Lhokha, to the south of the Tsangpo.

As the sun is setting, the family returns home. The animals are in their pens, the door is bolted, and everyone gathers in the kitchen, or the rooms next to it, for the evening meal. The locked house is guarded by mastiffs, great tawny or black sheepdogs, something between a wolf and a bear, which leap towards an unknown caller with such rage and savage growls that they seem about to break the heavy chains which always secure them. To make them more fearsome and ferocious looking, their owners put great collars on them, made with the long hair from a yak, dyed red.

But the Tibetan does not go straight to bed in the evening; his natural inclination to cheerfulness and lightheartedness comes to the fore now that the family is all together after the day's work. The rich play dice or dominoes, with frequent interruptions for *chhang* between the games. A very common amusement is the asking of riddles, an ancient occupation which at one time had a sacramental quality, remaining to a certain extent in some wedding songs. The riddles are often in verse, in which case the answers must be, too. The peasants are fond of dancing and singing, the performances taking place in the courtyard or the kitchen, depending on the season. The songs are an ancient cultural heritage, passed down from generation to generation, and showing in the process how customs and ideas have changed. They are learned from childhood, and songs from another village may be written down, with the spelling

70. The buddha Vajradhara (Dorje-chhang), his crossed hands emblematic of the symbolic marriage of Wisdom and Means.

133

mistakes to be expected, because the pronunciation of Tibetan differs widely from the spelling. Sometimes the songs are improvised, for example during the chhang parties much enjoyed by the better-educated classes or the nobility. Stories of saints or from epic literature may be told by the old people.

Then follows night, the most dangerous time, but fortunately the gods are guarding the house and from the post in the courtyard wave the banners inscribed with sacred words. Everyone's conscience is clear as, of course, the *sang* has been offered that morning. Each member of the family bows three times before the household altar and the older ones will recite prayers before settling down for the night, on the floor or on the carpet-covered cushions which served as seats during the day.

Now come the hours of sleep when an indication of the future is mysteriously given in dreams. Some of these are easily explained on the theory of Humours: they are caused by too much or too little to eat. Like those dreams which come in the early hours of the night they have no significance. But the dreams which come during the last hours of sleep can provide serious omens. Here the inherited beliefs of the Tibetan have been added to by dream-lore brought from China and India. A dream of a tooth falling out means a death in the family, dreams of unclean or repulsive things are an extremly good omen. It is also lucky to dream of a man or woman richly dressed, or of going up a mountain, of singing or playing musical instruments or of listening to agreeable stories, discovering hidden treasure or overcoming an enemy.

It is a bad omen to dream of the sun or the moon setting, of the house falling down or burning, of being naked, falling from a hill, riding a horse or a donkey without a saddle, darkness and storms. The content of dreams is a subject which furnishes material for conversation when the family gets up, or even for the rest of the day, but can also give rise to anxiety, in which case the lama specializing in astrology must be consulted for an explanation.

Figs 5 & 6. Tibetan coin.
Broad flan early style *c.* 1790.

Tibetans do not change their clothes often. They have one set for everyday wear, and another kept for feast-days, when they also flaunt their jewellery. The women all wear aprons as part of their costume. They are made of wool or sometimes of silk for the aristocracy, in bands of bright colours such as red, blue and green.

The gown, or *chhuba*, usually dark red, almost purple, is worn by all. It reaches the ankles and during working hours it is hitched up to just below the knee, and is always tied round the waist with a coloured sash, often red. The nomads and shepherds wear chhubas and trousers made of sheepskin. In warmer weather the right arm is kept free of the gown the sleeve hanging down empty, and in winter trimmings of fox or some other fur protect the wrists and neck. Both men and women wear a cotton or linen shirt, which comes down to the waist and has very long sleeves, and they have adopted a Chinese type of sleeveless jacket, buttoned on the right. Boots are soled with white yak-hide, and have a rounded toe that often curves upwards; the insteps and uppers are made of cloth or leather, and coloured red for lamas. Hats vary in shape, from the high-crowned, wide-brimmed felt ones to the tapering round ones made of wool. Of recent years, however, European styles have been fashionable. But on ceremonial occasions and feast-days, hats are a mark of office and rank, and strict rules, dating back to the fifth Dalai Lama, establish the type of hat to be worn. The nobility at Lhasa favours the wearing of brocaded garments from China.

Monks are shaved according to the rules; the lay population has long hair worn in a single plait falling over the shoulders and pulled over the left shoulder to hang over the chest when a person of superior rank is addressed.

Nomad and peasant women dress their hair in a number of small plaits (cf. pl. 7), hanging over the shoulders and tied up with strips of wool, decorated with silver medallions set with turquoise stones or coral. In some districts they wear a head-dress consisting of a long piece of felt hanging down to the thighs or even to the ankles, and decorated with silver, coral and turquoise medallions, together with Indian or Chinese coins, and they are very proud of their collection. In some nomad tribes two more strips ending in fringes are added, to reach the thighs. In Lo, the Tibetan-speaking part of upland Nepal, the head-dress is a thin sheet of silver, slightly curved. But those seen in Tsang and Ü are the most typical. A kind of wooden diadem, lacquered or covered with material and fixed to the crown of the head is worn by Tsang women.

Ear-rings, long and heavy and made of gold and turquoises hang from the hair on either side of the forehead, not from the ears themselves (cf. pl. 19). The lower part frequently has the shape of a leaf, although there is a great variety of design, and the turquoise decorating the leaf-shape is similar to that seen on the *gau*, the silver or gold box encrusted with turquoise which hangs from the neck to form an ornament and a talisman containing sacred writings of a protective character (cf. pl. 22).

Fig 6.

Jewellery is also worn by the men and frequently shows their rank. A gold and turquoise brooch fastens their hair at the top of their heads (cf. pl. 65), and government officials wear a single ear-ring on the left ear, made of cylindrical pieces of turquoise ending in a long drop-shaped piece. No Tibetan is too poor to possess a ring, in silver or some other metal, set with a turquoise or a piece of coral, and some wear large jadeite rings on their thumbs.

There are occasions when the home and everyday tasks must be left and a journey undertaken, perhaps for business reasons or as a pilgrimage. It is usually the men who face the risks of travelling over difficult country, with the danger of falling among bandits, but they are sometimes accompanied by women and children. The most favourable day and hour for setting off are carefully checked beforehand and the traveller watches out for bad omens at the moment of his departure. On particularly important occasions the *tra* takes place first; questions concerning the success or failure of a proposed journey are asked of women who fall into a trance, possessed by a god, and so are able to predict the future. It is advisable to carry a turquoise ring, as the turquoise is a lucky stone and protects the wearer from accidents. The traveller is of course armed, a dagger or a sword is thrust in his belt, and he may carry a gun of some sort, so that he himself is not unlike a bandit when seen from a distance on the lonely path. Merchants travel in caravans, their goods packed in wooden chests covered with skins, or in bags made of yak hide. The most usual beast of burden is the yak, which might be called the emblem of Tibet, for one could not imagine life there without it. Sturdy and long-haired, the yak has been domesticated since ancient times and withstands the climate admirably. In the warm season he is left to graze at will on the highest plains, as he does not tolerate long periods of labour. Neither can he cover too long a distance in a day; with a load on his back, ten or twelve miles is his average. And the animals must be rested at regular intervals on the way. This of course gives a general picture, as the resistance of the animal varies according to the kind of country being crossed and the quality of the pasture. In western Tibet, where the land is high, the paths are extremely difficult, winding continually up and down, and the grazing rather poor, so the yaks are easily fatigued. On one of my journeys, before I was really familiar with the habits of the country, I left nearly half of my yaks sick, exhausted or dead on the wayside, but I was doing what were forced marches when compared with the Tibetan's speed of progress.

The yak is more than a beast of burden and a means of transport, it forms one of the principal resources of the country. Its hair is spun and woven into material suitable for the black tents which are the home of the nomads and the refuge of travellers; the hair of the tail is used with a religious significance to decorate the peculiar cylinders erected on the roofs of monasteries. Its hide has a variety of uses; the copious bags where the traveller keeps his tsampa are made of yak hide, dyed red and decorated with *appliqués* of the same material, arabesques to bring luck or designs painted in various colours. Cases covered in yak hide are used for storage at home as well as on journeys, and the hide is used for belts and to tie up books. Yak meat is one of the Tibetan's staple foods; but it is always a sin to kill any animal and also to eat its flesh, although this rule is glossed over. Because of this Tibetans prefer to kill larger animals, such as the yak, and not smaller ones like chickens, as then there will be meat enough for several days and the crime of killing need be repeated less often.

Popular literature abounds in legends about yaks; there are accounts of the hunts which used to take place in pursuit of the wild yak, of the hostility between the horse and the yak, tales of demons which at one time took the form of the yak, and of ancient battles with the yak which are perhaps the Tibetan equivalent of bull-fighting or the sacred hunts of former times. Since becoming a domestic animal the yak has grown smaller; the wild yak, lone and unsociable, could be seen as a formidable black shadow, on the edge of the snow-fields, to retreat at the first sign of the approach of man.

Butter made from yak's or dzo's milk is an essential food for the Tibetan, and it is one of the ingredients used in making tea; it is patted into a ball and stored in a container made of untanned goatskin. The monasteries use an enormous amount every day as fuel for the lamps burning in front of the statues and for other religious purposes, so mountains of it are kept in their storerooms.

The hide of yaks is also used to make boats, the skins being stretched over a frame of willow or birch branches. At the bottom of the boat the branches are laid criss-cross and close together, for greater solidity, and the sides are high enough to give some protection to the passengers and luggage. The boats are about nine to twelve feet long and six feet wide. They are pushed out into the water by one of the boatmen, so that they immediately catch the current, and then the passengers jump in. The boat's uncertain path through the rapidly-flowing water is guided by a steersman who crouches in the prow, holding a primitive kind of oar. The current can suddenly become strong, causing the boat to rock and shudder. The journey is accompanied by the boatmen shouting to each other as they keep the boat in the fastest stream. In quieter waters the journey becomes slower and more peaceful, the boat moving noiselessly through smooth, languid water, past green villages and silent monasteries, with mountains on each side. Everything is restful and calm, and the boatmen bring out their flutes from the folds of their gowns and play mournful tunes which echo in the silence all around. Accidents are not infrequent, owing to the rapids, over-loading or the condition of the boat. Passengers and luggage are often thrown into the water, and before such a journey the boatmen will be sure to warn you of this; if, in fact, an accident does happen he will not omit to remind you of his words, possibly enriching his story with a few extra details.

Boats are usually hired out between landing-points on terms agreed for the trip. At the end of the journey the boatmen take the boat out of the water, let it dry and

71. Wrathful aspect of a buddha or bodhisattva.

136

return to their village on foot, the boat on their shoulders, as it is impossible to row against the current. The boats are extremely light and no burden.

Rivers less frighteningly wide than the Tsangpo are crossed at fords at suitable points, on foot, on horseback or yak. If the river is full or the current strong and it seems too risky to remain in the saddle, the rider leads his animal across the river by the bridle; yaks are relieved of their burdens and guided across with shouts and sling-stones. Then the men take up the loads and carry them across the river on their backs, walking in single file, hand in hand. The way in which Tibetans can deal with such situations even on their own is admirable. They provide themselves with a sturdy staff, pull up their clothes as high as they can and, throwing stones in front of them to ascertain the depth of the water, they wade obliquely through the most deadly currents with apparent unconcern and indifference to cold. Some bridges exist, mainly on the most frequented routes. The introduction of bridges made of iron is attributed to the famous ascetic Thangtong-gyelpo. Suspension bridges are common. Made of strips of wood joined together they span the abyss above the river, which roars and boils below. In the south and the south-east, these bridges are made of tied bamboo rods with a rope hand-rail; they are unsteady and sway fearfully in space.

In wilder places bridges become still more slender in construction, consisting of a saddle slung between two ropes so that the traveller can slide from one side to the other. Sometimes the two ropes are at a distance from each other, one for each way across. Firmly attached to blocks of stone or stakes on either side, the ropes hang loosely over the gorge in a great arc, with a tube or half cylinder of bamboo which slides over them. The traveller must lash himself to the piece of bamboo and gripping this saddle with both hands allow himself to hurtle along the rope until his flight is stopped by the upward curve of the rope on the other side, when he heaves himself the rest of the way using his hands and his crossed feet. The ropes are usually made from entwined creepers or yak's hair, and not infrequently the traveller is halted by a knot which he must somehow negotiate. Baggage is, of course, carried on the back while the crossing is made, and it can happen that the rope gives way and the unfortunate traveller hurtles down into the rocky, tumbling waters below.

The worst dangers a traveller could encounter were those involved in crossing rivers, not those presented by mountain passes or inclement weather. Where the river banks are not too far apart great steep walls would be built, supporting beams of wood firmly attached to them in layers, each projecting a little further than the one under it, until the two sides were near enough for planks to be laid across.

Travelling between valleys is less hazardous since paths follow the lie of the land. They are improved more by long use than by conscious effort, being the only possible route or the easiest track to a mountain pass. On the plains the paths widen and branch out into parallel trails where caravans wearily thread their way over the vast distances. But in places, even here, there are difficulties: a cliff will appear, like a barrier put up expressly by jealous Nature, and the traveller must patiently cut steps in the smooth hard rock in order to reach the top; or he can drive wooden palings into the cliff face, to give himself a fragile support.

At times the path runs below rocks which may break off, in parts where the mountains tend to crumble, and come roaring down in a landslide without warning. When faced with any of these dangers, the Tibetan is not helped by technology but rather by representations of the compassionate deities Drölma and Chenrêsik carved on the rock face to save their devotees from danger, or by banners inscribed with prayers waving from the tops of stone cairns, and the sacred words Om maṇi-padme hūm cut

72. Hevajra, one of the esoteric deities of the Tantric schools.

on boulders (cf. pl. 61). Hundreds of Buddha figures are carved or traced on rock, sometimes placed at the entrance to a dangerous path.

Faith in these images and invocations takes the place of civil engineering devices. Man is disputed ground between two powers, good and evil, and he calls upon the benign forces for help, confident that good will triumph; if an accident does happen, it is due to the inevitable ripening of the victim's karma.

Owing to the survival of the nomad way of life, there are no caravanserai for the comfort of travellers at the end of a day's journey, as there are in the deserts of Iran and Afghanistan or in other parts of Asia. Tibetans sleep out in the open, wrapped in their robes and in woollen blankets. Their resistance to the rigours of the climate and to the intense cold of the starry nights is a source of wonder to the non-Tibetan, as is their calm in the face of danger, but they are a people used to the unexpected, living as they do in magnificent but potentially menacing natural surroundings. Travellers generally use the same stopping places, near running water and grazing land. Fuel, otherwise difficult to come by if the place is rocky or in the sandy areas, is found on these sites, as the animals of the last caravan to pass that way will have left dung which can be burnt by those that follow.

On arriving at a mountain pass the traveller pauses. It will be the dwelling place of a spirit, a *lha* or *sadak*, marked by a pile of stones on the ridge of the pass, with branches pushed into it; banners with sacred words on them and scraps of material and coloured wool are tied to the branches, and the traveller, as soon as he arrives at the top (cf. pl. 86), adds another stone to the pile, shouting the ancient words, '*La so so, lha gyelo*', or 'the god is victorious'. He then proceeds on his way, keeping the heap of stones to his right, sure of his safety as he makes the descent, in the knowledge that he has paid the necessary homage to the god of the mountain. This custom is a legacy of an older religion which Buddhism has not been able to eradicate.

Those who travelled on affairs of state or in the course of their duties were entitled to ask for means of transport and food on their way as part of the state service owed by the village. The few foreign travellers, who had obtained the necessary pass were given the same kind of help, but in return for payment made at fixed rates. The headman of the village, or *genpo*, was responsible for these arrangements in both cases. He was usually elected every year by the villagers and might be reappointed. We never encountered any difficulties during our travels in Tibet.

Other travellers are sometimes seen on the journey; apart from the caravans one may meet lamas visiting their monasteries, civil servants going to take up their appointments, travelling monks and exorcists, and pilgrims. Caravans wind slowly over the great silent stretches of land, while the travellers chatter or turn their prayer-wheels. Or perhaps they pass the time by spinning wool, and sometimes they play the flute.

An ecclesiastical dignitary is a particularly impressive sight. Preceded by a servant holding the bridle he is mounted on a caparisoned horse, bright with silver and gold. Alone or attended by his assistants, the priest wears a red tunic and a yellow jerkin and a gold lacquered hat, so that on the horizon he looks like some magical bloom bursting out of the arid soil. Itinerant lamas wear a big topknot padded with false hair to make it more imposing, after the fashion of some Indian sādhus. Sometimes, like them, they carry a trident, and always a *damaru*, a little drum of shamanic origin, made of the tops of two skulls put together hollow side out, with skin (sometimes human skin) stretched over the two concavities. Two cords with little balls at the ends are attached to the drum, and strike it rhythmically when swung. The damaru is used to accompany the lama's chants and prayers.

73. Wayside *chhörten* near Bod Kharbu, Ladakh.

74. Mulbek village and monastery, Ladakh.

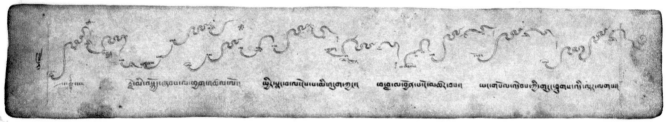

75

7

Other travellers may be beggars, dressed in rags and patches, often a whole family together with no other roof but the sky, living entirely on the charity of others. Pilgrims carry their belongings, a change of clothing, prayer books and their teapot in a canvas or wicker basket on their backs. They walk from dawn to dusk, carrying their boots in their left hands while they turn their prayer wheels with their right hands, willing exiles in search of signs that divine beings have left on earth.

On these endless journeys, the pilgrim's trust is placed in his own strength and in his karma. His pilgrimage is a courageous assertion of man's aloneness, a voluntary renunciation of life in society with others, a complete abandoning of himself to whatever may come. He has nothing with which to defend himself and no medicines. Treacherous paths, rope bridges, avalanches, sickness or hunger are not dangers in themselves, but are the means through which the evil or supernatural beings which populate the earth proclaim their power: nature is indifferent to man. The pilgrim, at the start of his journey, puts himself in the hands of the benign gods and tries to protect himself from the others with prayers and rites and by taking care not to offend them. If he falls sick, he relies on sacred words or his own good karma and the intervention of forces capable of overcoming the evil ones that have struck him. Once, on a journey in western Tibet, I fell ill at night in the middle of a comfortless desert. We had seen no villages for days, and the medicines I had with me had no effect. We were at an altitude of 15,000 feet, perhaps more. I could only wait until I got better. Then a caravan of nomads came by, always a pleasant break in the monotony of a journey. The leader courteously enquired about my state of health, and, being an expert in such matters, offered to help. He recited prayers and carried out a long ceremony and finally told me his conclusions. I had pitched my tent right over the dwelling place of a spirit of the soil, thus offending him, and this was the cause of my sickness. There was only one thing to be done, to move the tent a few yards. He himself chose the most favourable spot, and this was done. The next day, as luck would have it, my fever was gone. This is the way of all pilgrims, and if there is no exorcist, they rely on themselves. But it is on one's own karma that the ultimate result depends.

In those provinces with only a small settled population bandits and raiders are the greatest source of danger. Nearly all the raiders come from Kham or from the north and possess large herds and flocks. They are families or groups of families who migrate according to the weather and the need to find new pastures, camping in the most suitable places. They rustle animals from the local population and do not hesitate to resort to violence. Armed with antique or modern guns they can be a danger to the solitary traveller, although bandits are even more to be feared. They haunt the usual routes and are pitiless when offered the slightest resistance. Sometimes they form bands of such numbers and attack so frequently that the government intervenes. An armed conflict takes place and the bandits who are captured are severely punished. The bandits were found, above all, around the passes leading to the monasteries where people would go to have ceremonies performed for themselves or for deceased relatives, or to present a donation, or else near the villages where commerce was carried on. When I was in Samyê there was a gun-battle between the monks and bandits, resulting in many dead and injured on both sides.

This more or less regular life was interrupted by religious or seasonal festivals. The dates of these, some fixed, some moveable, were contained in the calendar published every year by the astrologers (*tsipa*), together with the phases of the moon and other information necessary for the Tibetan to consult in order to reach his decisions.

75. Pages from a manuscript, with Tibetan musical notation accompanying some of the words. Note the intricate nature of the liturgical chant. The illustrations are: *Left:* Mila-rêpa; *centre:* Marpa, the translator; *right:* Gampopa.

76. Pages from a medical work. The illustrations are: (a) Śākyamuni; Bhaiṣajyaguru; (b) & (c) herbs.

The Tibetan calendar is based on a cycle of twelve years, distinguished not by numbers but by the names of animals; the mouse, the ox, the tiger, the hare, the dragon, the snake, the horse, the sheep, the monkey, the bird, the dog and the pig. Each of the five elements, wood, fire, earth, iron and water also applies to two successive years, and in this way we arrive at a cycle of sixty years in all, called a *rapchung*, in the course of which each animal is combined with each element. It is easy to work out the year according to our calendar if one remembers that the number of the first year of the first rapchung was 1027, and one knows the number of the rapchung in which the given year falls.

When asked his age, the Tibetan will say he was born in the year of the mouse or of the ox and so on, and if he states what element was in conjunction with the animal at the time, it is a simple matter to tell how old he is.

The beginning of the year generally falls in February; there are twelve lunar months, in some years thirteen, and weeks that correspond to our own—the names of the days being taken from the planets: thus, the planet (*za*) Sun for Sunday, the **Moon** (*dawa*) for Monday, 'Red Eyes' (*migmar*) or Mars for Tuesday, *lhakpa* or Mercury for Wednesday, *phurbu* or Jupiter for Thursday, *pasang* or Venus for Friday, and *penpa* or Saturn for Saturday. The day is divided into twelve *khyim*, in turn divided into five *chhutshö*, the word nowadays used as the translation for 'hour'.

It is therefore obvious that any reference to dates or the order of events is inconclusive unless the number of the sixty-year cycle is mentioned or the period in which the date falls can be ascertained in some other way. The naming of the years and their grouping under an element are not done solely for the purpose of marking the passage of time, but also to enable the Tibetan to determine his natal influences so that he can decide the course of action to be taken at critical moments in his life, his good or bad luck depending on the stars. The calendar is of the greatest importance in the lives of all as, by indicating the passing of the days, the coming of the seasons and the positions of the planets, it informs the whole community, and especially the monks, of feast days, the celebration of which is a religious duty.

The New Year festival, the *losar*, is perhaps the most important event of the year, and is preceded by a number of preparatory ceremonies to wind up the old year and begin the new one. The element of risk in changing from one period to another makes this a very important time, when all feel a certain anxiety in case the cycle is not renewed and the miracle of rebirth does not take place, mixed with the hope that the new year will be better than the old. So the ceremonies at this time have the double aim of chasing away the evil elements that hover all around and of inspiring faith in the future. It is also necessary to see that there remains no trace of anything evil, unlucky or sinful from the previous year as this might mar the happiness of the year to follow. Everything must begin anew, in peace and tranquillity, and all that may be even indirectly unlucky must be carefully avoided. After the preparatory ceremonies are over full rein is given to the gaiety of the occasion.

The Feast begins on the 29th of the last month of the year with a ceremony called the 'collecting of the soot'. The soot which has gathered in the course of the year in the kitchen is carefully collected and placed in a stone jar with a black edge; it is then thrown on to a crossroads, or a meeting of three paths, places frequented, according to popular belief, by every kind of baneful spirit—especially those called *dre* or *dön* or *dü*, inclined to harm both men and animals. Rags, black seeds, and even money are thrown away with the soot as if to placate the hostile forces and buy off the calamities that they can cause. At the same time the kitchen is purified, as the *thaplha*

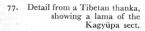
77. Detail from a Tibetan thanka, showing a lama of the Kagyüpa sect.

77

or hearth god resides there, and, although he protects the house, he is sensitive to any impurity which may sully his dwelling-place.

On the last day of the year the monks perform a certain ceremony, called the *tor-sor*, in order to exorcise the evil spirits that are invisibly present everywhere in the world of men, and so to ensure that the new year will be a happy one. Nine, nineteen, or twenty-nine offerings for the wrathful deities are prepared, and special representations, called *linga*, which are inhabited by evil spirits are thrown away, together with the offerings, to the accompaniment of shouting and gunshots or fire-crackers, and other festivities, while in the monasteries sacred dances are performed.

On the same day, eight loaves together with flour, butter and sugar, are prepared to be served at the midday meal. A different object is placed in each loaf—a piece of paper, a sliver of wood, a stone, a piece of coal or some salt, a piece of animal dung, some yak hair and some medicinal herbs. Each guest chooses a loaf and makes predictions about the future according to the object found in the bread. The person who has the piece of paper will become learned; the one finding the piece of wood will become poor and will go about supporting himself on a stick; animal dung means good luck; herbs, strength and victory over one's enemies. In central Tibet there are additional methods for chasing away the evil spirits and for purifying the houses. The people search their houses carrying torches, looking carefully in every corner, then they run out, as if following a thief that had been discovered, shouting the words 'Ki ho ho', a phrase believed to have exorcising powers. Shrieking and firing guns, they all run to the end of the village, where they throw down their torches.

Great importance is attached to the decoration of the houses on the last day of the year. Festoons of coloured material or paper are hung everywhere, or the walls of the verandah are adorned with drawings in white flour, showing such good-luck symbols as shells, a jewel, the sun, the moon and so on. It is customary to eat barley flour mixed with fresh butter and cheese, served in a wooden or metal bowl, and with a sun and a moon, made of different coloured butter, placed on top. This is considered a particularly auspicious dish.

On the first day of the year everyone rises early to draw water from the nearest spring or stream. First of all *sang* is offered; that is, juniper branches are burnt and the usual words are pronounced, 'the god is victorious'. When water has been drawn, the family return home, but stay outside the house where they wash and put on new clothes. They then enter the house, going to the chapel where lamps are lit and prayers said. The water is believed to be especially purifying and sanctifying on that day as it has been cleansed by the starlight of the night before and is in fact called *karchu* or 'star-water'.

The first day of the year is a new beginning, and all unfortunate words or meetings must be avoided. To ensure that the new year starts auspiciously the *Drekar* goes from house to house, wearing a goat-skin round his waist, a cotton mask on his face and with a stick in his hands. He greets each family with the appropriate words of good omen. All welcome him warmly, vying with one another in offering him food and money according to their means. It is a sign of ill-fortune if the Drekar misses out a house or is sent away. On the same day, other groups, called *Maṇi-pa*, also wander round the village, knocking on all the doors and repeating, *Oṁ maṇi-padme hūṁ*, the mystical invocation of Chenrêsik. Families visit one another, dressed in their best clothes and the women wear their finest ornaments. Tea is offered, served in cups with the rims decorated with lucky symbols made out of butter, and a special greeting is said at the same time:

78. Detail from a Tibetan thanka, showing lamas of the Geluk-pa lineage.
In the centre of the representation of the Buddha is the symbol of the reintegration process, evoked and realized by meditation.

Blessings, much happiness!
May the mother be blessed and her body enjoy good health,
May she ever be happy.

Or this (in Kham):

With this handful of flour and sugar, at this
gathering, our mouths are full,
May prosperity and merit increase,
joy last for ever:
u la lo ho—the god is victorious.

On the second and third days the celebrations continue with archery competitions, horse-racing, and dancing and religious plays. But the festivities centre round the unusually lavish meals, prepared with all the resources, modest though they may be, that the Tibetan cook can muster.

Life in the monasteries, too, is interrupted at this time, the monks being able to visit their homes, but not for long. After these family celebrations comes the feast of *Mönlam*, originated by Tsongkha-pa, at Lhasa. At first the 'yellow' sect assumed the leadership of this feast, directed towards the renewing of time, but later the government took it over.

In a country where magic rites are a dominating force and at the New Year when, by old tradition, the whole community concentrated on ensuring a period of happiness, that sect which had risen to power could do little else but attach ever-increasing importance to the end-of-year celebrations. For the first half of the month thousands of monks gathered at Lhasa from all over Tibet to perform religious services with special pomp, so that this dangerous period might be lived through safely. The city was controlled by monks chosen to govern temporarily, and the religious community reaffirmed its rights. Leading theologians gathered in the monasteries to hold public debates in logic and philosophy; others interpreted books of special interest to large gatherings of monks. Those who distinguished themselves were nominated to the Dalai Lama for a title of honour. The Mönlam finishes on the twenty-fifth day of the first month.

Summer is the time for relaxing, and monks and those of the lay community who are able to do so camp out in the *lingka*, parks or gardens near running water. Big tents of different colours with stylized versions of the Chinese characters for 'long life' and 'good luck' give new colour and life to the countryside (cf. pl. 39). Picnics and banquets take place in the shady gardens of the nobility.

The Tibetan's liking for festivities comes from a spirit of sociability. A festival is only partly a private affair: it is more a way of restoring the wholeness of the community, and it allows those from different walks of life to meet. And, as the Tibetan is also very fond of shows, there is nearly always a performance of a religious play which incorporates good deal of dancing.

The dance is not a diversion but a long-established rite in Tibet; it also plays a large part in the Bonpo ceremonies. The dance is generally regarded as a means by which new supernatural forces can come down to the world of men. An example of this is the *lha-chham*, which take place especially but not exclusively in the monasteries at the end of the year, with monks as the performers (cf. pls. 93, 94). These sacred dances always recall great events of the past, and in Tibetan Buddhism in particular.

The struggle between religion and evil powers is a customary theme, for example in the story of the persecution of Buddhism by king Langdarma and his assassination by Pelgyi-dorje.

The performers wear huge, monstrous masks, which do not just exaggerate the basic features of the human face, in order to portray wickedness; they are more the arbitrary product of an inflamed imagination, so that the face loses its normal proportions (cf. pl. 16).

The dances which form part of the plays are performed with a wild energy, although according to precise rules. The vigour that characterizes them is in marked contrast with the measured refinement of the Japanese Nō, for example. The Nō has a restrained quality but in Tibetan religious dances there is a feeling of primeval violence. The dancer's body seems possessed by an uncontrollable force which makes it leap and whirl and sway to the varying rhythms, now slow, now fast, of the music. These dances take us back to the time when the distance between men and spirits was small; man is no more than the temporary dwelling-place of a divine presence to whom he is lending his body so that the god might repeat his wonders. This does not mean that man becomes a god, he is rather the instrument of the powers for good and evil. The music which precedes and accompanies the dancing is intensely moving. A stronger version of the settings used in some religious services, it is like a symphony of pre-human sounds, or a tone-picture of the convulsions of nature; the roar of the great trumpets finds a reply in the thunder of the drums and their long silences are bridged only by the lament of the *gyaling* or clarinets.

These dramatic performances are common to all religious schools and take place outside the monastery or in some other place reserved for this purpose. Habit and yearly repetition do nothing to lessen the half-frightened enjoyment of the numerous spectators. Other dramatic performances are held after the harvest, but these are more like a thanksgiving ceremony, with professional actors instead of monks. Some of these companies of actors, such as the Kyomolung group, have the privilege of being permitted to perform before the Dalai Lama. This kind of drama is also indirectly religious in character, as it is inspired by popular Buddhist lore on the lives of saints. The actors wear masks, but they are different from the ones in the monastery plays. They are triangular in shape, edged with hair and hung with shells.

These dramatic performances illustrate the spirit of sacrifice which the Buddhist faith has inspired, and the resulting patience and acceptance of suffering or difficulties; or portray the struggle between good and evil with the unfailing triumph of truth; but at all times they encourage the people to practise the Dharma. The differences between the monastic and lay performances is in the underlying meaning; the monks are concerned with some event which once endangered the community and which is now re-lived so that the forces of evil may be overcome; the long-past battle is again fought so that good may again triumph, to show that attack by the powers of evil is not simply a past event but is ever-present. These dramas are like mystery-plays endowed with a liturgical significance and powers of exorcism to make quite sure that life continues in the usual way: they are a religious rite, even though they are intricate and spectacular and full of feeling, thus claiming the fervent attention of the lay public. Professional actors, on the other hand, set out principally to entertain and to break the monotony of everyday life, although at the same time their performances contain a religious element. The spectators are deeply involved in these plays, living with the characters in such a way that they weep and despair at misfortunes and become wild with joy when the happy ending comes.

The villagers frequently dance on other occasions, when the solemnity of religious feasts is absent. Springing of its own accord from the life of the fields there will be a brief burst of festivity, when the young men and women dance together, facing each other in two lines. Holding hands and taking turns to sing, they dance forward gradually till the two lines meet, then after a moment they return to their places. Sometimes it is only the women who dance, while the men watch. Their songs are a mixture of sacred and profane themes, telling of unrequited love and invoking the gods. I have watched this kind of dancing which takes place generally at full moon in western Tibet, in Lo on the border between Tibet proper and Nepal, and in Yarlung.

There are of course other religious feasts as well as seasonal ones. The lay community is involved in these celebrations, if only as spectators or supporting donors. The monastic calendar marks various feasts which are celebrated with special solemnity. Of great importance are the events in the life of the Buddha; at the New Year the miracle of Śrāvastī is commemorated, this being the occasion when the Buddha subdued heretics by multiplying himself, and causing water to flow from his feet and flames to leap from his shoulders. The seventh day of the fourth month is the Buddha's birthday, and on the fifteenth day of the same month there is the feast to celebrate the occasion when the Buddha attained supreme enlightenment, and his passing into the state of nirvana. On the fourth day of the sixth month the first sermon is recalled, and in the ninth month comes the remembrance of the descent from heaven. On the night of the twenty-fourth and twenty-fifth of the tenth month the special feast of the Geluk-pa is held; it is celebrated with great solemnity at Lhasa and in important monasteries of the same sect elsewhere to commemorate the death of Tsongkha-pa. Lhasa and the other cities where the 'yellow' sect is predominant are bright with lamps placed on the roofs of the houses and monasteries, twinkling like the distant stars. It is a feast reminiscent of the *diwāli* of India and which takes place at roughly the same time, perhaps inspired by the Indian custom. It is a day of great celebrations, when the rules of good behaviour are relaxed somewhat, and a day when monks are sent out from the monasteries to beg.

Equally important and just as picturesque is the feast which falls on the fifteenth of the first month. On this occasion big statues of the most venerated deities are made from butter kneaded with flour. They are made with the same care that would be given to the fashioning of statues of a more durable nature. They are lavishly painted and, so that they will not be damaged by the sun's heat, they are placed outside the monasteries at twilight, while thousands of lamps are lit in celebration. Some of the larger statues are constructed round lattice-work frames and at the end of the ceremony they are generally thrown away as an offering to the powers of evil. But it can happen that the poor take them for food.

There are plenty of occasions for festivities apart from these and many others are marked on the religious calendar. Any specially pleasing family event will be celebrated by parties, this custom being extended to perhaps unexpected occasions. For example, when a *geshé* or doctor of theology, the victor in a public discussion, is honoured with the coveted title of *Lharampa*, he is more or less obliged to celebrate in style by inviting the monks from the monastery to a liberal meal, all at his own expense, which can be extremely costly when his monastery is a large one housing several thousand monks.

Laymen have a similar problem. The sons of noblemen are entitled to an official career by birth, but when they come to take up their duties it is customary to give splendid banquets for a whole host of superiors and other colleagues. It is not uncom-

79. Detail from a Tibetan thanka of the Bonpos, showing some Bonpo masters worshipping the image of Shen-rap (the Bonpo revealer) appearing inside a *chhörten*.

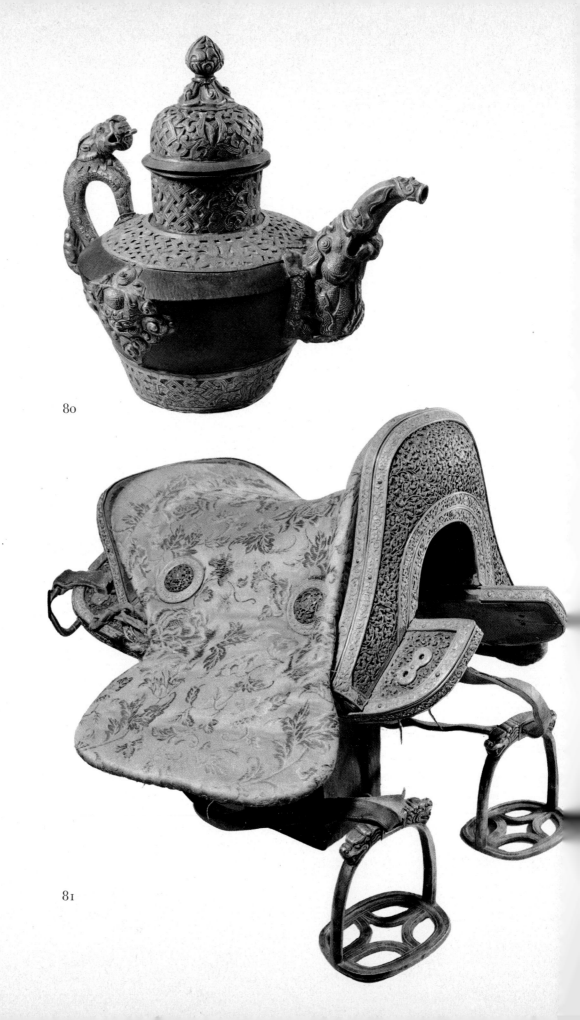

80

81

mon for several hundred guests to be invited, and none would dream of bringing less than two servants along to attend him.

Major festivals are often the occasion for all kinds of games and contests, and some of them, like horse-racing and archery, are *de rigueur* for the young official. These sports are time-honoured survivals of ancient ritual, from the days when Tibetan society had to be steeled in the rigours of war and the hazards of the chase. The competitor must try to hit the target at full gallop, with arrow or spear. The warlike significance has long disappeared, but such competitions kept the sporting spirit alive and gave people a chance to display dazzling costumes as splendid as those which had once graced the old Chinese aristocracy. On a smaller scale, events like this took place in other parts of Tibet besides Lhasa; and sports were especially in favour in Kham.

The upper classes enjoyed their own ways of passing time and could afford pleasures denied to the country folk buried in the poverty of their villages, or nomadic shepherds on the upland plains. Life could be monotonous even for the minor nobility shut up in their houses or ensconced in their remote estates, to share the flat succession of day upon day with their peasants, save when some pilgrimage, or trip to market or the capital, intervened. Once again, it was religion that broke the tedium with its ceremonial splendour, even though this could never equal the solemn magnificence of the performances mounted at Lhasa or in the chief monasteries.

Fig 7 Silver jewel box *c.* 19th century.

80. Tea-pot; iron with applied brass decoration.

81. Saddle for ceremonial use, with stirrups, silver, silver gilt and brocade. This saddle was the personal property of Surkhang Shapé, first Cabinet Minister to H. H. the Dalai Lama at the time of his escape.

Birth, marriage, sickness and death

FAMILY LIFE FOLLOWED the same pattern everywhere, varied only by those moments of joy, sadness or worry known to all of us. Birth, marriage, sickness and death were accompanied by their special customs, differing a little from place to place and according to the wealth of the family involved.

Childbirth was attended by none of the care and concern known in western countries. Birth was regarded as a completely natural function, and the physical strength necessary to the mother was not weakened by worries about hygiene.

Prayers and talismans would help to make the birth safe and easy, according to age-old custom, and the intervention of the exorcist or the village lama would frequently be requested, but doctors and midwives were unknown. The woman was left to herself, and only in rich families would she stay in bed, or be looked after, for a week or so. In the country she would resume her normal activities after two or three days. Neither would the new-born child receive the care and protection given in our society. It might be washed once in a while, and since fuel was scarce and expensive the water would as likely as not be cold, or else be slightly warmed by the mother, who would take a mouthful at a time and sprinkle it over the baby's body. Much faith was placed in the talismans and chantings of the lamas summoned to welcome the new-born child, but infant mortality was very high. Accurate information is difficult to come by, as there were no registrar's offices and no statistics, but it is probably no exaggeration to say that, up to the tenth year of life, it was over fifty per cent.

Male children were the favourites in Tibet, but owing to the high status enjoyed by women, the birth of a girl was in the end as joyful an occasion as the birth of a boy. Three or four days after the birth would come the celebration. Friends and relations would visit the family, bringing gifts of food and the usual silk or gauze scarf, a necessary part of any ceremony. But a few days later a much more important event occurred, the casting of the baby's horoscope. There was usually an astrologer, or *tsipa*, in every village. If by any chance there was none, the nearest one would be sent for. The hour, date and month of the birth were noted, so that the horoscope could be carefully cast, and the favourable and unfavourable moments in the life of the child accurately foretold, according to the influences of the Elements. Sometimes, especially in families of the poorer classes, the day when the child was born would give it its first name: for example, a boy born on Friday would be called Pasang, the Tibetan word for Friday. Other more personal names with an auspicious meaning might then be taken, such as Töndrup, 'he whose aims shall be achieved' or 'he who has fulfilled the wishes of his parents', a name having the double advantage of evoking that of the Buddha Śākyamuni who was called Sarvārthasiddha, its Sanskrit equivalent. These names were changed if later the boy entered a monastic order. Then a religious name would be given him, probably chosen from those of the great teachers of the sect he joined.

82. Stone inscribed
' om maṇi-padme hūm '.

83. Old inscriptions
on the obelisk of Samyê,
rom the time of the royal dynasty.

84. Amitāyus (Tshepamé),
the Buddha of Boundless
Life—another form of Ö-pamé,
the Buddha of Boundless Light.

82

83

86

87

The giving of a name and the casting of the horoscope were celebrated with much solemnity, not only because of the Tibetan's natural enjoyment of festivities, but also in order to create a happy and therefore auspicious atmosphere at the moment when the new-born child was assuming his proper place and asserting his own identity in the world.

Marriage was of course another event to be celebrated with solemnity. It must be noted that Tibetan women enjoyed considerable freedom and, in practice if not in theory, lived on the same level as the men. They were never segregated or expected to be bashful in the way law or custom decreed in other parts of the East. They were also fortunate in possessing marked practical ability. Many women helped their husbands in business affairs or even acted on their own account, and were more likely to increase the family fortunes than to squander them, because of this business sense. It was not unheard of for a civil servant to find some excuse to stay at home and direct his own affairs, sending his wife off to the office to do his work in his absence. I have myself frequently met the wives of local governors who were temporarily carrying out their husbands' duties, and I have always admired the strictly ordered way in which they ran their own houses as well as the way in which they conducted their business affairs. In the family, the mother had great authority, being responsible for the up-bringing of the children and the household expenditure. Even when the sons of the family brought home wives, the mother would remain the central figure.

Much has been written on the subject of polyandry, or the practice of a woman taking more than one husband by marrying not only the man she has been betrothed to but also his brothers. This custom did exist in every part of Tibet, but it was not as common as is generally believed. Many explanations for it have been given; perhaps it arose because more females than males died in infancy, or many women as well as men entered monastic orders, or because it was desirable to keep the family and the property undivided, especially among the richer families. But monogamous marriages were the rule in all classes of society. The children of a polyandrous union were considered to be the issue of the eldest brother, to whom the mother was first married, and his brothers, even if they were in fact the fathers of some of the children, would be called uncle by all. In such a union it was generally arranged so that only one of the brothers was at home at any one time, the others being absent on business or for other reasons. In some parts of Tibet, when the wife retired with one of the men, his boots were left outside the door.

Because of the position of women and the flexibility of family life, young couples were always acquainted before marriage, although the consent of the parents was a necessary formality. Girls being free to go out and meet young men in the course of the day's work or at a celebration, the choice of a partner rested with the young people and depended on mutual attraction. Sometimes the girl was already a mother. In the case of rich families, however, marriage became more of a contract as the financial interests of the parents were involved, as well as the feelings of the couple, and the desire to save a heritage in peril could override the preferences of the children.

The marriage ceremony had none of the complexity found in India. The lamas participated, but only because their presence was necessary on all occasions in life. The wedding itself was perhaps the most secular event of all, accompanied by no religious rites. Certain preliminaries were necessary. First of all, it had to be established that there was no close kinship between the two families. Marriage between cousins was frowned on, causing a scandal when it did occur, but a man could marry his brother's widow, or even his father's, provided, of course, that she was not his

85. Fierce guardian deity. Her saddle is a flayed human, or demonic, skin.

86. A *lhatho*, heap of stones and abode of a mountain god on the top of a mountain pass.

87. A huge shrine containing an image of Chenrêsik, the god who protects from the eight kinds of danger. In front are the stones or pebbles which pilgrims throw there after invocation.

mother. Many of the rules which so severely govern marriage in India were completely absent in Tibet. The horoscopes of the couple were studied to ensure that they were not incompatible: in the case of any serious clashes the marriage would not take place. There were, however, certain difficulties that could be smoothed over by consulting astrological manuals. The astrologer was all-important during this preliminary phase, and when the first decisions had been taken, the intermediary was called in. He was either a member of the family or a professional go-between, and his duty was to obtain the permission of the bride's family, to negotiate her dowry and to establish the kind of presents, jewels and clothes that the bridegroom would give on the day of the wedding. When agreement had been reached, the bride's family would accept the chhang which the intermediary had brought with him to offer at this moment. This meeting did no more than confirm an already existing agreement but it gave an air of solemnity to the proceedings. The intermediary's job was sometimes deliberately made to appear more difficult than it was in fact, as this treating between the two families, the long discussions, the banquets and the exchanging of chhang were a welcome break in the monotony of everyday life and no one was anxious to hasten things unduly. Sometimes the discussions were spread over a number of days, difficulties and obstacles being artificially created to give an air of drama. Chhang was of importance throughout the negotiations and had an almost religious significance at the wedding ceremony. Words which could bring to mind others, similar but with a different, unlucky meaning, were carefully avoided at this time, but objects with auspicious names were freely exchanged, so that a joyful harmonious atmosphere was preserved. It was seen that no sterile woman approached during the ceremonies as her presence could be unlucky and mean that the couple would be childless.

The wedding day was chosen by the astrologer and the eve spent in banqueting and drinking chhang, friends of the two families and the intermediary all participating. The bride's mother would put the finishing touches to her daughter's dress and the necessary rites were performed to ensure that the phuklha would not desert the bride's family and follow her to her new dwelling. In addition to the advice and warnings given to the bride by her mother, in rich families long sermons on the duties of married life were often delivered by some eloquent lama.

The marriage procession started off at dawn, led by a man dressed in white, mounted on a white horse and carrying the *si pa ho* to ward off evil. This was a square sheet of paper bearing a picture of a tortoise with its limbs clasping a circle. In the circle, symbols would be drawn to show the course of time and astrological combinations causing good or evil events. The position of the planets at the bride's birth was also shown, so as to identify her place in the cosmic order and portend the favourable or unfavourable events in her life. Then came the bride, also on horseback, dressed magnificently in many coloured garments and wearing her finest trinkets, but with her face covered by a white scarf as a sign of the modesty every girl of good family was supposed to show at her wedding. It was customary for her to weep as she left her family, while the procession set off, with everyone shouting 'Trashi-delek,' 'May it be auspicious and well'. The procession stopped outside the bridegroom's house. Now came the most dramatic moment of all. The house was locked and barred and a long dialogue ensued during which questions and answers were exchanged in order to establish a state of complete mutual trust so that the uncertainty of the waiting period might be replaced by one of calm and happiness. Finally the door was opened and the bride admitted, to be received by her parents-in-law and to take her place on the chair reserved for her. The contract was sealed by

88. A monk musician of the Nyingma-pa sect at the Palace Monastery, Gangtok, Sikkim. He is playing the big cymbals. To his right is the great drum, held by a single support. In the background is the road to Tibet.

the exchange of scarves and copious servings of chhang and celebrations were soon in full swing.

The bride had not come to live in the house of the bridegroom for good, however. She remained there for three to seven days after the ceremony, and then returned to her parents' home. There was no fixed time for her to take up permanent residence with her husband, this depending on the age of the couple and local custom.

Considering the absence of a binding civil or religious marriage ceremony and the freedom of Tibetan women, it is hardly surprising that divorce was not uncommon, taking place by mutual consent. Long discussions were necessary to resolve the most important problem, the division of the property. The woman, if no blame was attached to her, would ask for the return of her dowry, and was entitled to claim some of the husband's possessions if she took the children of the marriage with her, as was her right. The village buzzed momentarily with the gossip, but it was soon forgotten since such events were not unexpected.

A man is a man the world over, and the Tibetan did not take it kindly if his wife committed adultery, for all the independence she might have. On discovering that his wife was unfaithful, the husband had the right to cut off the tip of her nose. The victim would try to heal the wound by putting a black covering over it. It was, therefore, customary to say, when something arousing scorn took place, 'It's a case for cutting noses'. Wife-murder was not infrequent; but in this case the law took over and the culprit had to pay blood-money.

The Tibetan approached illness with a mixture of religious convictions and a belief in magic together with the most advanced medical ideas from India, China and Iran —and even Galen had been heard of—all countries where research into medicine and pharmacology had been pursued in a constructive fashion. In India there is a substantial body of writings on medicine, which reached Tibet together with sacred literature and aroused widespread interest. Various manuals, which also included treatments and theories from China, helped to disseminate medical knowledge.

But medicines, drugs and surgery were effective only up to a point. If the right prayers were not said and divine intervention was refused, then no medicine would bring about a cure. At the end of every book on medicine, as its conclusion, there was a section on the 'mantras', or phrases to be recited by the sick man himself or by the lama, to invoke divine power to enter the patient and the drugs he was taking. The medical manuals state that cures can be effected by the use of medicine, dieting, courses of treatment, bleeding and exorcisms and religious ceremonies, thus affirming that the psychological element was an essential one for the Tibetan. No clear demarcation was made between the body and the soul; the two were one, so that the soul, helped by the right religious and magic utterances, was able to act on the body and re-establish the right balance of humours, the disturbance of which had caused the illness in the first place. My friend, Lopsang Tenpa, the president of the Mentsikhang Medical College in Lhasa, once told me that in his opinion western medicine, which he knew a little about from his travels in India, was of course incomplete, as it was built entirely on human knowledge and discoveries which were frequently misunderstood. 'But our own', he continued with great certainty, 'has the advantage of being revealed to us. The Great Physician, the Doctor who cures body and soul at once, the Buddha, who is a manifestation of cosmic consciousness and absolute wisdom, has shown it to man'.

The famous medical school of Chakpori in Lhasa was therefore primarily a temple,

89. Detail from a Tibetan thanka, showing the symbolic union of a deity with his consort.

with images ranged on the altars around the 'God of the colour of lapis-lazuli', the chief of eight divinities called the *Menlha*. These were the supreme doctors, since they taught men how to cure sin, the most powerful disharmony causing physical infirmity.

At Mentsikhang there was an extensive array of herbs and drugs of all kinds, roots, powders and plants, some from India and China as well as from Tibet itself. Medicines were usually made up in the form of pills, which were appropriately blessed before being distributed to those in need of them, with instructions not only on the dose to be taken, but on the times of day they were to be swallowed and the prayers that were to be said with them. Medicine did not isolate man from the universe but he was considered to be so bound up with the elements that any treatment which did not take these into account would be not only ineffective but positively harmful. Cosmic harmony had to be preserved, as the most important factor in good health.

Most of the herbs used as medicine were gathered on a mountain to the north of Lhasa, near the monastery of Sera. This mountain was the Garden of Aesculapius to Tibetan doctors and great care was taken in the choice of the plants, which could be beneficial or harmful, more or less effective, depending on the season, or whether they grew on sunlit or northern slopes. Not all medicines were extracted from herbs: sometimes metals, particularly gold, silver, zinc, iron and mercury, or stones, were used, as was the custom in India. Other remedies were based on the belief in strange analogies between certain substances and parts of the body, as in the folk-medicine of any other country. So the gall of oxen was used to treat weaknesses of the eyes, the spleen for abscesses, the tongue of a dog was often used to heal wounds and the liver of a dog was a remedy for leprosy.

The basis of Tibetan medicine was the Indian theory of Humours, which in turn springs from the ethical concept that physical imbalance is associated with spiritual imbalance. In other words, it is the work of karma, which controls the course of human life. Sickness, which originates in sin, is born with karma, and as soon as sin begins to trouble the human conscience, tainting man's original innocence and serenity, evil gives rise to illness. Karma operates under three guises, as greed, wrath and torpor. These three defects have their parallels in the three humours, wind, bile and phlegm. The theory and practice of medicine were based on this fundamental scheme, and by means of endless classifications and ramifications the whole system of interconnected causes, signs, symptoms and cures of the various kinds of sickness could be shown.

These three humours permeate the whole body, but they govern, above all, the brain, the abdomen and the bowels respectively. When one of the humours prevails over the others, illness results. Wind influences the bones, ears, skin, flesh and arteries; bile governs the blood, sweat, eyes, liver and intestines; and phlegm has its effect on the chyle, flesh, fat, marrow and semen, the nose, tongue, lungs, spleen, liver, kidneys, stomach and bladder.

Surgery was rarely resorted to, and then only in the case of wounds, abscesses and the like. Even here it was necessary to establish the cause of the disability. Cauterization was the treatment for malfunctioning of wind, blood-letting and cold compresses for disorders of the bile, cauterization and hot compresses for disorders of phlegm. Surgical instruments were few; the lance, the cautery, the *mebum*—a vessel in which paper was burnt and which was then applied to the part of the body to be bled—and the 'sucking-horn', which drew blood off by suction.

The time comes when no medicine is effective, meaning that the patient is the victim of his karma, and the sum of his sins is overtaking him, or else that demons have gained possession of him, amongst them the planets, always believed to be hostile.

Some diseases are, in fact, caused exclusively by them, for instance, epilepsy and apoplexy. The *lu* and the *sadak*, spirits from beneath the earth, are also easily offended and most vindictive. A slight upset, even involuntary, can call down extreme wrath on man. Then medicine is no use and the doctor becomes an exorcist.

The reading of any book whose subject matter seemed particularly apt, or of sacred texts in general, helped in such cases, for they represented the Buddha's 'verbal plane', embodied in sounds. The mere recitation of these writings had a strange but positive magical power, as of light dispelling darkness. Monks from the temple or the village lama were called to the sick man's bedside to read or murmur the recommended books, the comprehension of which was immaterial. Even the lama did not always fully understand the text he was reading. The act of reciting the appropriate words was, in itself, effective through the magical power of the sound produced. In this way the divine presence was evoked and healing would result. Another method was to buy from the butcher a goat or a sheep about to be slaughtered. The animal was then set free after a red ribbon had been tied round its neck. As long as the ribbon lasted, the animal was safe from recapture, and the saving of life in this way was also the saving of the sick man.

The moment of death was a decisive one, governing the future destiny of the victim. In case there was no immediate attainment of nirvana there was a limit of forty-nine days between the end of one life and the beginning of another, and the dying man's fate depended on his clear awareness in the moments preceeding his end. Acts are important according to Buddhism, but only conscious acts, as consciousness gives responsibility to the action, and this responsibility will bring the action to fruition. An involuntary action can bring no positive result. Buddhism acknowledges no soul, but in Tibet certain old beliefs persisted and it was thought that a certain spiritual entity analogous with the soul existed, so that Buddhism there was occasionally tinged with these superstitions among some people of lower doctrinal experience. The continuance of our personality, which is destined to dissolve at death, is entrusted to the *namparshé*, or consciousness. This preserves within itself the karmic remains of past existences, modified according to the kind of life led, which have determined the conditions of our present life. This consciousness, enriched by its new experiences, orders our future life at the moment of death, for it then has the power to project itself into a new set of components of the physical personality, such as every living being possesses. Whether these are real or illusory is a question for the Buddhist metaphysicians.

This new future depends on us, on our karma. So, on his deathbed, it was necessary to draw the dying man's attention, or rather, that of his consciousness, which contains his personality, to a consideration of what was about to befall him. There were existences far worse than that of a human being in store for sinners: rebirth as an animal, descent into various hells, or becoming one of the *yidak*, wretched beings who perpetually wander through space, tormented by thirst and hunger.

Terrible visions of hell, where the damned suffer indescribable torments, had been brought from India. It was thought that these wretched beings believed they suffered, rather than that they suffered in fact, for everything is merely a product of the imagination, though to the uninitiated it has the value of reality. The Tibetan, with his tendency to the macabre, drew an even grimmer picture of hot and cold hells and frightful tortures, which are dwelt on at length in a hair-raising literature, the *dêlo*. This is a series of accounts given by those who, on the brink of death, caught a glimpse of life beyond the tomb, but then returned to tell of the terrifying things they saw.

An idea prevalent in Indian religious thinking is found also in Tibet. The luminous awareness of what we are and what awaits us acts, at the moment of departure, as a factor for our salvation since, as we see in the *Song of the Blessed One*, 'the dying man attains the same level as his thoughts occupied in his last moment'. To this end, a lama specialized in these rites would read an appropriate book, whispering the words into the ear of the dying man or of the corpse. It mattered little if the man was already dead or not, as his consciousness would remain hovering about his body for several days. The book is called the *Bardo-thödröl*, 'the book whose mere recitation, when heard by the dead man during the period of his intermediate existence between the life he has left and the one he is to enter in forty-nine days' time, will lead him to salvation'. None of this applied, of course, to the saintly who, at the moment of death, were absorbed, in full consciousness, into the wonderful clear light which is the Absolute itself made manifest, or who vanished into the sky in the splendour of a rainbow.

For more ordinary beings the intermediate state with its attendant dangers began. Apparitions were perceived by the dead man's consciousness, the most exalted being flashes of contrasting light, which dazzled or invited him, a tumultuous roaring, shapes which frightened or allured him. Then came seven days during which the five primary forces were revealed in the form of the five supreme Buddhas, the fivefold source of everything that exists. The five Buddhas each appear with a 'Mother', coupled with whom they become manifest in the universe with all its variety. They were arranged in the form of a cross, representing infinite space, divided by two intersecting axes to mark the five directions of divine experience: the centre, east, south, west and north. The secret of their mysterious works was revealed and the dead man's consciousness was made aware of their true meaning. The forces thus represented are present in all of us and go to make up our personality of which they form the underlying pattern; they are therefore also the means of salvation, when our gnosis, on understanding their nature, absorbs them. This is the knowledge that annihilates, bringing us back from the apparent to the real, a return to our origin.

When this salvation through recognition did not take place, a progressive decline set in; visions of deities, which the dead man should think of as springing from his own body, would appear. He must win the conviction that all images, including the divine, are the creation of his own mind, emerging from and returning to himself. The man who was not saved by such recognition would then see six lights which corresponded to six kinds of existence, those of gods, of men, of demons, of animals, of ghosts (*yidak*) and of beings in hell. These lights are pleasing and attractive; and he who surrendered to their persuasion, unmindful of what they represented, would be caught up in that existence whose light most forcefully struck or attracted him. This happened because desire would take over in this welter of images and volition, unless the purifying of gnosis intervened; what we are is the effect of the ideas in which we believe.

The fearsome gods would appear and had to be disposed of in the same way. When recognition was absent, such visions would be regarded as the god of death, and death would be believed to be a reality, and the dead man caught up in the succeeding phases of the karmic process, since all events are caused by our own will. Whatever can death be, let alone the god of death, in a philosophy which reduces everything to a nebulous set of images? How can there be anyone that dies, or causes to die, from the point of view of this doctrine, according to which everything dissolves into the colourless, motionless light of cosmic consciousness?

90. Detail from a Tibetan thanka, showing the god of Good Fortune, or Wealth, with a mongoose in his left hand.

166

After the thirteenth day, the dead man's consciousness, which up to now had stayed in the vicinity of the corpse, harried by the wind of karma, and occupying a slender body in a state of unrest, began to wander about in profound grief. After trying nine times in vain to re-enter the recently abandoned body, it vainly attempted to enter another. Frightening visions disturbed it and chased it from place to place. Liberation must be found in the knowledge that these visions too are illusory. Divine mercy had only to be invoked for them to flee away, provided that the mind could remain in a state of complete tranquillity during the ordeal.

Many creatures would be saved, but many others would be led by their karma to embark on a new incarnation. In this case new visions of rebirth now appeared before the consciousness and corresponded to the four continents into which the word is divided according to Indo-Tibetan cosmology. So a man had to be able to distinguish the signs of Jambudvīpa, the continent blessed with regular appearances of the Buddha, from those of the other worlds where the teachings of the Buddha have not spread. He could, alternatively, allow himself to be drawn towards the heavens, the habitation of the gods, but would have to flee the deceitful images of the world of the demons, of animals, the hungry ghosts, or hell. And he would have to be alert and wary, as karma would call up frightening visions to tempt him to take refuge in caves or lotus flowers, where he might expect to find escape from the turmoil surrounding him and the demons pursuing him. These places of shelter would only be the entrances to unhappy forms of existence, during which he would have to expiate his past misdeeds.

But not all was lost even in this sad situation since, by composing one's mind and meditating on the god Tamdrin, there were still two courses open: one was to reach a paradise of the Buddha, the other, the choice of the womb. The first goal was attained by concentrating the will towards this miraculous rebirth with complete and undivided faith. The second course was embarked on after the continent had been chosen, and it was not impossible to be born into a good family, so as to live to the advantage of one's fellow-creatures, if this was desired with real sincerity and determination. No further effort was to be made, and a desire for one particular womb or a feeling of aversion for another were avoided, as such feelings could reflect badly on the coming existence and would favour the development of karma. Once the wish had been formed, the mind was left to rest in the thought of the three Sacred Gems, the Buddha, the Law, and the Monastic Community.

Such then was the way of salvation, except in the case of saints. The consciousness left the body through a tiny hole at the point where the cranial bones meet on the top of the head, the lama pulling out a hair to provide the way of escape. Since it was believed that the consciousness wandered in the vicinity for several days, the corpse was left in the hourse for a period of three to seven days, or even longer. The dead man was dressed in his best clothes and placed in a sitting position, his hands crossed on his lap. Only the bodies of highly esteemed lamas were washed, and then this was done with water made fragrant with herbs. The dead man was not left in the room where he died but was taken to another room where the picture of his personal deity (*yi dam*) was hung above him. He could not be touched for three days. If a member of the family were to touch his feet, for example, the deceased would run the risk of going to hell. A lama would remain near him for several days, reading aloud from a sacred book and reciting the prayers for the dead: the rich would send for seven or fourteen monks from the nearest monastery to perform this rite. Those who were very wealthy would make a generous gift to the monastery, so that a funeral

91. Detail from a Tibetan thanka, showing the Buddha Ö-pamé (Amitābha) in his Western Paradise of Dewachen (Sukhāvati). Below is a retinue of *changchupsempas*.

service could be held with the participation of all the monks, and alms would be given to the poor. Meanwhile the astrologer would establish the most appropriate time for the burial, after consulting the dead man's horoscope and each day a funeral meal would be eaten by the members of the family, friends, and the officiating lama. Some of the food was put in front of the corpse or his image. This food offering was placed before the image of the dead man for forty-nine days, the whole of the period of the intermediate existence. The image itself consisted of a piece of paper with the Sanskrit syllable *nri* ('man') and the word *tshelêdêpa* (dead) written on it, followed by the name of the deceased. Every seven days the piece of paper was burnt and another put in its place, and from the colour of the flames the lama was able to infer what new form of existence the dead man was progressing towards. The ashes were carefully collected and mixed with water to make little conical stūpas, like the tshatsha mentioned previously, and put on the household altar or in a place set aside for the purpose. On the appointed day, the corpse was taken to the cemetery. A further banquet brought the family together again and the last prayers were said, while the dead man was warned not to come near the house any more nor to bring misfortune to other members of the family. In some places a white scarf was tied to the corpse's feet, the other end being held by the lama. Then the body was carried out of the house by the *Ragyapas*, whose job it was to see to the last funeral rites.

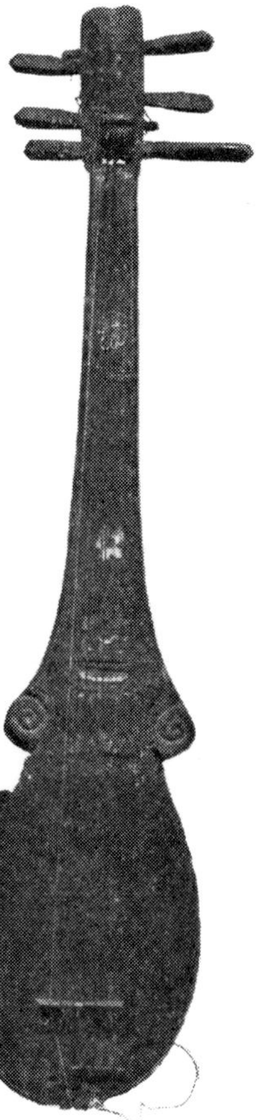

There was no general method of disposing of the body, the custom varying from place to place and with the climate. In places where fuel was scarce one common method was to take the body to the top of a mountain reserved for the purpose. It was then left to the vultures or beasts of prey, after the Ragyapas had cut it up to make it easier for the animals to consume. They even stripped off the flesh with their large knives, and threw it to the crows and vultures, or broke the bones in pieces. A few days later the area was visited again and the remaining bones were crushed to a powder so that nothing of the body was left. In places where fuel was plentiful, the corpse was cremated; in other parts it was thrown into a river. This is an old custom and sometimes, where the body was disposed of on a mountain-top, an effigy was made of the dead man, which was clothed and thrown into the river in place of the actual corpse.

In the case of venerated lamas and also the Dalai Lamas and Panchen Lamas, the remains were placed in the hollow interior of chhörtens.

The lama would assist the members of the dead man's family to purify the house, death being a contamination, calling down supernatural, harmful forces. There was also a danger that the dead man himself might return to his earthly home to take vengeance for some offence, but the lamas performed the necessary rites to restore sanctity to the house and put everything to rights.

Fig 8. Tibetan banjo *c.*
19th century

92. Beer jug in damascened iron;
    Derge work.

93

94

Tibetan literature

WE HAVE NOTICED more than once how religion dominates the Tibetan's cultural upbringing, and it is plain that there can be no literary work that does not reflect this concern. On the other hand, there has always been an active folk literature, consisting of work-songs, the good-natured anonymous expression of grievances against the rulers, and the spontaneous improvizations of parties and weddings. Every agricultural task or caravan journey is accompanied by these songs, handed down from generation to generation and constantly enlarged with new contributions which the people at once make their own. Each job has its own song with its appropriate setting. On holidays when the 'chhang parties' take place, there are poetic contests between the guests. Favourite themes are the forgetting of cares in chhang, and allusions to love. Love not only inspired the bulk of the folk songs to which villagers dance when their work in the fields is over, but was also treated by so unlikely a figure—in Tibet—as the sixth Dalai Lama, obliged to follow a life that did not exactly suit him. A collection of love-songs attributed to him is in the folk idiom, but is not without literary echoes.

> This girl was perhaps not born of a mother,
> But blossomed in a peach tree:
> Her love fades
> Quicker than peach-flowers.
> Although I know her soft body
> I cannot sound out her heart;
> Yet we have but to mark a few lines on a chart
> And the distance of the farthest stars
> In the sky can be measured.

So the primacy of literature dealing with religious topics has not meant a total lack of secular writings—merely that they cannot stand on the same footing. In any case their authors were normally monks, who were not forbidden to take an interest in matters only indirectly connected with religion, as a minor activity. This secular literature deals with sciences like medicine and astrology, on which there were countless treatises. The *Vaidūrya karpo* with its commentary the *Vaidūrya yasel*, concerning astrology, and the *Vaidūrya ngönpo*, on medicine, were amongst the most widely known. All three works were written by Sanggyê-gyatso (1653-1705).

Then there are the *jikten-tenchö*, manuals dealing with activities that were particularly the province of laymen (*jikten-pa*), such as *zorik*, workmanship, which ranges from architecture, sculpture and painting to the making of weapons and so on. But even these works were nearly always written by monks.

A religious subject was the one most likely to interest a Tibetan. He was attracted by tales or legends that provided some satisfaction for his sense of the sacred and his

93. Sacred *chham* dance.

94. Sacred *chham* dance.

173

belief in marvels. Nearly all the books that fed his desire for knowledge came from monasteries, for only in the monasteries did facilities for printing exist. The books that roused most interest and had a large circulation were the lives of saints or great miracle-workers—not surprisingly, since these accounts dwelt on the wonders attributed to them, their feats of asceticism, and the final victory over adversity.

These biographies are called *namthar*, which means 'liberation'. They relate how this liberation—salvation in nirvāna—was pursued, and hence how one should live in order finally to overcome the cycle of births and deaths. In fact, the object of these works is to offer an example to be followed. They set out to edify the faithful, not to portray the historical background or supply a precise biography based on verified facts. Their historical value is rare and indirect.

It may be asserted, accordingly, that the popularity of these works did not depend on their documentary or literary value, which was usually rather modest, but on their miracle content. The author was seldom so outstandingly gifted as to cast the spell of a true work of art upon this rather monotonous content. One of the few books that stands out above the rest is the biography of Mila-rêpa (1040-1123), who is one of the most famous and popular saints and poets of Tibet. Unfortunately we do not know who wrote it, or when. In the colophons with which the book ends the author is referred to by an epithet, but not by his own name. At all events whoever wrote this biography, which also contains Mila-rêpa's songs, certainly possessed great literary talent, and there is no denying that he found a subject suited to him. Mila-rêpa's life starts out dramatically. He loses his father when still very young and his mother suffers at the hands of unscrupulous relatives. The boy grows up in the bleakest poverty, his mind torn between love for his mother and hatred for the relatives. Burning for revenge he studies under certain magicians with the intention of becoming expert in the arts that will enable him to exterminate his enemies by gaining power over demonic forces. He succeeds in his aim, and makes a house collapse on his kinsmen who have gathered there for a celebration, but is assailed by the feeling that life is empty. He renounces magical arts wishing, through Buddhism, to find comfort and redemption in overcoming the passions, and the way to cross over from the plane of samsāric existence to the plane of Being. He becomes a disciple of Marpa (1012-97). the famous master and the translator of sacred texts brought by himself from India (cf. pl. 15). Marpa was an excellent psychologist: he does not miss the uneasy restlessness in the mind of the young man entrusting himself to him, and proceeds to break down his impetuous character. He obliges Mila-rêpa to build and demolish over and over again a nine-storied building, or rather a defence tower for his own land, and refuses to initiate him into the great mysteries until his spirit, tamed forever, grows calm in the light of wisdom. Mila-rêpa's rebirth is then complete. Having now achieved complete detachment, he returns to his mother's home but finds only her bones. Not even his sister is there, for she has become a beggar.

When I had learnt for certain that my old mother was dead and my sister begging, I grieved much and until the sun neared its setting I stopped in a secluded spot, weeping. As soon as the sun grew wholly red I went off to where once my village was. In a dream, as it seemed, grass grew high in the fields; the house once equal to a temple was in ruins. I entered and saw the books of the Holy Law scattered about, disfigured by water and covered with heaps of earth—birds and mice had made their nests and holes in them. Then, making for the inner part I came upon a pile of earth and rags over which grass had sprouted. I started rummaging and uncovered white human bones, and understood they were my mother's. On account

95. The *geshé* Jampel Senggé (the author's assistant in Rome) with ritual objects and a teacup, with stand and lid (to the left of the bell).

96. A bronze gilt lion from a Bonpo temple.

97. The Buddha in his 'earth-touching' pose, reminiscent of non-Tibetan Buddhist styles.

99

100

of the vivid memory of my mother and my unbearable grief I could no longer either think or speak, and remained for a long time in this state of unawareness. Suddenly I remembered my Master's teachings. I joined my mother's conscious principle with my mind and then with the spirit of the Masters of my school. I made a cushion of my mother's bones and with no wavering of the three planes —mental, physical and verbal—I remained in meditation of the [inner] light.

To have won the certainty that all is vain and nothing exists outside the supreme ineffable reality does not, however, at once succeed in calming his sadness, which overflows in a song where the remorseless emptiness of human hopes is stated once again:

1. According to the prophecy of Marpa the translator,
   My compassionate lord
   Of one essence with Mikyoba,
   My ancestral village, prison of demons,
   Is transformed into a Master who teaches me
   That all is ephemeral illusion.
   May this benign Master
   Grant me the grace of certitude.
2. In general all that appears,
   And all the things of the world,
   Are neither eternal nor lasting;
   In particular the cycle
   Of births and deaths is insubstantial;
   After serving that which has no substance,
   I shall go now to serve that which has substance, the Law.
3. Before, when the father was there, the son was not;
   Now that the son is, the father is not.
   The coexistence of the two is without substance.
   I, the son, shall go now to serve that which has substance, the Law,
   And shall go to meditate at Drakar-tazo.
4. When the mother was there, the son was not;
   Now that the son has arrived, the old mother is dead:
   The coexistence of the two is without substance, etc.
5. When my sister was there, her brother was not;
   Now that the brother has arrived, the sister is not there;
   The coexistence of the two is without substance, etc.
6. When, in this house, there were the books of the Law, no one rendered them due honour;
   Now that one has arrived who can render them due honour the books have been destroyed by water:
   Their coexistence is without substance, etc.
7. When the house was there, the owner was not;
   Now the owner has arrived the house is destroyed:
   Their coexistence is without substance, etc.
8. When the lands were fruitful the owner was not there;
   Now the owner has arrived, the high grass has grown:
   Their coexistence is without substance, etc.

98. The female bodhisattva Tārā (Drölma), classed in the family of Ö-pamé, hence the figure of him over her head.

99. The divine Yoginī, invoked by Tantric meditators.

100. Ritual headdress bearing Buddha-figures in five hand-poses symbolizing the five buddha-families, with a sixth above to embrace them all.

9. My village, house and paternal lands
Are an example of the non-substantiality of the things of the saṃsāric world:
They have taken from me all delight in unsubstantial creatures.
I am now a yogin and shall go to bring about my liberation.

Then Mila-rêpa begins his life's journey. A ceaseless wanderer, he halts in the loneliest places to meditate, and is stimulated by contemplating the vast spread of the landscape. The joy of ecstasy bursts into harmonious songs, which pour out the theory of Indian yoga and extol the bliss of winning enlightenment.

Like the followers of the unconventional Siddha schools in India, Mila-rêpa disliked logicians. The charges levelled by his Indian precursors were repeated again by him: 'The masters of logic split logic into four, but they are full of passion and envy. In monasteries they ensnare the novices. For a cup of tea they would sell their robes'.

Mila-rêpa's biography, with its alternation of lively narrative and mystical songs, is not always easy. Many songs referring to yoga techniques and the experiences they give rise to read obscurely to one not familiar with these doctrines. Accordingly, simplified abridgements of the biography were written, which anyone could grasp. The life of Mila-rêpa's Master, Marpa, received similar treatment. It tells of his travels in India, and also the lamentable end of his son, Darma-dodé, who was thrown by a restive horse on his way back from a party and died. Marpa thereupon performed the transference of his conscious principle into the body of a pigeon. The biography relates how the pigeon flew off towards India where Darma-dodé's conscious principle—his soul as we might say—carried out its own transference into the body of a young brahmin who had just died and was being taken to the funeral pyre, thus bringing the body back to life.

These biographies are also of considerable interest for the light they shed on Tibetan society and customs. Marpa was a yogin and we are used to thinking of yogins as strict ascetics, which is not always true. Marpa, like so many of his school, belonged to that body of initiates which required the presence of a woman (*chhagya*, Sanskrit *mudrā*) for the performance of certain rites and he availed himself of such. But he had in addition a wife, who developed a special liking for Mila-rêpa. These yogins were also very fond of money: Buddhism throve on the donations of the wealthy classes and spread with the support of merchants. Marpa was very jealous of his own wealth—he had lands and knew how to defend and increase them. He granted no one initiation unless they offered what, in the Indian fashion, was not to be looked upon as a payment—for teaching has no price—but as a gift or sign of devotion. His biography is a magnificent record of this symbiosis of spiritual and worldly interests which underlay the whole development of Lamaism.

One of the biographies which is somewhat out of the ordinary, probably through being a verbal account related to a disciple, by whom it was at once written down without too much concern for literature, is that of Urgyen-pa. He lived in the thirteenth century and, before going to China where he met Khubilai Khan, he travelled to Swat. This country, which the Tibetans call Urgyen (from the Sanskrit Uddiyāna), became for them a holy land, for two reasons—because Padmasambhava was born there and because it was regarded in India and elsewhere as the land of flying fairies, *dākinīs* and *yoginīs*, who could perform all sorts of miracles and magic. Despite the country's long conversion to Islam the tradition still survives there. But for *Vajrayāna* Buddhists like Urgyen-pa, seeing a ḍākinī—and to him all the women in Swat were

dākinīs—with one's own eyes meant coming into contact with divine beings of extra-
ordinary magical powers. His encounters with witches and sorceresses, whom he
takes in good faith for dākinīs, uplift him because he genuinely expects to derive great
spiritual benefits from them.

Reality is transformed under his credulous eyes, which turn every object or event
into a marvel. Like all travelling ascetics, whether Indian or Tibetan, he is always
full of cunning and resourcefulness. The following extracts from a description of his
travels show a mixture of possible adventures and strange events.

We went to the village of Rajahur for alms, and when it was time to eat we noticed
that all the fruit had turned into ants and worms. I showed them to my companion
Pêyé, who felt sick and was unable to take a mouthful. I closed my eyes and said
'Eat': the remaining food had turned into fruits and grapes. But he did not mind
going hungry and did not eat.

West of this village is the river Sindhu (Indus). Holding tight to each other
we went down to the ferry and entered the boat. I said to the ferryman, 'Go ahead'.
And he answered, 'Certainly I can. But when you have crossed the river the
Mongols are there, and there is the danger that they will kill you.' I answered
that I was not afraid of dying and he pushed the boat out...

Having forded the Sindhu one comes to a country called Kalapur. We reached
it at dusk and the villagers, believing that we were Mongols, greeted us with a
shower of stones. We hid amongst the trees and they dispersed, thinking that as
it was night we could not go away. But that night a great storm came and without
anyone noticing it we ran off along a bypath...

We slept before a sandalwood image of Maṅgala-devī, a divine work not made
by man. But I learnt in a dream that some danger was about to come upon us.
So I told Pêyé to make himself a staff, but he paid no attention. Next morning
we were at a meeting of three ways and he took the path leading north. I went
to collect alms along the other which turned south, and I met a woman who came
up to me, cast flowers over me, put a mark on my forehead with vermilion and
made symbolic gestures explained by the Tantras—so that my strength was
increased, and my vitality improved. But Pêyé was surrounded by a group of
armed men wanting to kill him. I ran and said he was my friend, and they let
him go. In that place all the women can perform miracles. If you ask them 'Who
are you?' they answer 'I am a fairy [yoginī]'. As I was about to lie down by the
image of Maṅgala-devī a woman said to me 'Lie with me', but I hit her with my
staff and she ran away.

In the morning a woman came and burnt incense, scattered flowers on us and
did honour to us. This was the reward for having kept the rules. In this place
there is a woman with three eyes. Another had a fleshy excrescence on her head,
like a swastika painted in red. She said she was a fairy. A Mongol who was present
told her, 'If you are really a fairy, show me something from my country'. Scarcely
had he said it, when there appeared a bow and a hat of Mongol style. They said
that this woman was the wife of King of Gyumatala... After three days we arrived
at Cikhrota where there is a big river that gushes from a rock. There a merchant
fell ill and started to fight his servants, killing two of them and wounding another.
Then I invoked the meditation of Sangwa-düpa and fixed him with a terrifying
look, and he immediately died. Had I not done so, they would all have been killed
fighting one another.

Urgyen-pa is not the only pilgrim to have left us an account of his travels. One of his imitators was Taktsang-rêpa, a contemporary of King Senggé-namgyel of Ladakh (died about 1640) and reputed founder of the monastery of Hemis in Ladakh, who also made a pilgrimage to Swat after the new foundation had been properly established.

Another Tibetan who visited India during 1236 and 1237 wrote a much more highflown narrative than Urgyen-pa's of his journey to Bodhgayā and Nālandā, places in which all trace of Buddhism however was extinct. His name was Chhörje-pel, but he is better known as the Translator of Chak, from the name of the monastery where he lived. Some of his information on places he visited or individuals he met is important but his book, too, abounds in the miraculous stories he was told, which he takes pleasure in retelling with ingenuous credulity. Now it will be the story of the block-head married off to the king's daughter by a trick, who went on to become, by the grace of the gods, the great Indian poet Kālidāsa; now that of a Buddhist master induced by the Hindus to pay homage to the statue of Śiva, which split into four parts as soon as he bent his knee before it—so that even in this travel-diary fact mingles with the fantastic in pages that are nevertheless of meagre literary value.

Perhaps the most interesting of all the books in this genre is that which Tāranātha (born in 1575) wrote about the travels of the restless Buddhagupta, one of the last of the Buddhist sādhus, who finally reached Tibet and became his master. Tāranātha diligently collected together the information he supplied, and this resulted in the first reasonably accurate account in Tibetan of the geography of the outside world. For in his wanderings Buddhagupta had toured nearly all of southern Asia; he had been to Swat, Afghanistan, Khorasan, Rangoon, had pushed on to Thailand and Indonesia and even to Zanzibar and Madagascar, which he actually calls by the name the Portuguese had given it, the Isle of St Lawrence. Buddhagupta told the astonished Tāranātha about the Catholic missionaries he had met in India, how they dressed in black and drank wine. And the two Buddhists agreed in taking them for followers of Padmasambhava.

This book is also interesting because it supplied the third Panchen Lama, Lopsang Pelden-yeshé (died 1780) with much material for a treatise on another country which attracted the attention and devotion of Tibetans—the mysterious Śambhala, where the Buddha is said to have revealed the *Wheel of Time*, a Tantra of astrological content that was especially successful in Tibet. Lopsang Pelden-yeshé, wishing to speak of Śambhala and the roads that lead to it, made it the pretext for a description of the world, for which he made use not only of Buddhagupta's travel-book, but also of other information that had reached Tibet from China, where the presence of European missionaries, from Matteo Ricci on, had introduced reasonably accurate geographical knowledge.

Mention must also be made of the various biographies of Guru-rinpoché Pema-jungnê (Padmasambhava), which relate the famous miracle-worker's previous incarnations, and his victories over the Bonpo deities through feats of magic. The tale of these marvels is interwoven with the shy narrative of the triumph of the new religion. Later, when the exorcising ceremonies for the consecration of Samyê are over, court intrigues and slanders against the master arise, accusing him of a secret affair with the queen. At this point the story moves on from miracles to a more human background, and becomes almost a novel, combining sacred and profane.

A religious epic cycle has thus grown up around this interesting and mysterious figure, consisting of two main texts: the *Kathang De-nga*, in five sections, and the *Pema Thang-yik*, of which several variants are known. Although both works are regarded

101

102

105

as *terma*, books hidden in the days of the master or his immediate disciples and then brought to light again by the 'terma revealers', there seems no doubt that the former is the older and contains some fragments that go back to ancient times. The other is relatively recent.

Although this literature is concerned with the myths relating to a figure whose historical reality is hard to determine, it forms an inexhaustible source for the study of Tibet's customs as well as her religious beliefs. It also contains numerous prophecies (*lungten*) written after the events foretold. The tone of the *Thang-yik* narrative is rather popular and plain-spoken, without the archaisms one meets in the *Kathang De-nga*, making the latter hard to understand at times. Here is a sample.

Vairocana, forced to flee on account of the queen's false accusations, says good-bye to his horse and to the disciples who have come to see him off. The scene is modelled on Śākyamuni's farewell to his groom and his horse Kahṇtaka, after giving up his kingdom.

'You must not follow me, for such is not your Master's order. To kill in one moment all the creatures in the triple world is a lesser sin than to violate one's Master's word. This is a sure cause of birth in the hells, even if a person has been spotlessly virtuous since the beginning of time, so that his equal is unheard of. Mount this horse, which is as though it were myself, and go before the Master. This black horse was the Master's messenger to the ten points of space, and when the time comes to leave its mortal body it will obtain liberation and be reborn in Tön-yö at Phen-yü to propagate the Law and win the Knowledge that saves.' (Chapter VI)

The repentant king pursues Vairocana to bring him back to his kingdom.

And king Trhisong-detsen, his mind in turmoil, his head covered, went out of his room at sunrise as though his heart had been plucked from him, intending to bring Vairocana back. He went to Yamalung in Trakmar, but did not find him there, and then he went towards Hara. The beasts of prey, game, birds and men were all looking northwards and weeping. The king-according-to-the-Law Trhisong-detsen was also afflicted and felt as though his bones were being torn from his flesh. In remorse he returned to his wife and said, 'Heed what the Master wishes and says. I give my word that when I reach him, if he so desires, I shall offer you yourself to him.' So saying he mounted Shukden and rode off in search of the Master. By Donkar he came across a black man, a smith, who was laughing and laughing. The king asked, 'You who are laughing so, what have you gained to be so happy? Have you perhaps seen a man go past here?' And the black man, the smith, replied, 'You who have suddenly come riding a white horse like quicksilver, whither are you running and who is pursuing you? What are you doing here? Very far has gone the man who went past here. I am cheerful because I have been given a bow and arrow—that is why I laugh and am happy.' The king bestirred himself and set off swiftly. As they arrived together before the river Kyichu, the Master was over the river in three strides and vanished beyond a mountain in an instant. The sun was about to set and the king had still not caught up with him. He glimpsed the Master on the far side of the water's spray, but the river was wide, there was no ferryman to get across to the other shore, darkness was falling, there was no town to go to. He got down from his horse and said

104. The golden roof of the Jokhang, the great temple of 'Jo' or Lord Buddha, which is regarded as the centre of all Tibet and is believed to have been founded in 652.

105. Conch tumpet, the shell mounted in brass.

106. Jampel Senggé (the author's assistant in Rome) in Tibetan layman's dress.

with hands joined, 'O my chaplain Vairocana, why have you forsaken me? Where are you going? I offer you my wife for your companion if you wish. Return, I pray you, O my chaplain.'

Thus he spoke, but the Master answered from the river's northern bank, 'Faithful king and lord, the works of women are like the poison *hala*, whoever eats which dies. The works of women are like the demon, whoever meets which dies. The works of women are mud: whoever walks over it gets it stuck to him. The works of women are like the prison of saṁsāra: he who is stained with them fails to gain salvation. The works of women are the evil of Māra: he who is touched by them suffers immeasurable pain. There is no seed of passion in my heart—and if there is none in my heart, how could there be in my body? The queen has schemed against our friendship; but the time will come when it will be seen that it is blameless. I can return no more to your country, O king. You must find yourself another chaplain.'

So saying he dismounted and handed the reins to his two companions. The horse neighed, overcome with grief; and from its eyes fell tears as large as eggs.

'All creatures in the universe put their hope in the Master, lamp of the teaching. I, as his substitute, now leave for China and will take charge of a hermitage pleasing to the mind. There is no place where I can go on horseback.'

Whilst tales like this are extremely popular and nearly everyone knows them, the subject-matter of others leads to their circulation amongst the followers of particular schools—as is the case with the life of Tsongkha-pa and those of other masters of the reformed sect. It is clear that by means of hagiographic literature, which was intended to appeal to the people for it satisfied their interests and answered their demands, the monastic class also plainly succeeded in keeping the masses concerned with religious questions. Even though the technique and subtlety of the teaching of theory are not to be found here, this literature takes its inspiration from religion. Laymen's lives are never, or hardly ever, recounted, simply because earthly interests seem unworthy of literary treatment. One of the few exceptions is the biography of Pholanê Têji (eighteenth century), a leading figure in the early period of Chinese political penetration in Tibet.

Then there exists an epic cycle whose central figure is an east Tibetan king, Kesar of Ling, to which the legends and story tales from all parts of Tibet as well as neighbouring countries have contributed whatever most impressed Tibetans in them.

This saga is recited by itinerant bards who often have paintings which they unroll, bearing representations of the episodes related, to add life to their tale. These paintings are designed to help them remember the succession of episodes and provide the hearers with a visual depiction of the world they describe. The bards can command a large public and even though they keep fairly closely to a traditional story-line they are not averse to improvising whenever the occasion offers. In versions that often differ considerably, this extraordinarily successful cycle has travelled throughout the country, and as far as Mongolia and Gilgit.

In all the versions one finds the same mixture of sacred and profane—bold borrowings from the legend of Guru-rinpoché; pious injunctions as in our own mediaeval narratives; heroic exploits that no human being could possibly have undertaken; opposing camps of good and evil; the wiles of the wicked and the hero's victorious simplicity; and the strange world of the popular religion, neither pure Buddhism nor Bon but a bit of both.

The same applies to the Tibetan theatre, whose religious performances may be likened to the mystery-plays of mediaeval Europe. The scripts were usually handwritten, and passed down from father to son in the actors' guilds. But now and then, thanks to the lay public's interest in them, they received the attention of monks, who polished up their language and even had them printed. The plots, with few exceptions, are taken from Buddhist or general Indian fables and stories. For example, in the drama of Sugi-nyima a parrot is the unheeded giver of good advice, who finally falls victim to his own wisdom. Although the scenes are played out in India, against an Indian background, by characters and in places with Indian names, the facts of geography and history are lost in a vagueness that leaves characters and setting devoid of concrete reality, and raises the audience to a kind of religious rapture where emotion rather than reason predominates.

The compilers of these works addressed the heart, not the mind, of simple folk who, though incapable of understanding the baffling subtleties of Buddhist doctrine, are all overwhelmingly moved by the display and the events enacted. Drama thus took its place in the spiritual teaching that Buddhism regards as its highest mission. Instead of sermons that have to follow a model logical structure and deploy their doctrines in due sequence, the Tibetan masters used deep-rooted feeling as their lever: Buddhism preaches love and charity, and here are heroic feats of both, acted out on the stage.

To relieve the tension, of course, impromptu buffoonery and allusions to unpopular persons and situations were included in the course of the show. Criticisms, often general, of those in power were slipped in, giving an outlet to the grievances of the downtrodden and the government tolerated this.

> The king's pride is like a mountain
> Which rises amidst the ocean of universal woe:
> That mountain is surrounded by greedy, covetous people;
> The gaze of the great rests upon its slopes
> But at the bottom it weighs down the heads of the small:
> And *there* is the root of evil.

Elsewhere we find descriptions of temporary epiphanies of deities, who come down among men to spread the Law. This is what happens in the miracle-play of Drowa-sangmo, who is incarnated on earth and married to a king to whom she bears two children, a boy and a girl. But soon she is opposed by the jealousy and intrigues of the king's other wife, embodiment of the forces of evil. Drowa-sangmo then returns to the celestial regions and the other wife seizes power. The king goes mad because of a magic potion administered to him. The queen and her counsellors try every means of doing away with his son and daughter, but the two butchers and two fishermen entrusted with the dirty work are moved to pity and have not the heart to carry out their orders. For a long time the two children wander through fearsome forests, always pursued by their stepmother. The boy is thrown from the top of a cliff but is miraculously saved by his mother, who takes on various shapes to protect her children. Finally he becomes king of a country bordering on his father's. His sister, convinced of his death, drifts disconsolately from place to place begging alms. She eventually reaches the country ruled by her brother, there is a recognition scene, the stepmother rushes to an exorcist to satisfy her thirst for revenge but is killed in battle by the young king, and all ends happily.

This miracle-play again moves in an unreal world. The unlucky prince and princess, its protagonists, are aged five and three, but they talk and act as only Bodhisattvas could, with an intellectual maturity and a degree of wisdom that deprives them of reality. They are abstract examples of the highest virtues of Buddhism, watched over from heaven by a mother ready with miraculous aid, transporting the spectators to a fairy-tale world. The stepmother sees all from the top of her palace—not only what goes on in the royal household, but what is happening far away, even in other countries. One moves in a dream situation that sometimes becomes outright hallucination, as when, to heighten the audience's emotion, the horrible cemeteries where the butchers take Sugi-nyima to kill her are described with morbid insistence. A peculiar blend of the frightful and the piteous, cruelty and compassion, is the outcome.

> 'Let her therefore be entrusted to three butchers and taken to the south-western limits of the land, where the terrible cemetery called "The Lake of Boiling Blood" lies. Wicked men and demons frequent it. It is full of hell-creatures who feed on human flesh, and horrible-looking ogres. By day there are whirlpools of blood and marrow, by night the burning pyres shine from all sides, and fearful cries of wolves, jackals, hyenas, savages and wild beasts are heard on every side. It is full of poisonous snakes whose breath condenses in a cloud, and of demons who snatch the soul of the living. It is strewn on every side with skeletons, corpses and rags. Let her be borne thither and banished there. And after she has been taken thither by the three butchers, let a third of the land of Ngari, which is the king's land, be given to those three'.
>
> When she was handed over to the three butchers the earth shook and split, obscuring the light of sun and moon. Newly opened lotus flowers and *udumbara* flowers stopped in their growth, and flowers and leaves and fruit, on trees in blossom and covered with fruit, withered. The lakes and rivers dried up. Birds that had chirped sweetly woefully lamented, crawling on the ground. Only wolves and jackals took notice and they began to howl at the crossroads of the city. Signs of ill-luck appeared from all quarters.

Some religious plays, slighter and of less literary substance, glorify certain famous figures in Tibet's history, and are meant more to amaze us with the protagonists' skill and intelligence than to move us. Such for example is the one devoted to king Songtsen-gampo, who is credited with the introduction of Buddhism to Tibet, though in fact the play celebrates the tricks and stratagems of the minister Gar, charged by the king with obtaining the daughters of the king of Nepal and of the emperor of China for him in marriage. Songtsen-gampo has only a secondary role, although he gives the play its name.

The unities of time and action are absent in these religious dramas. We jump from one place to another, and the connections between situations and events are hard to grasp—they are seen through a cloud, as it were, and have the vagueness of dreams. When the action takes place in Tibet, however, we breathe the homely air of everyday life.

Religious uplift perhaps reaches its pinnacle in the miracle-play devoted to the pathetic story of Trimé-künden—the Tibetan reworking of a celebrated Indian legend that extols the pious spirit of love and sacrifice of a previous incarnation of the Buddha in the hardest and most pitiful of his trials. Possessed by a boundless zeal for charity, Prince Trimé-künden is unable to refuse any request or favour, even the cruellest and most unjust. Accordingly, infatuated with mortification, he first of all gives away the precious gem on which the fortunes of his kingdom depend. Afterwards, when he is sent into exile in punishment for this improvident act of generosity, he has no hesitation in yielding his own sons and even his wife to Indra, who appears to him dressed as a brahmin. In the end, when he is at the height of his sacrifice, the spell is broken and the story ends in the glory of the Dharma.

In this instance the Tibetans had before them the models of a great Indian poet (Āryaśūra), whose work had been translated into their language some time earlier. But they did not follow the Indian text literally; they fashioned it to make it more suitable for performance and to get greater emotional effects from the dramatic situations offered.

An equally popular literary cycle is about a cuckoo's preaching of the Law to the birds—the story of Moon-blueneck. Naturally the cuckoo is a Changchup-sempa, who manifests himself in this way to spread the Buddhist teaching amongst flying creatures, since the Master's word is not reserved for men alone, but addressed to all beings.

Taking up Indian themes about the transference of the soul, this story tells how a very virtuous king aroused the jealousy of a lady in his harem by showing too much partiality for the queen. Vexed, she made up her mind to enthrone in his place the son of a minister whom she had taken a fancy to. The young man devised a stratagem to this end. One day, while walking with the king in a park through which ran a great river with a fine, deep forest on its further bank, he suggested that they should go and admire the wonders of the wood. Instead of taking a boat as the king would have liked, he picked up the bodies of two cuckoos that had just died, and urged his friend to perform transference into these little creatures. After some doubt on the king's part, from hesitation to use an art to which even yogins only resorted in very special cases, the pair of them animated the birds' bodies, crossed the river and, flying from tree to tree, enjoyed the delight of the woods. Unknown to his companion the young minister went back to the other bank, reanimated the king's body with his own consciousness, and threw his original body into the river; he sped to the palace, found an excuse to drive out the queen, and put his paramour in her place. Meanwhile the king-cuckoo, after a night of terror in the woods, with the storm raging and lightning flashing, was comforted at daybreak by the god Chenrêsik who appeared to him in cuckoo's shape and invited him to stay amongst the birds to preach the holy doctrine to them. For many years the king-cuckoo carried out his mission and then, finding his own body again, he reascended the throne. But by now the world had no more charm for him, and resigning his power he retired to the woods.

Preaching to the birds is the theme of another little book that is much read, *The precious garland of the Law among the birds*, a charming and delightful summary of Buddhist doctrine. The topic of the insubstantiality of the world is returned to again and again,

for in it, all is like a magical illusion, a dream, a rainbow, a mirage. The only hope is in the Law. Rid yourselves of all desire, for death arrives swiftly. Be not attached to anything, for soon you will be separated from all that is dear to you. Take nothing as real, for all is merely illusion.

Also very prominent is *gnomic* literature—rules of life, moral precepts, advice to statesmen, a collection of golden rules for the layman's guidance, so that within his own sphere of activity he may uphold a moral dignity that guarantees the triumph of the Law. For life goes on along two paths, seemingly divergent but closely bound up with one another—*si* and *chhö*, the rules that apply in secular life (*si*) and those belonging to religion (*chhö*). But the latter can only thrive in a soil already prepared for it by daily observance of a moral discipline without which religion's flower would fade.

So there is constant interchange between the two aspects of life, one the necessary preparation for the other. Gnomic literature helps us to this end—to behave in such a way that all our days have the fragrance of virtue, in the sense of lay virtue, the groundwork of the religious life. Such at any rate was the aim, but as we all know there is a world of difference between intentions and practice. One of the most widely circulated gnomic booklets is that written by Khaché-phalu Jowo. The very name, particularly the suffix *jowo* (an honorific form corresponding to Kashmiri *joo*) gives us a clear indication that the author is a Kashmiri (Khaché)—a Muslim, perhaps, or one steeped in Islamic doctrines (even the name of God he uses is the Arabic *Khoda*). But many Tibetans, in their esteem for the wisdom it contains, have not let these facts deter them from ascribing it to the fifth Dalai Lama who, on account of his great renown in Tibet, is commonly credited with far more books than he actually wrote. The maxims are all of a more general character than those attributed to Sakya Panchen (1182-1251), who wrote a famous treatise of moral and social rules, mainly for princes to follow. In Khaché-phalu one finds admonishments of wider application, written with poetic fervour and full of deep spirituality.

> Religion and the world are quite different things;
> Mind and body are unlike one another.
> If the mind is distressed it wants to go on,
> But if the body has eaten tasty food it wants to stay put.
> The mind's troubles are troubles that keep growing:
> If you desire the mind's happiness, the body is afflicted;
> If you think of the body it is the mind that suffers.
> If you would hearken to me, be sure to keep mind and body distinct.
> Although a girl is decked out with jewels and clothes,
> She can never become the wife of King Norsang:
> If the mind has not understood [the nature of things], even though you [apparently] follow the Law,
> In the land of darkness, upon the mirror [of the Judge of the Underworld], there will not be light.
> When the eyes of the ox that turns the mill are bandaged,
> Even though he moves all day, at evening he will still be in the same place.
> If you do not loose from your foot the noose of desire,
> Even though you say you have followed the Law, yours is [an assertion] empty of sense.
> If you tie its wings with a silken thread,
> Even an eagle cannot cleave the high heavens.
> A great king is the ornament of his country:
> If he rules by the laws, the state will be mighty;
> If the laws prevail, the things he desires will be accomplished.
> If he casts himself down before the laws, prosperity will be perfect.
> When the lake is troubled, the fish is still more so;

When the country is poor, still more so is the king.
Entrust the work to him that knows it well:
It is not fitting that a joiner be employed as a painter;
What pleases the wolf does not suit the shepherd.
Entrust command to people efficient in action;
Let not the lamb fall into the wolf's mouth.
If you would get the better of your foe at the first opportunity,
For the time being it is better to be friendly to him:
If the object can be attained by some expedient,
Only a madman resorts to arms.

Alongside this fairly easily comprehensible literature flourishes that reserved for the monks, with its foundations of theory based on texts translated from Indian originals, which are to be found in the great collections already mentioned, the *Kangyur* and *Tengyur*. Naturally the veneration in which this tradition was held prevented the Tibetans from going outside the path it taught—Tibetan literature is largely one of clarification and glosses. The greater Tibetan masters made an impressive contribution along two main lines: dogmatics proper, and liturgy. Their methodology, however, modelled on the teaching of the famous Buddhist universities of India, consists of classifications, and subtle and profound discussions without much originality. The figures of the first Sakya-pa abbots, of Pu-tön, Tsongkha-pa, the Panchens of Trashi-lhünpo, and the Dalai Lamas stand out in this enormous literature—thousands of volumes in which the same arguments recur, with the same care to keep the schools' teachings and practice within the bounds of orthodoxy, to unravel the abstruse doctrine, and to put forward more effective liturgical methods. The merit of this rather unvaried literature, the subject matter of which makes it unalluring, lies in facilitating a better understanding of *Mahāyāna* Buddhism as it was interpreted in India.

This is not the place to take up so vast a topic. Suffice it to mention, by way of example, Tsongkha-pa's two greatest works, the *Lam-rim* and the *Ngag-rim*, which were completed in 1403 and comprise a summa of Lamaism as interpreted by that great master. The first is an account of the gradual journey to salvation, following the system of a well-known Indian work (the *Abhisamayālaṅkāra*), and the second expounds the esoteric teachings, i.e. the path of gnosis as understood and defined by the new school. Both are works of unusual profundity, in which the author summarizes, respectively, Buddhist dogma and Tantric liturgy—the path of reason and the mystic path, working together to the same end—as clearly as the intrinsic difficulty of the subject allows.

In this the Geluk-pas repeated the example of Gampo-pa (1079-1153)—a pupil of Mila-rêpa—who had written a Lam-rim of his own, an epitome of the holy scriptures, which it quotes copiously, to give Tibetans access to essential *Mahāyāna* doctrine. But in Tsongkha-pa there is something more, a thoroughgoing analysis and systematization which supplied the school he founded with its individuality and the basis of its teaching.

Unlike the Indians, the Tibetans had a special fondness for history. Like the Chinese, they began quite early to write chronicles, month-by-month and year-by-year records of the chief occurrences, compiled by court officials. There were lists of kings and ministers. Later came the so-called *chhönjung*—histories of the Law—telling how the Dharma was preached and afterwards propagated, both in India and Tibet.

Human events play a subordinate part in these books, in that the course of history is regarded merely as a preordained or foreseen succession of events, with whose aid we may follow the establishment of the Law, or note its setbacks and revivals. This considerable historical literature combines the narration of events and edifying discourse: general histories like those of Pawo-tsuglak (born 1566), Putön (1290-1364), and Tāranātha (born 1575), or the *Gyêrap-selwê-melong* (fourteenth century); histories that stress the fortunes of the sect their writer belongs to, like that of Pema-karpo (born 1527); historical synopses like that of Sumpa-khenpo (1704-88), and others all written by indefatigable scholars. Of these, Pawo-tsuglak deserves special consideration, for he diligently assembles the greatest number of sources and confines himself to recording facts and events without bending them to ideological patterns. Naturally each author shows a preference for the events and masters of his own school and its outlook. Tāranātha's interest is mainly in the Tantric trends. Putön keeps to the limits he has set out to follow and establish, namely what schools and masters had authoritatively continued the ancient teachings and how they were linked up with these. The *Depther ngönpo* ('Blue Annals') of Shönnu-pel (1392-1481) chronicle the transmission of the teaching from master to disciple in the various schools. The fifth Dalai Lama, with whom we are already familiar, merits a special place here. His history implicitly propounds a justification of his policies, taking these as the realization of Tibet's process of unification which began with the kings, broke up on the collapse of the dynasty, was tried again temporarily by the Sakya-pas and Phagmotru-pas, and was carried to completion by himself. This work further deserves mention for the courtly language in which it is written, in common with most of his other works, and its professed adherence to Indian models and the rules of rhetoric.

Changchub-gyentsen enlarged the palace of Neudong, so that it seemed like Indra's palace, called Vijayantī, come down to earth. Shortly thereafter a conflict broke out with the lord of Yasang. He belonged, as regards religion, to the spiritual descent of Phag-tru; as far as political relations were concerned he should have been subject to the Phagmotru-pas, who were of those who belonged to [the Mongol emperor] Hulagu. Yet driven on by the force of his misdeeds he came to grief, as was said of another:

Being of great intelligence he followed the mistaken path
And embraced the mad practices of Wangchuk,
Supreme teacher of the heretics.

Accordingly several times he attacked Phag-tru with his troops, and since the prince of Tshê was behind him and the *Pönchens* were not loyal, the lord of Yasang repeatedly came off best. Then the *Pönchen* Wangchuk-pa called both Yasang and Phag-tru before him to be judged, and although Phag-tru was in the right, through intriguing of the *Pönchen* Kündor the case was won by Yasang. Shortly thereafter the *Pönchen* Wangtsön invited Situ Changchup-gyentsen to a feast in Duglumpa and resorted to all kinds of deceits and tricks to make him hand over the tiger-headed diploma [which the Mongol emperor had given him as a sign of investiture], and for thirteen days shut him up in prison at Gungthang. Further events, however-proved the point that:

The wise man, even though he is tricked,
Does not lose his way, and knows what should be done;
The ant of the steppes, though he has no eyes,
Is faster than the others that have.

The character of these historical works, too, takes them out of the sphere of monastic literature. They are kept in private libraries and are read by the laity, and may be said to form one aspect of their education and culture.

But how was this enormous literature, on matters sacred and profane, published? Where was it printed? In the monasteries. Every foundation of any importance had its own press. This consisted of rooms of varying size, according to the quantity of books printed there, in which were kept the wooden printing-blocks—sometimes, in Kham, they were made of copper—on which the separate pages were carved (in reverse, of course). In some cases, as in the great printing-house at Narthang from which we get one of the best-known editions of the *Kangyur* and *Tengyur*, hundreds of thousands of such blocks were piled up on the shelves. Smaller establishments elsewhere printed the works of the more famous monks who had lived in them, or lives of saints particularly honoured by the sect to which the monastery belonged, or liturgical manuals. And almost everywhere there were the *karchak* or *nêyik*, 'guides' for the use of pilgrims, containing the history and praises of the monastery, or of the sacred places of the region. These little works are also to be classed among the Tibetans' favourite reading matter: every pilgrim or traveller obtained a copy for himself when visiting a monastery, and took it away with him to deposit in his own shrine and re-read for his edification—for these guides, too, are always centred round miracles.

Anyone who wanted a copy of a work ordered it from the monastery where the blocks were stored. Paper could be supplied direct by the monastery or by the person who commissioned the printing. The monks in the printing-shop ran an ink-moistened roller over the blocks, and the pages of the work came off one after another, clear and legible or otherwise according to the degree of wear of the blocks and the quality of the paper. Then the pages were put together again in the order of the numbers on their left-hand margin, pressed well, and trimmed all round. The resulting volumes often had red or yellow colouring applied to their edges according to the school they came from.

Even laymen, of course, deposited sacred texts by the images in their private shrines —as many of them as they desired, the limit being set only by their financial resources. The texts they did not read or understand could be used by lamas invited to perform any prayers and rites the patron wished; in any case, as verbal embodiments of the Buddha, they would imbue the place with sanctity and ensure the protection of its inhabitants by simply being there. This fact explains the great devotion Tibetans have to books, whether they can read or not: the book is a divine presence, and so must be treated with the utmost respect. There is a whole set of rules on how it should be opened and shut. No book should be allowed to touch the ground, but must rest upon one's knees or the table at which one sits. To touch it with the feet or step over it is a grievous sin. When one makes a gift of a book, the recipient must take it with outstretched hands and rest it reverently on his head to receive its blessing. Books are oblong in shape, on the pattern of Indian palm-leaf manuscripts. They are held together by silk tapes or leather straps with metal buckles, and are often kept between wooden boards which have figures of deities or decorative motifs carved on them in the case of works of great value or spiritual significance.

The book trade, though humble, also existed. The retailers of books thronged to the scene of fairs and festivals. Squatting on the ground they laid out their books before them on pieces of material and offered them to the public. They had had them printed in monasteries on their own account, and sold them on these special occasions for a modest profit. Naturally they only stocked up with works of interest to the laity—lives of the saints, accounts of visions of the other world, guides to holy places—but sometimes I have also seen more exacting works, as difficult as Tsongkha-pa's *Lamrim-chhenmo*. Be that as it may, the booksellers were very much to the fore at the time of village festivals, perhaps because their presence symbolically confirmed the Law's unending watch over every occupation. Anonymous folk-songs urge us not to lose the opportunity of showing homage to the Doctrine, when it comes, and not to let the strolling book-sellers go away disappointed.

> When dawn rises in the eastern quarter
> In the sluggishness of awakening,
> Tomorrow, the sellers of books of the Holy Doctrine will come out.
> Each of you should buy a book of the Doctrine.
> If each of you does not buy a book of the Doctrine,
> Tomorrow the sellers of books of the Holy Doctrine will go back.
> When the sellers of books of the Holy Doctrine have gone back,
> What reason will the mind have to repent?
> How can your spirit waver?

Fig 9 Hinged gilt collar with Langshe inscription *c.* 19th century

Administration

IN SUCH A WILD and mountainous land where in many areas stockraising was still the main source of livelihood, it may come as a surprise that the state organization was based on landed property. However, as we have already said, ownership of land determined the part that members of the public were expected to play in government, and controlled social obligations. Land ownership was of three kinds: state (*shung*), noble (*ger*), and monastic (*chhö*).

It was the duty of every nobleman owning land to put his sons into public service. The state, on its side, hardly ever paid its servants a salary, but granted them land concessions, some of the income from which became due to the state in return. The basic principle of Tibetan political organization was the obligation to serve the government. A list of the noble families, all of whom were liable to perform such duties, was therefore published annually by the Council of Ministers (*Kashag*).

This aristocracy which, together with the monks, ruled Tibet, varies in its origins. Some of its families boast ancient lineage and claim to go back to the time of the kings, while others came to the fore during the troubles that plagued Tibet for many centuries, from the fall of the dynasty onwards. More recently, since the institution of the Dalai Lamas, this ancient nobility has been extended by the inclusion of families in which Dalai Lamas have been incarnated.

The labourer was in complete subordination to the landowner, to such an extent that the latter had judicial powers over his peasants, within certain limits laid down by the law. This situation could lead to conflict between the two sides, in which case the prefect (district governor) or *dzongpön* might intervene, but his decision could be contested by either of the parties involved, who then had the right to appeal to a higher authority.

The position with regard to monasteries was similar, but neither lay landowners nor the monasteries themselves were exempt from the legislative measures of the state, generally taken for serious, usually political, reasons. In fact, it was known for property to be confiscated from both groups.

With the institution of the Dalai Lamas finally established and the 'yellow-hats' assured of overriding control of the country, the state organization of Tibet came to centre on the figure of the Dalai Lama himself, in whom spiritual authority and political power were combined. One should not, however, assume that the advent of the Dalai Lamas represented a revolution in the country's social and administrative organization. The old patterns persisted, especially as far as the state structure was concerned, though of course in the context of a new situation, brought about by the pre-eminence of monastic over feudal power. The theory of repeated incarnations of the same person presented a working compromise between hereditary succession and overt choice, entirely to the advantage of the ruling monastic class and the continuance of its sway. The Dalai Lama—the one now in exile in India is the fourteenth incarnation—is regarded as the earthly presence of Chenrêsik, patron of Tibet and embodiment of compassion, who has personally chosen him to carry out his mission of salvation: thus upholding the ancient tradition that affirms his periodical descent to the Land of Snows for the specific purpose of watching over the spiritual destinies of its inhabitants. As a *changchup-sempa* or bodhisattva, and one of those most highly worshipped in *Mahāyāna* Buddhism, he renounces the opportunity of vanishing into indefinable nirvāna; so that by taking human form and undergoing birth, death, all the vicissitudes mankind is subject to, he may illumine with words and example the creatures he protects, and thus swiftly lead them to that state of spiritual perfection which assures them paradise or liberation, within the bounds of their ability, keenness and karma.

After the Dalai Lama's death—which, for reasons given above, is justified as an accommodation to the human lot, since men are susceptible only to a teacher who divests himself of any transcendent character and goes through the same life as themselves—he returns to his paradise to decide in what place, family and condition he should be reborn. Here, in other words, we have a fresh repetition of the event in the story of the Buddha when, before being incarnated as the son of Śuddhodana in Kapilavastu, he cast his gaze over the world eight times to determine where he should descend. It reproduces a pattern to which faith and scriptural authority give the status of dogma. The difficulties of identifying the new incarnation are resolved according to detailed rules of investigation. First of all, on the strength of answers given by the Nêchung oracle (the state oracle resorted to on the most serious occasions in the life of the nation) the chief religious authorities ascertain the region in which the new return to earth has taken place. Then in the train of rainbows, dreams, and similar indications and portents, both earthly and celestial, the divine child is discovered. He is recognized by various signs which must distinguish every changchup-sempa. As soon as these signs have been verified by a commission of high religious dignitaries whose task it is to confirm the choice, the decisive moment is reached: the child who unquestionably possesses the qualifications required is recognized as the Dalai Lama's incarnation. He is taken to Lhasa, where he must still undergo a final test to confirm the validity of his selection beyond all dispute: he must be able to pick out from a number of similar objects, both ritual and personal, those he made use of in the previous incarnation. His subsequent education will be conducted under the guidance of the Trhi-rinpoché of Ganden and other monks universally recognized as great teachers of the holy scriptures.

This system has on the whole borne good results. The choice has usually fallen on influential families, except for two cases in which the families were poor but highly respected. If the incarnation were to appear in an unworthy family, this would run counter to the supposition that worldly fortune and well-being result from the performance of good works. But of course in theory anything may happen, since the ways of compassion are numberless. Nor should one forget that a selection sanctioned by leading ecclesiastics as outlined above, is not so easy as it might appear. Since the Dalai Lama has political as well as religious authority various other considerations of expediency or advantage are naturally involved when the choice is made; although these are kept hidden from the people. One must agree, however, that the choice has always been fortunate, with the exception of the sixth Dalai Lama, who does not appear to have been particularly given to the contemplative life. In that very difficult period which followed the death of the fifth Dalai Lama (cf. pl. 5), with its resulting disorders which, as we have said, gradually led to Tibet's subjugation to China, his successor showed inclinations that were neither political nor mystical. Similar examples are not unknown in the case of the many *trülku* or incarnations to be found in Tibetan monasteries. I myself, in the course of my travels, have come across examples of mistaken incarnations. Nevertheless, one can on the whole state that the system has functioned extremely well, which is evidence of the caution and circumspection with which the choice is made, and still more of the course of instruction the trülku in general and the Dalai Lamas in particular have to undergo. This is a relentless system which prepares the candidates for the great responsibility that is to be theirs, obliges them to forgo the joys of boyhood, keeps them under the continual surveillance of elderly tutors who instil in them wisdom and experience.

Until the Dalai Lama reaches the prescribed age for governing on his own, power is in the hands of a regent, who in recent times has been a lama. He is elected by the national assembly. Between the Dalai Lama and the Council there may be a prime minister, who in fact represents a kind of liaison officer between the two.

When the Dalai Lama is enthroned at the age of eighteen, the regent's task is finished and the Dalai Lama assumes sole responsibility for public affairs. This does not mean that he has absolute power. His authority is restricted and watched over in a number of ways. Not all questions to be decided come before him, or they do not reach him in their true form. In other words the Dalai Lama's power, though theoretically absolute, is restricted chiefly by the high authorities that surround him —the monks in particular—and only outstanding individuals such as the fifth and thirteenth Dalai Lamas have succeeded in assuming full control of public affairs.

The two main bodies which assisted the Dalai Lama in the exercise of his functions were the council of ministers and the assembly. The Council of Ministers was composed of four members, three of them laymen and one a monk, who was considered *primus inter pares*. These were the four pillars (*kapshi*) on which the government structure rested. They were nominated by the Dalai Lama. The authority of the Council of Ministers extended to administration, justice and political decisions. In fact, the use of the term 'ministers' is inexact, since although each one of them might devote his attention to a particular field (as happened, for example, in the case of Surkhang Shapé who dealt with foreign affairs, though this was an office only instituted in 1940), decisions and responsibilities were collective. The Council of Ministers appointed the various ecclesiastical officials (on the recommendation of the Office for Religious Affairs) as well as civil servants, or presented them to the Dalai Lama by proclamation. It also received the various petitions, which could be presented by anyone, against decisions taken by the provincial governors, or relating to disputes between great families. In cases of greater importance, or when the Council's decisions failed to satisfy the interested parties, the latter could make a further appeal to the Dalai Lama himself, who was the supreme judge. Naturally the latter's decision would be dependent on the manner in which the case has been presented to him.

The other body that exercised major responsibility, though only intermittently and in special cases, was the Grand Assembly (*gyadzom*), to which belonged religious dignitaries, civil servants, members of the aristocracy and even representatives of the merchants and artisans. The Assembly reached its decisions by majority vote: those who disagreed with a proposal remained seated. Although primarily a consultative body with no power over the executive, it was nevertheless invested with the most binding authority: its decisions were final. Clearly this was not an arrangement borrowed or imitated from similar systems in the West, but a survival from or adaptation of those national assemblies of which ancient sources give evidence and which find a parallel in the *khuriltai* of the Mongols and the *jirga* of the Pashtu tribes. One of the most important assemblies of this type was convened when Genghis Khan menaced Tibet. The assembly satisfactorily met the needs of a country which, despite the political unity it had achieved, still contained a considerable diversity of interests: ranging from the comparatively independent rule certain families were able to maintain over the inhabitants of their own territory to the existence in East Tibet of actual principalities, such as Dergé, and to the relative autonomy of the large monasteries. Members of the Council did not as a rule attend sessions of the Assembly, but these were presided over by the *tsipöns* or the *trungyiks*.

The executive was represented by the *tsikhang*, consisting of four members called *tsipön*, with the function of controlling and inspecting the public administration, excluding religious affairs, of course. Their main task was to manage the country's resources and to check and apportion the revenue from taxes, duties and other sources, for which they kept the records, though the actual collection of taxes was not within their province but fell to local and provincial officials. The tsipöns also saw to the recruitment of laymen for official service.

Running parallel to this secular branch was the monastic administration headed by the *chikhyap chenpo*, to whom the religious officials were subordinate. He had the power to decide controversial cases that had been put up to him directly, save in exceptional circumstances when they had to be submitted to the Dalai Lama. His functions were many and varied, and through being in daily contact with the Dalai Lama his authority was of course considerable, though he ranked after the members of the council. His principal colleague was the *drönyer chenpo*, who could be described as chief of protocol.

Immediately below him came the *yik-tshang*, a Council of four monks who were known as *trungyik-chenpo*. These were not only charged with promulgating and carrying out the Dalai Lama's orders, but also with the appointment and transfer of monk civil servants, such as the religious counterparts of the civil governors in each district, and with hearing the petitions and appeals of monks and monasteries. They also supervised the administration of the monasteries, but there were four Treasurers below them, corresponding to the tsipön of the lay administration. Three ecclesiastics and one layman, they administered the Palace (*labrang*) treasure made up of all state revenue in goods, from butter to grain, from cloth to jewels. This office was also authorized to make loans, interest on which amounted to about 15 per cent. Another department, called the *tsechang*, supervised the profits derived from trade (for example, that with India and Nepal through the western provinces), precious metals (especially gold from Ngari in West Tibet) and gifts offered to the Dalai Lama. But it also provided for the needs of the Dalai Lama himself and paid the expenses incurred by the Palace for purposes of representation and protocol.

Besides these two offices there was a third which had to look after what could be regarded as the nation's reserve fund—real treasure accumulated over the centuries, untouchable but kept ready in case of need.

As one can see, the administration of the state followed two separate but often converging lines: civil officials (*trungkhor*) and monk officials (*tsetrung*), who frequently assisted one another. For the latter reason one cannot speak in terms of dual power and indeed the lay and ecclesiastical officials all came from the same social class.

How were such officials recruited? There was a school in Lhasa to take care of this, of which there were naturally two branches: one reserved for those seeking a career as monk officials, which was supervised by one of the *trungyik-chenmo* or members of the ecclesiastical office, and the other run by a member of the tsikhang.

In order to be admitted to either school the prospective candidate had to make an application and possess various qualifications including physical ones: no boy who had any deformity was accepted. The youths had to belong to the nobility, and those who aspired to an ecclesiastical career were admitted for preference, though not exclusively, from monasteries. The schools were separate and had different names. The age of admission varied between fourteen and twenty years for both of them, and the course of study normally lasted three or four years, depending on the ability of the pupil, who had to take several examinations every year and was carefully watched over and supervised. The number of places available was generally limited. Once they had passed their examinations and were considered capable of holding office, the appointments of the successful students were officially proclaimed during the New Year festival.

In the course of the centuries Tibet has been subject to many changes, but since the days of Mongol supremacy it has been divided into three great regions, Kham, Domè, and Ü-Tsang, together with the far western province of Ngari. The whole territory was subdivided into about a hundred prefectural districts (dzong), of which the most important at least were administered by two officials, one a layman and the other a monk. The authority of these dzongpön was very wide, inasmuch as they were responsible for the collection of taxes, the administration of justice and overall superintendance of their subjects.

But human nature is the same everywhere: the further the district governors were from the centre, and the less subject to its control, the more they were inclined to abuse their power. Since all officials, whether they followed a civil or an ecclesiastical career, belonged to the nobility, they were always able to set the influence of friends at Lhasa in motion if any complaint was made against them. Despite the fact that the central government had often issued orders prohibiting any abuse and threatening severe disciplinary measures in the case of infringement, habits did not change in practice. The local governor, especially in those provinces on the borders of the country and therefore close to commercial centres and trade routes, could be certain of securing financial advantages. The collection of taxes and duties was often carried out less honestly than it should have been, and laws not applied impartially. To this should be added the fact that a person appointed to the office of dzongpön was only in theory obliged to reside in the place where he was to carry out his duties. More often he remained in Lhasa where it was easy to pull strings and attend to other more lucrative affairs; or he simply stayed on his estate and sent his wife to perform his duties, or entrusted his functions to his steward.

In the administration of justice the local governor was bound to follow the penal code first drawn up by Songtsen-gampo, later revised on several occasions and produced in its final version in the first half of the nineteenth century. The maximum penalty he was allowed to inflict, after judgment had been passed, was a flogging, to be carried out in accordance with certain definite regulations, and the application of the cangue or of chains for a limited number of years. But even in these cases abuses were not uncommon.

In spite of the respect for human life which Buddhism teaches, the penal laws of Tibet were extremely severe, and retained some of the original harshness which religion had not entirely succeeded in softening; this may in any case be due to an unavoidable need to check anarchy and wrongdoing by the fear of punishment. One of Tibet's worst evils was brigandage. Armed bands roamed from one part of the country to another, stealing cattle, and attacking travellers and pilgrims. When one of their members fell into the hands of the law he remained for a considerable time shut up in a vile prison where no one could communicate with him. If he was brought out alive his neck was put in a cangue and his feet in chains. His life went on in this way—depending on the charity of others, and obliged to remain in the district where he had been tried, since this made it easier to keep an eye on him—for the number of years laid down by the judges. Then he was exiled to some border region, among the Mön tribes of the south, where the difference of climate made his existence even more precarious. In cases of proven theft, flogging was the usual penalty, followed by a term of imprisonment whose length varied according to the seriousness of the crime. It was not infrequent for a habitual criminal to have his foot or his right hand amputated, although such mutilations had been prohibited by the thirteenth Dalai Lama. It was easier, however, to atone for theft by paying ransom and restoring the sum or goods stolen, after agreement had been reached between the injured party's family and that of the accused. The same applied in the case of murder. Here again the course of justice could be halted if the murderer's family paid adequate compensation to the victim's. But in such cases a considerable role was played by the connections or influence of either party. In certain provinces like Kham, moreover, the penal code carried less weight since, on account of the unruly character of the people and their tradition of fighting, cases were usually dealt with by the village heads. This did not succeed in ending the vendettas that inevitably developed after the first act of violence, and which were inherited from generation to generation.

For political crimes the penalties were even more severe. The guilty vanished into the state prisons, fearsome underground pits from which few could hope to come out alive. They were often blinded. According to custom, even in the case of monks guilty of serious crimes the punishments were most severe. On several occasions I was told of the exemplary punishments inflicted on temple guardians who had sold sacred objects for personal profit. Pepper was pushed under their eyelids, or spikes were driven under their fingernails.

The army existed more in theory than in fact. It consisted of a few regular regiments (four), which appear never to have exceeded some ten thousand men in all, whose main task it was to parade at the Tibetan New Year festival.

These troops were only nominally regular, since once their occasional duties had been carried out they were free to return to their own occupations. Alongside them there existed an irregular army or militia (*yümak*) supplied by the landowners, who were obliged to send a certain number of fit men under arms, according to the size of their estates.

The nobility had to supply not only the men but their clothes, and to guarantee the family of the departing soldier sufficient cultivable land for its support.

This military service was not particularly arduous, since the men were called up two or three times a year, and for only a few days at a time. The training they received was very variable, as was their equipment. They had no uniforms, save in the case of the troops assigned to protect the Dalai Lama (the *kusung*). Even the monasteries provided troops, and soldier monks were not uncommon. Some of them, like the monks of Sera, had the reputation of being especially fierce fighters. A law passed in the time of the thirteenth Dalai Lama envisaged a general levy of all fit men between the ages of eighteen and sixty, but this was never resorted to. A few military detachments were stationed, however, in provinces considered the hardest to govern and those near to the frontiers: at Shigatsé, Gyantsé, Tingri and Nyarong. There were two officials known as *phokpön* at the head of the military administration, one an ecclesiastic and the other a layman. They held the titles of *Dzasa* and *Thêji*, and hence ranked above the *tsipön* in the hierarchy. The regimental commanders were called *makpön*.

The organization was rudimentary, as can be seen, and neither demanded nor offered effective training. Like so many things in Tibet, it reflected ancient customs and traditions that no longer applied in the modern world.

This assessment of Tibet's military organization, which may not sound very flattering and is of course based on our own conception of what an army should be, is not intended as any slight upon the fighting qualities of the Tibetans. The lack of true political unity was evinced in the survival of special relationships between the great families and their subjects, with the consequent tendency to regionalism, and in the continued opposition between supporters of the 'yellow' and the 'red' monasteries, after so many historical upheavals had riven the country with internecine strife. All these are factors that helped to break up the sense of national oneness which had made Tibetan military power and organization something for the Chinese themselves to dread in the time of the Dynasty.

A spirit of partisanship gradually came into being, which prevented any concerting of counsels even when China and Nepal invaded the country. To this must be added the Tibetan's natural individualism: accustomed as he is by feudal and monastic tradition to show great regard for outward form and notable courtliness in his manners, he has nevertheless not forgotten his instinctive spirit of independence, a legacy of his primeval nomadism that centuries of sedentary life have by no means done away with. His powers of organization, in fact, have never been able to exercise a clear and dominant role, or taken definite shape. However ceremonious and respectful of authority, the individual has never given up his freedom. From this, too, stems the openness of the Tibetan, who seldom hides his feelings.

When situations arise that excite his resentment, however, the Tibetan is quick to react decisively. He will not fight in highly organized bodies, for this is a form of discipline with no appeal for him: but fight he will, to the death, with a devotion and obstinacy which he will not give up till the uselessness of his effort is obvious. This explains the fanaticism the monks themselves have given proof of, time and again —the monks of Sera for instance—and the determination and courage with which a few of the faithful succeeded in bringing the thirteenth and fourteenth Dalai Lamas to safety when they were being harried by the Chinese. Indeed, the fighting spirit, the capacity for self-sacrifice and the contempt of danger which led the Tibetans to wage war against the Chinese Empire, often victoriously, may not be entirely dead. On several occasions there have been signs that this spirit is ready to rise again, even though it then made itself felt in a disorganized form. Despite the Buddhist religion, the Tibetan has remained a fine fighter at heart, much as the Bushido spirit, in Japan, was nurtured and refined by Zen Buddhism.

Even recent events have shown that the Tibetans, lacking as they are in suitable equipment, and ignorant of the techniques of modern warfare, can nevertheless sustain a dogged and effective guerilla campaign, sufficient to hinder and delay Chinese penetration and actually endanger their occupation of certain provinces.

Short bibliography

BACOT, J., *Trois mystères tibétains*, Paris, 1921 (translated into English by H.I. Woolf: *Three Tibetan Mysteries*, London, 1924).
— *La vie de Marpa le ' traducteur '*, Paris, 1937.
BELL, Sir Charles, *Tibet: Past and Present*, Oxford, 1924.
— *The People of Tibet*, Oxford, 1928.
— *The Religion of Tibet*, Oxford, 1931.
BLEICHSTEINER, R., *Die Gelbe Kirche*, Wien, 1937 (also in French: *L'Eglise Jaune*, Paris, 1937).
CARRASCO, P., *Land and Polity in Tibet*, Seattle, 1959.
CHAPMAN, F. S., *Lhasa, the Holy City*, London, 1938.
COMBE, G. A., *A Tibetan on Tibet*, London, 1926.
DAS, S. C., *Journey to Lhasa and Central Tibet*, edited by W. W. Rockhill, London, 1902.
DAVID-NEEL, L.A.E.M., *Mystiques et magiciens du Thibet*, Paris, 1929 (translated into English: *With Mystics and Magicians in Tibet*, London, 1931).
— *Initiations lamaïques, des théories, des pratiques, des hommes*, Paris, 1930 (translated into English by F. Rothwell: *Initiations and Initiates in Tibet*, London, 1931).
— *La vie surhumaine de Guésar de Ling*, Paris, 1931 (translated into English: *The Superhuman Life of Gesar of Ling*, London, 1933).
— *Textes tibétains inédits*, Paris, 1952.
DUNCAN, M. H., *Harvest Festival Dramas of Tibet*, Hong Kong, 1955.
— *Customs and Superstitions of Tibetans*, London, 1964.
EBERHARD, W., *Kultur und Siedlung der Randvölker Chinas*, Leiden, 1942.
EKVALL, R. B., *Tibetan Skylines*, London, 1952.
— *Religious Observances in Tibet; Patterns and Function*, Chicago, 1964.
EVANS-WENTZ, W. Y., *Tibet's Great Yogi Milarepa*, London, 1951.
— *The Tibetan Book of the Great Liberation*, London, 1954.
— *The Tibetan Book of the Dead*, London, 1957.
FILCHNER, W., *Kumbum Dschamba Ling*, Leipzig, 1933.
GETTY, A., *The Gods of Northern Buddhism*, Oxford, 1928.
GORDON, A.K., *The Iconography of Tibetan Lamaism*, 2nd Ed., Ruthland, Tokyo, 1959.
GUENTHER, H. V., *Gam-po-pa, the Jewel Ornament of Liberation*, London, 1959.
— *The Life and Teaching of Nāropa*, Oxford, 1963.
HERMANNS, M., *Die Nomaden von Tibet*, Wien, 1949.
— *Mythen und Mysterien der Tibeter*, Köln, 1956.
HOFFMAN, H., *Quellen zur Geschichte der tibetischen Bon-Religion*, Wiesbaden, 1950.
— *The Religions of Tibet*, London, 1961.

KAWAGUCHI, E., *Three Years in Tibet*, Madras, 1909.
LALOU, M., *Les religions du Tibet*, Paris, 1957.
MACDONALD, D., *The Land of the Lama*, London, 1929.
NEBESKY-WOJKOWITZ, R., *Oracles and Demons of Tibet*, The Hague, 1956.
OBERMILLER, E., *History of Buddhism;* translated from the Tibetan text of Pu-ston, Heidelberg, 1931.
PELLIOT, P., *Histoire ancienne du Tibet*, Paris, 1961.
PETECH, L., *A Study on the Chronicles of Ladakh*, Calcutta, 1939.
— *I missionari italiani nel Tibet e nel Nepal*, Rome, 1956.
RIBBACH, B. H., *Drogpa Namgyal. Ein Tibeterleben*, München, 1940.
RICHARDSON, H. E., *Tibet and its History*, London, 1962.
ROCK, J. F., *The Na-khi Nāga Cult and related Ceremonies*, Rome, 1952.
— *The Amnye Ma-Chhen Range and Adjacent Regions*, Rome, 1956.
ROCKHILL, W. W., *Land of the Lama*, New York, 1891.
— ' Notes on the Ethnology of Tibet ', *Smithsonian Institution*, Washington, No. 2/1895, pp. 665-747.
ROERICH, G. (RERIKH), *Sur les Pistes de l'Asie Centrale*, Paris, 1933.
— *The Blue Annals*, Calcutta, vol. 1 1949, vol. 2 1963.
SCHMID, T., *The Cotton-clad Mila: The Tibetan Poet-Saint's Life in Picture*, Stockholm, 1952.
— *The Eighty-five Siddhas*, Stockholm, 1958.
SCHULEMANN, G., *Die Geschichte der Dalailamas*, 2nd Ed., Leipzig, 1958.
SHEN, Ts. L. and LIU Sh. C., *Tibet and the Tibetans*, Stanford, 1953.
SNELLGROVE, D., *Buddhist Himālaya*, Oxford, 1957.
STEIN, R. A. ' L'habitat, le monde et le corps humain en Extrême-Orient et en Haute-Asie ', *Journal Asiatique*, Tome CCXLVI/1, 1957, pp. 37-74.
— *Recherches sur l'épopée et le barde du Tibet*, Paris, 1959.
— *Les tribus anciennes des marches sino-tibétaines*, Paris, 1959.
TOUSSAINT, G. C., *Le dict de Padma*, Paris, 1933.
TUCCI, G., *Indo-Tibetica*, Rome, 1932-41.
— *Tibetan Painted Scrolls*, Rome, 1949.
— *The Tombs of the Tibetan Kings*, Rome, 1950.
— *To Lhasa and Beyond*, translated by Mario Carelli, Rome, 1956.
— *The Theory and Practice of the Mandala*, translated by Alan Houghton Brodrick, London, 1961.
— *Tibetan Folk-Songs*, Ascona, 1966.
WADDELL, L. A., *The Buddhism of Tibet, or Lamaism*, London, 1895.

Index of Tibetan Terms

Kangyur	*bka' 'gyur*
kapshi	*ka bži*
karchak	*dkar čhag*
karchu	*skar čhu*
kashak	*bka' śag*
Kathang De-nga	*bka' thaṅ sde lṅa*
Kelsang-gyatso	*skal bzaṅ rgya mcho*
Kham	*khams*
khata	*kha btags*
khenpo	*mkan po*
Khê-trup	*mkhas grub*
khyim	*khyim*
Kongjo	*koṅ jo*
Künga-sangpo	*kun dga' bzaṅ po*
kusung	*kus sruṅ*
kyang	*rkyaṅ*
kyangchhak	*brkyaṅ phyag*
labrang	*bla braṅ*
lama	*bla ma*
Lam-rim	*lam rim*
Langdarma	*glaṅ dar ma*
lha-chham	*lha čham*
lha khang	*lha khaṅ*
lhakpa	*lhag pa*
lharampa	*lha čham*
lha Thothori	*lha tho tho ri*
Lopsang-Chhökyi-gyentsen	*blo bzaṅ čhos kyi rgyal mchan*
Lopsang-gyatso	*blo bzaṅ rhya mcho*
Lopsang Pelden-yeshé	*blo bzaṅ dpal ldan ye śes*
Lopsang Tenpa	*blo bzaṅ bstan pa*
losang	*lo bsaṅs*
lotsawa	*loccha ba (locā ba)*
lu	*klu*
lungta	*rluṅ rta*
lungten	*luṅ bstan*
Makpön	*dmag dpon*
mangja	*maṅ ja*
mani-pa	*ma ṇi pa*
Marpa	*mar pa*
Mé Aktsom	*mes ag tshom*
Menlha	*sman lha*
Migmar	*mig dmar*
Mikyoba	*mi skyo ba*
Mila-rêpa	*mi(d) la ras pa*
Mi-trhukpa	*mi 'khrugs pa*
Miwo Shenrap	*mi bo gśen rab*
momo	*mog mog*
mönlam	*smon lam*
namparshé	*rnam par śes*
Namparnangdzè	*rnam par snaṅ mjad*
namthar	*rnam thar*
Namtrhi	*ngam khri*
nangpa	*naṅ pa*
nêyik	*gnas yig*
Ngag-rim	*sṅags rim*

Ngarikorsum	*mṅa' ris skor gsum*
Norsang	*nor bzaṅ*
Nyaktak Sangpo-pel	*ñag thag bzaṅ po dpal*
nyamchung	*ñam čhuṅ*
nyangenlê-dè	*mya ṅan las 'das*
nyen	*gñan*
nyerpa	*gñer pa*
nyingje	*rñiṅ rǰe*
nyingma	*rñiṅ ma*
Pawo-tsuglak	*dpa' bo gcug lag*
Pelgyi-dorje	*dpal gyi rdo rǰe*
Pèma-karpo	*padma dkar po*
Pèma Thang-yik	*padma thaṅ yig*
penpa	*spen pa*
Phagmotru	*phag mo gru*
Phakpa	*'phags pa*
phokpön	*phog dpon*
pönchen	*dpon čhen*
Putön	*Bu ston*
ragyapa	*ro rgyag pa*
rapchung	*rab byuṅ*
Rapten-künsang-phapa	*rab brtan kun bzaṅ 'phags pa*
rêpa	*ras pa*
Rêpachen	*ral pa čan*
rê-rimo	*ras ri mo*
Reting	*ra sgreṅ*
rê-tri	*ras bris*
Rinchen-jungden	*rin čhen 'byun ldan*
Rinchen-sangpo	*rin čhen bzaṅ po*
ri-nga	*rigs lṅa*
rongpa	*roṅ pa*
ru	*ru*
Sadak	*sa bdag*
Sakya (Penchen)	*sa skya (paṅ čhen)*
Samdruptsé	*bsam 'grub rce*
sang	*bsaṅs*
Sangwa-düpa	*gsaṅ ba 'dus pa*
Sangyê-gyatso	*saṅs rgyas rgya mcho*
Senggé-namgyel	*seṅ ge rnam rgyal*
serthang	*gser thaṅ*
Shakya-thuppa	*śākya thub pa*
Shalu	*ža lu*
Shang	*śaṅs*
Shangshung	*žaṅ žuṅ*
Shen	*gśen*
Sherap-gyentsen	*śes rab rgyal mchan*
shé-tra	*bśad grva*
shung	*gžuṅ*
Situ Changchup-gyentsen	*si tu byaṅ čhub rgyal mchan*
Shönnu-pel	*gžon nu dpal*
Sok	*srog*
Sönam-gyatso	*bsod nams rgya mcho*
Sönan-sengé	*bsod nams seṅ ge*
Songtsen-gampo	*sroṅ bcan sgam po*
Sugi-nyima	*gzugs kyi ñi ma*

Sumpa-khenpo	*sum pa mkhan po*	Tshangyang-gyatso	*chaṅs dbyaṅs rgya mcho*
sungma	*sruṅ ma*	Tshê	*shal*
		tshelêdêpa	*che las 'das pa*
Taktsang-rêpa	*stag chaṅ ras pa*	Tshe-pamé	*che dpag med*
Tamdrin	*rta mgrin*	Tshering	*che riṅ*
Tengyur	*bstan 'gyur*	tshokchen	*chogs čhen*
tenma	*brtan ma*	tshokkhang	*chogs khaṅ*
thanggo	*thaṅ sgo*	tsipa	*rcis pa*
Thangtong-gyelpo	*thaṅ stoṅ rgyal po*	tsipön	*rcis dpon*
thanka	*thaṅ ka*	tsowo	*gco bo*
thapkhang	*thab khaṅ*	tummo	*gtum mo*
thaplha	*thab lha*	Tüsum-khyenpa	*dus gsum mkhyen pa*
Thupten-gyatso	*thub bstan rgya mcho*		
Töndrup-gyatso	*don grub rgya mcho*	Ü	*dbus*
tongpanyi	*stoṅ pa ñid*	ula'	*'u lag*
Tongtsen Yalsung	*stoṅ bcan yul zuṅ*	Urgyen-pa	*u rgyan pa*
Tön-yö-truppa	*don yod grub pa*	Utsé-nyingpa	*dbu rce rñiṅ pa*
Trashi-lhünpo	*bkra śis lhun po*		
tr'a-trhê	*grva khral*	Wangchuk-pa	*dbaṅ phyug pa*
Trhikor	*khri skor*		
Trhi-rinpoché	*khri rin po čhe*	yak	*gYag*
Trhisong-detsen	*khri sroṅ lde bcan*	yidak	*yi dvags*
Trimé-künden	*dri med kun ldan*	yidam	*yi dam*
trülku	*sprul sku*	yik-tshang	*yig chaṅ*
trungkor	*druṅ skor*	yoga	*gYog gla*
trungyik	*druṅ yig*	Yönten-gyatso	*yon tan rgya mcho*
trup	*grub*	yümak	*yul dmag*
trupla	*grub bla*	yura	*yur ba*
Tsang	*gcan*		
tsen	*bcan*	za	*gza'*
tsetrung	*rce druṅ*	zorik	*bzo rig*

Index